MEL OTT

MEL OTT

The Little Giant of Baseball

by FRED STEIN

McFarland & Company, Inc., Publishers
JEFFERSON, NORTH CAROLINA, AND LONDON

In loving memory of my sister, Shirley Young,
who passed away just before this book was published.
She had a profound impact for the good in my life
in the years covered by this book and in the years since.

COVER: Mel Ott, 1942 (author's collection)

British Library Cataloguing-in-Publication data are available

Library of Congress Cataloguing-in-Publication Data

Stein, Fred.
    Mel Ott : the little giant of baseball / by Fred Stein.
       p.   cm.
    Includes bibliographical references and index.
    ISBN 0-7864-0658-5 (sewn softcover : 50# alkaline paper) ∞
    1. Ott, Mel, 1909–1958. 2. Baseball players—United
States—Biography. 3. New York Giants (Baseball team)—
History. I. Title.
GV865.O8S84 1999
796.357'092—dc21
[b]   98-53750
                                              CIP

Manufactured in the United States of America

*McFarland & Company, Inc., Publishers
  Box 611, Jefferson, North Carolina 28640*

CONTENTS

Author Fred Stein chats with former Giants manager Bill Terry in 1987.

INTRODUCTION

Mel Ott began his major league career in 1925, three-quarters of a century ago. He played in his last major league game in 1947, a half a century ago. So, the reader is entitled to ask: Why a book about Mel Ott, and who was this fellow whose name is recognizable to many people today only because its six letters fit so nicely into crossword puzzles?

Well, to begin with, Mel Ott had a truly unusual and remarkable career. An undersized rookie, he became a fixture with the New York Giants at age 17. He was a player clearly headed for greatness at age 20 after having arguably the finest year anyone of that tender age has ever had. He was a pillar of strength in the 1930s when he, along with fellow Hall of Famers Bill Terry and Carl Hubbell, carried the Giants to three pennant wins. He was a manager of the Giants who had the misfortune of taking over the job just five days before Pearl Harbor. A deeply beloved figure, he was replaced by a Brooklyn Dodger manager who was widely disliked by Giant fans. To enhance the irony, that unloved man attained managerial success with the Giants which eluded Mel Ott, baseball's renowned "nice guy." And, in a final irony, a fatal car crash took his life just before he was eligible to receive a generous baseball pension and the well-deserved fruits of a healthy, financially secure middle age.

Mel Ott's saga is the captivating story of an unprepossessing, naive, unknown teenager from a small town who rose to great heights in the country's most forbidding and hard-boiled city. He gained his enormous popularity and success despite having what used to be called a "passion for anonymity." Boy scout modest, unassuming, and gentlemanly, his success was gained entirely upon merit, on the ability of big, brassy New York to appreciate the quality of a man who was neither big nor brassy, and not the least on self-aggrandizement.

We live in an era in which Mel Ott's storybook career could not happen. It is no longer possible in today's high-powered, big money baseball scene for a callow, inexperienced 17 year old to be retained by a major league team as an apprentice instead of being sent out for minor league seasoning. It is also highly unlikely that such a diamond in the rough would be paid a minimal bonus and salary and, in today's season-by-season money grab, that a player would remain with his original team for 22 years.

This is also the story of baseball as it was played, and followed by fans, in the years before and just after World War II. This was the period long before television made it possible for a fan to follow each game as it was being played. The baseball devotee of that day relied either upon the radio to learn the score and skeletal details of that day's game, or upon the next day's paper. It also was the time when a fan could give full loyalty to a home team and its individual players, secure in the knowledge that the team, or a favorite player having a poor season, would most likely be back the next year. This is the story of what the Polo Grounds was like from a fan's vantage point. It also describes Ott's life off the field, both as a teenager in New York and as an older player with a family.

And I have a personal reason for recounting the life of Mel Ott. I first became aware of Ott when I was nine and the radio informed me of his winning home runs in the 1933 World Series. More than the usual case of hero worship, his exploits buoyed my spirits and helped carry me through a crushing emotional period in the mid-thirties when my brother and 47-year-old mother died in successive years. The baseball writers adored Ott, and they extolled his virtues as a true sportsman as well as a wonderful player. I took their praise of Mel's character and sportsmanship very seriously because I am old-fashioned enough to like my heroes to be exemplary off the field as well as on it. Mel Ott certainly filled that bill.

I can recall the wonderful feeling of escape from my personal travail when I took the subway or a bus down Broadway from my home in upper Manhattan to the Polo Grounds. I used to sit in the right field bleachers near my favorite fellow fan, Louie, whose words of wisdom I have set down in Chapters 22 and 23. Sitting out there with Louie and my other friends on those sunny afternoons gave me a heaven-on-earth feeling that I remember so vividly 60 years later.

Those were unforgettable days and it is a pleasure to share them as we recall the life and times of Mel Ott.

Chapter 1

MEL OTT ARRIVES

Legendary New York Giants manager John McGraw sat at his Polo Grounds desk on the morning of September 5, 1925. The scrappy, grey-haired manager was in an unhappy mood as he talked to a group of baseball writers. His team had just returned from a road trip well off the pennant pace. After having won four straight National League pennants, from 1921 through 1924, the Giants were slipping fast behind the Pittsburgh Pirates who would go on to win the flag by eight and a half games.

A clubhouse man knocked timidly on the door. "There's a kid out here who gave me a letter for you," he told McGraw. The letter was brief. It read:

Aug. 1, 1925

> *The bearer, M. Ott, is the young catcher whom you asked me to send you in September. We have just finished our season and this young-ster has shown up remarkably well. He is, as I told you, inexperienced and green, but seems to be a natural hitter and receiver. You, of course, will know what you want done with him, and I would appreciate hear-ing from you at a later date what you think of him.*

Yours sincerely,

H.P. Williams

The Williams who had sent the young man to McGraw was a millionaire lumberman in Louisiana. His chief claim to fame, outside of Louisiana at least, was his marriage to Marguerite Clark, a prominent silent screen actress.

McGraw shouted, "Send the kid in."

A nervous, stocky teenager walked into the office. McGraw looked at him and whispered to a nearby reporter, "Cradle-robbing. This kid is too young even to play college ball."

"I'm Melvin Ott," the baby-faced adolescent said in a tremulous voice. "I'm the fellow Mr. Williams wrote you about." He wore an inexpensive, hand-me-down suit and looked even younger than his 16½ years.

McGraw suddenly remembered his conversation with Williams. He bellowed, "Where were you? Harry told me you'd be up here before this." Then his beefy, red face softened and broke into a smile as he looked at the handsome, guileless, brown-eyed youngster. Young Melvin smiled back. The tension was broken.

"How old are you, son?" asked McGraw. In the best Hollywood actress tradition, Mel lied, "I'm seventeen, Mr. McGraw." Years later Ott told a reporter, "Mr. McGraw never would have given me a tryout if I told him I was only sixteen."

"I have a high regard for Mr. Williams' judgment and we'll look you over," said McGraw. "The clubhouse man will give you a uniform. Report here at ten tomorrow morning. Meanwhile," he continued, "how are you fixed for money and a place to stay?"

Before Mel left the office, he had been given $50 and a lodging at the Ansonia Hotel in Manhattan. Mel remembered years later that he had been frightened at being alone in a strange hotel that first night, so frightened that the youngster piled all the furniture in the room against the door for protection. Ott laughed in recalling it. He told a writer, "I'll never forget that pile of furniture. I stacked it nearly to the ceiling. Talk about a busher!"

A few days later a Giant player called a Washington Heights dentist who had put up ballplayers in the past. He had a room to rent. Mel moved in with him and lived with the family during the next several seasons until he married.

Mel arrived at the Polo Grounds at 8:30 the next morning with his battered catcher's mitt in hand. He waited anxiously for McGraw who showed up at 10:30. The paunchy manager told him, "I want you to catch batting practice and then hit."

Mel looked around for a mask and chest protector. McGraw pounced on him like a hawk. "You're supposed to be a catcher and you come out here without equipment," he scolded. "Go to the clubhouse and get ready. And, remember, a carpenter can't build a house without a hammer and nails."

A mortified Ott raced for the clubhouse and hustled back behind the plate, still red-faced with embarrassment. Jack Scott, a big, fastballing righthander was pitching to the hitters. This was the era well before night games and the entire Giant squad was on hand for the morning workout. They stood around the batting cage—Ross Youngs, Bill Terry, George Kelly, Travis Jackson, Frankie Frisch, and the other regulars—fully expecting the stocky youngster to be handcuffed by Scott's powerful pitches. But Mel conquered his nervousness and caught the deliveries of Scott and the next pitcher, lefthander Jack Bentley, with ease.

After the regulars hit, McGraw barked, "O.K., Ott, grab a bat and get up there." Virgil Barnes, another righthander, stared in at the somber, heavy-legged teenager, all 5 feet 7 and 150 pounds of him. Mel stood at the plate, his nervousness gone, his legs well spread and swinging his bat in a smooth, level plane. It was similar to the stance that baseball fans would enjoy in future years, but with one important exception. The young man lifted his front (right) leg slightly before the pitch came to him, but he had not yet developed his signature high leg kick.

Ott impressed the onlookers immediately. Frankie Frisch vividly remembered Ott's first time at the plate. He recalled, "Mel stepped into Barnes' first few pitches and smashed them solidly through the infield. Then he hit several deep into the outfield, and finally he parked a number of fastballs and curves high against the advertising signs on the right field wall." After a few more minutes of impressive hitting, McGraw called a halt, shouting, "All right, Ott, that's enough. Go on out to the bullpen and warm up the other pitchers."

With Mel out of earshot, a beaming McGraw told a writer, "That kid is remarkable. He's like a golfer; his body moves, but he keeps his head still with his eyes fixed on the ball. He's got the most natural swing I've seen in years." He continued enthusiastically, "This lad is going to be one of the greatest lefthand hitters the National League has seen."

Ott was awed by the historic, bathtub-shaped Polo Grounds. The ballpark had been modified and expanded since it was first built in the 1890s. It eventually was demolished in 1963 to make way for a large housing development. The park was situated in a hollow overlooked by a mini-cliff known as Coogan's Bluff. It was located near 155th Street in Manhattan, just across the Harlem River from the Yankee Stadium. The Polo Grounds was bounded on its home plate side by Coogan's Bluff and the "Speedway" (now the Harlem River Drive), a picturesque road running along the Harlem River from 155th Street to 200th Street in upper Manhattan. Outside its first base and right field stands was an enormous lot used by local cricket teams. The area outside the third base and left field stands was bounded by subway train yards, and the street bordering the center field area was sun-sheltered by an IRT elevated station.

The green, double-decked, horseshoe-shaped stands seated about 56,000. The unusual configuration included high fences, 257 feet down the right field line and 279 feet down the left field line, and a pasture-like center field which terminated 483 feet from the plate at the base of the clubhouse. Right and left field bleachers, fronted by large, green "batters' background" screens some 460 feet from the plate, were separated by about 25 feet of open space extending from the screens back to the clubhouse. Each inner bleacher side had a flight of stairs, one flight leading to the Giants' half of the clubhouse on the right field side, and the other flight leading to the visiting team's dressing room on the left field side. The bullpens were in the outfield corners of the playing field. The Giants' owner had an office above the clubhouse and a large clock was situated above this office.

As Ott would demonstrate in future years, the Polo Grounds was ideal for hitters capable of pulling drives directly down the foul lines. But the distances from the plate to the fences increased sharply from the foul lines out towards center field, and many long drives not hit close enough to the foul lines were converted into easy outs. The narrowness of the field also permitted outfielders to play relatively close to each other, thereby reducing the chances of hitting balls between the outfielders into the power alleys for extra-base hits.

The outfield walls were probably the most difficult to play of those in any other major league park, and not only because of their sharp angles. The right field wall was a solid stretch of concrete where most drives struck. Accordingly, a hard smash off the wall was likely to rebound back towards the infield. Balls hit not quite so hard most often caromed off towards center field, and softer drives, particularly those that hit near the base of the wall, often rolled near the wall toward deep right field.

The left field wall was even more difficult to play. Compounding the problems encountered in playing caroms, the left wall had a corrugated iron door on its gate which caused even more unpredictable rebounds. Judgment of fly balls was complicated further because this was the sun field. In addition, the upper deck extended well out past the lower deck. This meant that in cases where fly balls just missed the upper deck there was a split second during which the left fielder lost sight of the ball.

The outfield walls, as in most of the older ballparks, were covered with advertising (GEM razor blades, Stahl-Meyer frankfurters, Botany clothes, etc.). The advertisements would remain until 1948 when the walls were painted a restful green to conform with the rest of the park. This displeased accomplished outfielders who used letters in the advertisements as reference points in playing rebounds off the walls.

There was only one point outside the Polo Grounds from which any field action could be seen. This was an area high above Coogan's Bluff where a small sector of the field—the second base area and a small outfield patch—was visible. An experienced viewer could have a good idea of what was taking place on the field simply by observing this sector and listening to the changing crowd noises.

Mel Ott arrived in New York from New Orleans a few days before he met John McGraw. Many years later he described the events preceding his first meeting with McGraw. Ott recounted, "Harry Williams was on his way to Europe in the late summer of 1925 and he stopped off to visit Mr. McGraw (Ott always referred to his mentor as "Mr. McGraw") in New York. He told Mr. McGraw about me and Mr. McGraw told him to send him this kid. Williams sent me a penny post card telling me to go to New York. Of course I thought it was a joke, and I threw the card away." Ott smiled at the thought. "Just suppose that card never reached me and Williams had stayed in Europe longer. He wouldn't have known. You know," Ott continued, "I thought that postcard was a joke, and I didn't go to New York until Williams returned home and found me there. He gave me hell for not following orders, and then he financed my train trip to New York."

Mel was thrown for a loss as soon as he left Penn Station after arriving in New York. He recalled, "I got a cab at the station and gave the driver the number of the Giants' office on 42nd Street." He laughed and continued, "And, of all things, the cabby said he couldn't find the address. That's never happened to me since, but it had to happen to me that first time when I needed help so badly. Do you know what that fellow did? He dumped me out at 42nd and Fifth, right at that busy corner. He told me to ask a cop. There I was, a country kid with a big bag in each hand, tramping the streets of Manhattan."

Mel finally found the Giants' office, and fell into the hands of Jim Tierney, the Giants' traveling secretary. Ott remembered, "Jim took me to the window and showed me the Sixth Avenue elevated, which then ran beneath the Giants' windows. He told me in which direction to take a train. I finally got to the Polo Grounds, but the Giants were on the road. All I did for a couple of days was play catch with another young player, Buddy Crump. I stayed with Buddy until the Giants returned home."

Following Ott's eye-opening hitting exhibition, McGraw kept him under wraps. Ott recalled, "He had me practice with the team each morning for the rest of the season. Then I watched the games from the press box." Ott chuckled, "This was pretty deluxe treatment for a raw, 16-year-old kid."

After the season, McGraw gave the youngster a $400 bonus and told him that he would be sent a contract for the 1926 season. Reflecting on that time, Ott told a writer, "I was a happy young fellow all that winter but even happier when the contract arrived in January."

Chapter 2

THE EARLY YEARS

Melvin Thomas Ott came into the world in a big way, a whopping infant weighing in at 12 pounds. He was born to Charles and Carrie (Caroline) Ott, a hard-working couple of Dutch descent, at about 7 P.M. on March 2, 1909, in the Ott family's small cottage in Gretna, Louisiana. The Otts had one other child at the time, a daughter Marguerite, and later a second son, Charles, was born. The three children were brought up in the small cottage on Newton Street in Gretna, just across the street from Carrie's brother, George (Moo Cow) Miller. George, along with Mel's father, played an important early role in Ott's baseball career.

Charles Ott worked long, arduous hours as a laborer at the Southern Cottonseed Oil Company in Gretna. He supported his family on a small salary, but nevertheless the family lived comfortably and well. Long-time Gretna residents who knew the Otts recalled that it would be hard to find a happier, thriftier family. The Otts lived a life of simple pleasures and church-related activities, typical of a small-town, Southern family of that period.

Gretna, a town of 8,000 at that time, is just a short distance across the Mississippi River from New Orleans. It was a fine place for a young boy to spend his early years, and Charles Ott, an avid hunter and fisherman, spent many days in nearby woods and at local streams with his sons. The elder Ott had been a semi-professional pitcher, and he was an enthusiastic baseball fan.

Mel had an active interest in all sports at an early age. As a small child, his intense interest in shooting marbles earned him the derogatory nickname, "Mary Ott." A boyhood friend told of the time that Carrie Ott twice called Mel home from playing marbles to do his homework only to have him ignore her both times. Carrie decided to teach him a lesson. She dragged him in the house and dressed him in sister Marguerite's blouse and skirt. But Mel, undeterred by the feminine attire, rushed out to continue his marble game. For some time later he was met with neighborhood taunts such as "Here comes Mary Ott."

Despite his short, stocky build, young Mel was a gifted all-around athlete. He was an effective shooter and ballhandling field general for McDonough-Jefferson High School's (later renamed Gretna High School) basketball team. The high school did not have a football team when Mel was a student, but he played a couple of seasons with an independent Gretna football team. He was a center and a halfback and many years later he recalled the lingering effects of being tackled by a 230-pound lineman on a team representing Algiers, a neighboring township.

A boyhood friend remembered the time that a local family installed a tennis court. He recalled, "Mel came over to play tennis for the first time. He had never seen a tennis racket before but he beat everybody easily."

But baseball was Mel's passion from the start. His mother remembered his rolling a baseball along the floor before he was able to walk. His father and two uncles had a semi-pro team in Gretna called the Trans-Mississippi Terminals. That was a lot of name to put on the front of a baseball shirt, but that was the impressive name which fans saw in the small Louisiana towns where the Ott team played. Charles Ott was the team's catcher. Uncle George (Moo Cow) Miller, who worked in a local dairy, hence the nickname, was a pitcher whose enduring claim to fame was having hurled a 1–0 win over the Cleveland Indians in an exhibition game in 1921.

When Mel was old enough to travel, he was the team's mascot, and he went along on team trips. His small uniform also had the long name emblazoned on the tiny shirt front. In the lower grades in grammar school, Mel naturally knew more about baseball than the other kids. So he became the natural leader in all pickup games.

One day the boys talked it over and decided to organize a school team. They decided on the name "Red Devils" and turned to the task of obtaining suitable uniforms. They wanted gray shirts with "Red Devils" stitched in large letters on the shirt front. Like Charles Ott, many of the fathers of Ott's grammar school friends had played semi-pro ball, and Carrie Ott and the other mothers were busy for several days digging up old, musty uniforms. In this period, long before the Little League program was thought of, Mel's team was the envy of all the boys in Gretna and other nearby towns. It was a significant time in Mel Ott's career because, at age ten, that was his managerial debut.

The Red Devils practiced and played in Gretna's dusty streets and parks. Their baseball activities were concentrated in an area from Huey P. Long Avenue to Fifth Street. Emulating his father, Mel was the team catcher, and from the start he had the ability to hit the ball harder and longer than the other boys. Oldtimers recalled that the team won most of its games with Mel's hitting leading the way.

In high school Mel was again the catcher and leading hitter. The team played its home games in Gretna Park, today the site of a playground on Fried Street in Gretna. The ballpark had a short, right field fence, so short that a double was awarded on balls hit over it. Retired Judge L. Julian Samuels, a boyhood friend of Mel's, told the *Gretna-Picayune* in 1990: "Melvin was always good for a double. I played with him when I was a kid, but he was always so much better than the rest of us."

The high school team played two games a week and, often on other days, Mel played with a semi-pro team. Frank Baiamonte, a local barber, ran the semi-pro team for which Mel played when he was in high school. Baiamonte described his discovery of young Mel as follows:

> In 1923 (when Mel was 14) I had a team over in Gretna, and I was looking for another catcher in case my regular got hurt. I was watching a game over in City Park and I see this stocky little guy up at the plate. He gets hold of a pitch and powers it over the center fielder's head. I figure it had to be luck because nobody that small can hit a ball that far.

Baiamonte continued,

> So I wait until he comes up again and sure enough he sends another blast, this time to deep right center. Then I call him over and I ask him if he'd like to play for me. At the time he was playing for a team named Mothers Pies, and when I asked him how much he got paid, he looked surprised and said, "When we win I get a free pie to take home to Mama." When I told him I'd give him five bucks for every game he played, you'd have sworn I was giving him a pot fulla' loot. We got very close after that. I can still remember l'il Melvin sitting around my barber shop, just sitting and talking about baseball.

It was the custom around the local area that when a player's home run figured in a victory, a hat would be passed among the spectators to reward the hitter. So Mel Ott was earning money with his bat at the tender age of 14.

Ott's co-star on the high school team was his friend and battery mate, Les Rouprich, a righthanded pitcher with a fast ball that overpowered high school hitters. The New Orleans Pelicans, then a club in the Southern Association, was holding a tryout camp in March 1925. Although neither Mel or Les could graduate until June, both youngsters took a bus into New Orleans and tried out. Pelicans owner-manager Alex Heinemann liked Rouprich and offered him a contract.

Heinemann told Mel that he was too small and to come back after he had grown up. Larry Gilbert, also associated with the Pelicans, was impressed with Mel, but he failed to sign him because of his tender age (Mel was younger than Rouprich) and the red tape with which he would have had to deal. However, it was understood that Mel would play for the Pelicans at a later time. It is interesting to note that the Pelicans club was a farm team for the Cleveland Indians. Had Mel been offered a contract, he would very likely have played for the Indians.

At that time Harry Williams, the Louisiana lumberman, had a plant in Patterson, Louisiana, about 90 miles from New Orleans. He decided to organize a company team at Patterson. Williams asked Larry Gilbert if he could borrow a pitcher for one game and Gilbert suggested to Rouprich that he pitch a game for Williams. Rouprich agreed and asked, "Say, Mr. Gilbert, this kid Mel Ott who catches me is a better ballplayer than I am. Can he go with me?"

Gilbert agreed and he phoned Williams to tell him he was sending along a 16-year-old catcher who he was sure would be a first-rate player as soon as he grew a little. Gilbert told Williams he could keep Ott for a week or two but that he had to have Rouprich back sooner to join a lower minor league team. "I expect to get a lot of money for that Ott boy some day," Gilbert told Williams, "so take good care of him."

And that was how Mel Ott joined the Patterson Grays not long after his sixteenth birthday. Several months later, when Williams sent Ott to John McGraw in New York, Gilbert was justifiably angry. The two men had a falling out over the matter, but they eventually reconciled after Williams apologized to Gilbert.

Williams' club played against a crackerjack group of Louisiana teams featuring players who later made the major leagues. The Grays played teams representing such cities and towns as Baton Rouge, Alexandria, New Iberia, and Abbeville. Several years later these teams were organized to form the Evangeline League, a Class C minor league loop. The Grays included such players as first baseman Eddie Morgan and second baseman Carl Lind, future Cleveland Indians players, and Clay Hopper who managed Jackie Robinson when he played for the Montreal club prior to joining the Brooklyn Dodgers in 1947.

Mel had a sensational debut with the Grays, hitting a triple in his first at-bat and winning the game with a ninth inning homer. He was paid $150 a month with room and board, and he justified Williams' faith in him with a powerful display of hitting and very professional catching for a boy barely past his sixteenth birthday. Ott never forgot the marvelous treatment the members of the team received at the lumber camp.

Williams, for example, was such an enthusiastic owner and fan that he routinely gave bonuses to any player who made an exceptional play, either at bat or in the field.

Harry Williams was an old friend of John McGraw and, during the Giants' spring barnstorming trips, they spent a lot of time together. It was in the late spring of 1925 that Williams told McGraw about his sensational juvenile catcher, and he told McGraw that if young Mel had a good season, he would let the Giants manager know.

Carrie Ott had mixed feelings about Mel's success. She badly wanted him to complete his last high school term and graduate, but she was won over by her husband's strong support of Mel's decision to forgo high school and begin his professional baseball career.

In 1941 J.G. Taylor Spink, editor of *The Sporting News*, summed up Mel's situation as he left high school:

> The Ott family was not one of the better situated of the community financially, but it had a real nugget in Mel. At no stage of his boyhood was he a problem. Never unruly, always considerate of the family problems, always recognizing the fact that his dad was a day laborer and the family needed help, Mel was a gem as kids go.
>
> He nearly completed high school, and it took no small sacrifice to see him through the four-year course. He was a powerful kid, sturdy, and well able to work. And to work he wanted to go.
>
> As it turned out, Mel could have gone to college on a baseball scholarship. But he felt the time had come to pitch in.

The young man continued to hit home runs for the Grays, plus a number of lesser hits. In one game he drove in seven runs with a grand slam home run and two doubles. The next day the youngster beat Baton Rouge with a ninth-inning homer. In another game he drove in six runs in a 9–4 win over Abbeville.

Most of the money Mel earned, plus the additional money chipped in at games by appreciative fans, was sent back to the Ott family in Gretna. That, plus Mel's sheer enjoyment in playing a game he loved, made for a happy early summer. Even Carrie overcame her disappointment at his quitting school as she read favorable local news stories about her son's performance.

One day in July Mel received a telegram from Alex Heinemann who realized belatedly that he had dismissed Mel too hastily. He offered the youngster a $300 a month contract. An elated Ott showed the telegram to Harry Williams, fully expecting Williams to recommend that he accept the offer.

Williams responded, "Why, that cheap rascal is trying to steal my players. Mel," he continued, "it may sound like a lot of money to you, but I advise you to turn Heinemann down." Reading the disappointment in Mel's eyes, he said, "I have a better idea than your playing for Heinemann. Just give me some time." Mel agreed reluctantly to wait.

A week later Williams said goodbye to his players before heading on a six-week trip to Europe. He shook hands with Mel without a word on his plans for the youngster.

A week later Ott received a penny postcard from Williams which had been sent from New York. It read: "Sailing tomorrow. Report to McGraw in the Polo Grounds, New York."

Mel read the card and immediately tossed it into a wastepaper basket. Even though he was only 16, he was sure he knew when a joke was being played on him. Through the rest of July and August Mel traveled the dusty Louisiana roads with the Grays. He was lonely at times, and frustrated because of Williams' long absence. Nevertheless, he continued to spark the Grays at bat and behind the plate.

One day at the end of August Williams returned from his trip. He greeted his players warmly but was taken aback when he saw Mel.

"What are you doing here?" he shouted. "You should be in New York. Didn't you get my card?"

His eyes popping, Mel replied, "You mean you really sent that card?"

Williams said, "Of course I did. You're more than a month late already. I want you on a train to New York tomorrow. Now, pack up and go home and say goodbye to your folks." He continued, "I'm going to give you a letter for John McGraw. Send him my regards and do whatever he tells you to do."

Ott told a writer many years later, "It was just happenstance that I wound up with the Giants, rather than the Philadelphia Athletics. Williams was very friendly with Connie Mack as well as Mr. McGraw. What decided him on the Giants was the fact that he was in New York in the summer of 1925 and he happened to visit with Mr. McGraw at the Polo Grounds."

Chapter 3

ROOKIE YEAR

Accompanied by his father, young Mel went to his first spring training camp in Sarasota, Florida. They arrived in camp at the end of February, just a week before Mel's seventeenth birthday. On their first day in camp, the wide-eyed youngster and his father joined the entire team in a fishing trip in the Gulf of Mexico.

John McGraw welcomed his players, but much of his attention was devoted to a personal matter. Florida real estate at the time was bringing enormous prices. McGraw, never as shrewd a businessman as he was a baseball strategist, had become involved as a front man for a real estate development project in Sarasota. He had agreed to participate, and lend his name and prestige to, a project concocted by two get-rich-quick acquaintances. By early 1926 the project, imaginatively named Pennant Park, existed largely in the form of blueprints of streets named for ballplayers, mostly former and current Giants stars.

McGraw's role was to have his name mentioned prominently in full-page advertisements in each of New York City's morning newspapers in January. A press agent wrote a story about the project which recounted McGraw's career and which identified him as a prime mover in the project's development. There were plenty of eager customers; the real estate office was flooded with checks and money order down payments on lots. The prospects for the project appeared rosy at times, and McGraw talked glibly of sidewalks, sewers, and street lights soon to be installed. Of course, McGraw had no time for the project after spring training started.

McGraw's early appraisal of Ott was borne out as the youngster pounded the ball to the far corners of the palmetto-fringed field. But, watching Ott operating behind the plate, McGraw knew that he was not suited to be a major league catcher, at least not up to McGraw's standards. His legs were too thick and heavy and McGraw felt he would be slowed down to a walk from the continual crouching behind the plate. And while the youngster was still growing, at 5 feet 7 and 155 pounds, he probably would be too small to provide a good pitching target or to possess the size and stamina to stand up to the daily grind involved in catching.

One day McGraw and coach Roger Bresnahan stood near the dugout talking. They looked in Ott's direction as he caught batting practice. Ott recalled years later, "I could sense that they were talking about me. I was sure they were talking about sending me to the minors, especially when Mr. McGraw called me over."

McGraw asked Mel, "Did you ever play in the outfield?"

"Yes, sir," replied the 17-year-old youngster, "when I was a kid."

Suppressing a smile, McGraw said, "Well, I'll tell you what to do. Throw away that catcher's mitt, get yourself a fielder's glove, and start shagging flies. Because from now on you're an outfielder."

The first story about the little Giants player appeared in the *New York Times*. Written by sportswriter Harry Cross, the headline and story read as follows:

MANAGER MCGRAW CONSIDERS YOUNG OTT A "FIND"

Sarasota, Fla., March 14, 1926—Manager McGraw has made a remarkable discovery. He has found a young ballplayer in the Giants' camp who, he says, is as rare a baseball possibility at the age of seventeen as his experienced eyes ever rested upon. The lad is Melvin Ott, a high school catcher from Gretna, La.

He has been watching him, especially at bat, for a week, and he says that he has never seen a youth of his age and experience with such a perfect stance at the plate. As Ott is too small to measure up to McGraw's proportions for a catcher, the young find will be developed into an outfielder...

His attention has centered on Ott, and when during the past week Ott began to smash hits to left, center, and right fields, he concluded that this youthful bit of bric-a-brac was a great outfielder in the making. So hereafter Ott will put away his catcher's mitt and will be seen roaming the outgardens.

McGraw supervised Mel's development as though the boy were his own son, and very soon the writers began referring to Mel as "John McGraw's boy," along with the obvious appellation, "Master Melvin." Rud Rennie, of the New York *Herald-Tribune*, wrote, "It was almost as though McGraw were playing baseball again in the person of the youngster." Every batting technique, every outfielding trick, and every baserunning fine point were provided Mel. McGraw himself was among those who worked on Mel's hitting. And Ott's great predecessor, Ross (Pep) Youngs, worked for many hours with Mel on outfielding skills, and Giants leftfielder Emil (Irish) Meusel and coach Roger Bresnahan also were valuable tutors.

Ott had an uncommonly strong throwing arm despite his small size. A few days after his shift to the outfield, he threw from deep center field over home plate, a distance estimated at 400 feet. The widely recognized world baseball throwing record at the time was 426 feet.

The strength of Ott's throwing arm was not matched by its accuracy that early in his career. He had an especially rough time in one of his first games as a right fielder. He appeared to be aiming at one base and throwing to another and the Giants infielders were tired out chasing his wild heaves. In one of the late innings there was a runner at third and the next hitter hoisted a long fly out to Ott. The sturdy little fellow set himself to make the catch and get a quick throw away.

A spectator in the field box halfway down the third base line rose anxiously and was heard to address his companion, "Come on, Bill, let's get the hell out of here. That guy's got the ball again."

In addition to all of the personal instruction Mel received, he also had to be taught to run properly. His legs were thick but, as he had not yet fully matured, the muscles and tendons had not toughened. As he pounded around the outfield and the bases flat-footed or on his heels, he soon developed charley horses, severe knotting of his leg muscles. McGraw asked an old friend, Bernie Wefers, a well-known track coach, to come down from New York and teach Mel to run properly. Wefers put his pupil through exercises designed to keep him up on his toes as he ran. It was difficult, requiring a complete change in running style. But Mel was serious, ambitious, and willing to work hard to get the correct form.

Years later, Ott added a sidelight to the story. "Wefers damn near killed me. He had me spring up and down for hours at a time. I was supposed to run with my knees high, almost touching my chin. After a couple of weeks, I was ready to try it on the bases and Mr. McGraw was there to watch. I got as far as second base—going great guns—and then I kicked myself in the chin, tripped on the bag, and fell flat on my face." He continued, "When I got back to the dugout, Mr. McGraw told me 'You'll never go to the Olympics but at least you'll be able to come in on a ground ball.' But," Mel concluded, "it was one of the reasons I lasted as long as I did."

He also needed to improve his sliding. McGraw was a stickler on skidding correctly into a base. He wanted his players to not only hook-slide and roll away from a tag, but in potential double play situations to flatten an outfielder, or at least interfere with his throw to first base. Ott used to wad up pillows in his hotel room, charge across the room, and take off feet first. During a card game, with loud thumps coming from the room overhead, veteran Giants would grin knowingly and say, "Little Sunshine is stealing bases again."

By the end of spring training, Roger Bresnahan said of Mel: "That kid has a mind like a steel trap. You only have to tell him something once." McGraw was more impressed with his prodigy with each passing day. He wrote enthusiastically to Giants owner Charles Stoneham, "Ott is the best looking young player at bat in my 24 years with the club."

Mel became a particular favorite of the writers covering the Giants. They were attracted to the serious youngster although they found him a difficult subject to interview. "Trying to get him to tell you anything about himself is like getting blood from a stone," one of the writers commented. "He's a nice kid, but he hates to talk. He's too bashful, I guess." But the newspapermen could see that he was a well-brought-up, extremely pleasant, earnest teenager.

Many years later Daniel M. Daniel, a highly-respected baseball writer for the *New York World-Telegram*, wrote about interviewing Mel that spring. Daniel wrote:

> I came to know Mel Ott quite well that spring. He made instant appeal to the interviewer. Asked what his father did in Gretna, Mel offered no pretenses. "My dad is a poor day laborer, with a tough life which I would like to improve," the young man replied. Usually they say, "Pop is a contractor" instead of "a hod carrier." There was never anything phony about Mel Ott.

McGraw forbade Mel from fraternizing with the older players on the theory that the case-hardened veterans would "corrupt" the green teenager. Freddy Lindstrom, the Giants' 20-year-old third baseman, became Mel's roommate. Unlike Ott, Lindstrom was talkative and willing to resist authority. But the two young men hit it off well and Mel held his own with Lindstrom.

One day Lindstrom told a writer that baseball greats Tris Speaker and George Sisler had been his boyhood idols. And who had been Ott's boyhood favorite?

"Lindy here was my hero," answered Mel.

"What!" roared Lindstrom, "are you trying to make an old man out of me?"

"No," said Mel, "I'm serious. How old were you when you played in the 1924 World Series?"

"Eighteen," replied Lindstrom.

"O.K.," said Ott. "I was fifteen and in high school in Gretna. You were the hero of every high school kid that fall." Ott winked at a writer.

"Little did I think," he said, "that I'd grow up to room with the great Lindstrom."

"Nuts," said Lindstrom. "It's time were were getting to the ballpark. Come on, SONNY BOY."

Mel's teammates liked the quiet teenager from the start. They enjoyed teasing him and they even tried to acquaint him with the dubious delight of chewing tobacco. But that effort died quickly the first time Mel put a chaw in his mouth. It seems that shortly after Mel took his first few bites, a teammate bumped into him accidentally. Mel became violently sick, and he never chewed tobacco again.

Although Ott was so green and inexperienced, it was obvious that the 17 year old would eventually become a solid major leaguer if not a great player. Casey Stengel, then managing the Toledo club in the American Association, was in camp. He told McGraw, "I think I could develop that Ott kid for you." McGraw rebuffed him in no uncertain terms. "Case," McGraw said, "I'm not going to let any minor league manager, including you, take this kid over and ruin him. Forget it."

McGraw approached the start of the 1926 season with special concern. After four consecutive pennant wins in 1921 through 1924, the club had fallen to second place in 1925, eight and a half games off the pace. The writers covering the Giants had serious doubts about the Giants despite the presence of several fine players. First base was shared by George Kelly and Bill Terry. Team captain Frankie Frisch was at second, with Travis Jackson at shortstop, and Lindstrom at third base. Irish Meusel was the left fielder, journeyman Al Tyson the center fielder, and Ross Youngs was in right. Two weak hitters, Frank (Pancho) Snyder and Paul Florence, were the catchers. The starting pitchers were righthanders Jack Scott, screwballer (Fat Freddy) Fitzsimmons, Virgil Barnes and veteran lefthander Art Nehf.

The Giants opened the season in grand style, winning seven of their first eight. But a number of misfortunes struck the team, and it fell back in the standings. Terry, who hit .319 in his first year as a regular in 1925, held out for two weeks after Opening Day and then would play in only 98 games as he suffered a number of injuries. Jackson re-injured an already ailing knee and missed 40 games. Nehf, a pitching stalwart for the Giants since 1920, was completely ineffective and was sold to Cincinnati. Al Tyson broke an arm. And the high-strung McGraw criticized several of his veterans for exhibiting inadequate leadership and a lack of hustle. The only regular to escape the wrath of the frequently ill, harassed, and ill-tempered McGraw was Youngs, who had developed a serious kidney disease and was barely able to struggle through the 95 games he played.

The Pennant Park project had become a serious financial problem and a source of personal embarrassment to McGraw. By late summer the project had become a failure as orders for lots dwindled, and South Florida was hit by several devastating hurricanes which abruptly ended the real estate boom. McGraw was besieged by creditors and furious buyers, and the Giants manager discovered that the use of his name in promotions and sales could make him liable for fraud. As a result, McGraw had to sell a home he was building in Sarasota. He also spent more than his $50,000-a-year salary in satisfying his obligations.

Mel's continuing development as a player provided McGraw with the only bright spot as the Giants played under .500 ball. The manager decided to play Ott only in games in which the Giants were losing decisively to relieve him of any avoidable pressure. Ott made his first plate appearance against Philadelphia on April 27 as a pinch hitter for pitcher Jimmy Ring. Many years later he told a *Saturday Evening Post* writer about his debut:

> I was barely seventeen when Mr. McGraw said, "Ott, hit for Ring!" and launched me as a big leaguer. I doubt that any player, success or failure, had a worse start. My first fielding chance struck my right wrist and bounded over my shoulder for a two-base error. My first fly ball—a running catch which I thought perfection itself— brought me a bawling out from the pitcher, Virgil Barnes. He thought I should have been under it, waiting.
>
> But at the plate in Philadelphia, April 27, 1926, I was strictly a cold-storage proposition unable to move a muscle, and facing Wayland Dean. I was conscious only of a passing streak of white, a plunking sound and the umpire tolling off the fatal words. They say I swung at the last pitch, but I'm sure my bat slipped.
>
> Two days later in Boston, Mr. McGraw nodded to me again. I stood petrified at the plate as another fastball pitcher, Larry Benton, served up knee-high hard ones. Had he thrown at my head, I'd have been killed because I couldn't seem to move, and certainly didn't as the third strike went by unmolested to end the game.
>
> No one bawled me out, but Ross Youngs, recognizing my predicament, whispered words of wisdom and help. He said, "Always start swinging, kid, before rigor mortis sets in!"

Mel obtained his first major league hit on May 2 against righthander Dutch Ulrich of Philadelphia. It came on a hot smash off the third baseman's glove.

Later in the season McGraw was still using Mel mostly as a pinch hitter, and the youngster was having great success. At one point he ran off a string of five straight pinch-hits, then failed twice in succession. Renowned baseball writer Frederick G. Lieb happened to have dinner with the young Louisiana lad after the second failure. Lieb wrote:

> The boy was quite upset. "I just can't think what I'm doing wrong," he repeated over and over. "I hold the bat just the same way and swing it just the same way as when I made the hits, but I don't get the ball through anybody."

Lieb marveled, "Here he was hitting over .400, and the 17 year old couldn't figure out what he was doing wrong."

Mel made remarkable progress as an outfielder during his rookie season. His throwing accuracy improved as did his ability to get a jump on fly balls. Ross Youngs was a past master at playing caroms off the right field wall at the Polo Grounds, and Ott proved to be an apt pupil in learning from the veteran.

But young Mel's base running had its unfortunate moments during the season. He came to the plate one day with Lindstrom on first and Travis Jackson on second. Mel drove a liner into right center to score Jackson and, with his head down, he slid triumphantly into second base. Unfortunately, Lindstrom had held up at second base on the hit. Lindy looked down gravely at his youthful roommate and cracked, "A hell of a slide, kid, but one of us is out." Ott trotted back to the dugout, braced for the dressing down from the irate McGraw which followed.

Mel's apprenticeship under McGraw included more than playing in selected, non-pressure situations. It also included compulsory attendance sitting on the bench next to the high-strung manager during the entire game. Mel would have been happy to move down to the other end of the bench. But the portly McGraw insisted that the curly-haired teenager listen to his often profane, if educational, commentary on the game. Now and then, McGraw would forget himself and direct a number of epithets at Mel which were really meant for the blunderers on the field. Mel would protest in his soft, Southern drawl, "But Mr. McGraw, I'm not even playing." McGraw would respond, "I know, Ott, but I don't want you to make the same stupid mistakes as those dumb bastards out there."

On another afternoon, Mel sat on the bench, his 17-year-old mind not completely on the game. Suddenly McGraw barked: "Ott, what would you do if the next ball was to hit you?" Startled, Mel answered with the first thought that popped into his head, "I'd try to c-catch it, Mr. McGraw." McGraw normally would have followed such a response with a lecture but, in Mel's case, all he could do was stifle a grin. But he jumped all over Mel at other times.

One day Ott missed a coach's sign to keep on running to third base on a base hit and pulled up at second. The missed sign cost the Giants a run. After the game McGraw walked heavily into the clubhouse. He shouted, "Where is he? Where is that kid?"

"He's in the toilet," answered a player.

"Well," barked McGraw, "that's where he belongs. In the toilet!"

Mel wisely stayed there until McGraw calmed down.

With Ross Youngs unable to play because of his worsening illness, the Giants began a western trip on August 10 with a 56-51 record. They were in fourth place, but trailed the league-leading Pirates by only five and a half games. But they proceeded to lose their next nine games and fell 13½ games behind the Cardinals who had taken over the lead. The club wound up the season in fifth place.

As the Giants' fortunes declined during the western trip, McGraw became more choleric with each loss. During one of the losses in St. Louis, team captain Frankie Frisch missed a sign and McGraw, who often treated his club's captain as a whipping boy, berated him unmercifully in front of the entire team.

That evening at the Hotel Chase, Frisch decided that he had had enough of McGraw's abuse and that he was finished with the Giants. He left the team the next morning, taking the next train home to New York. It was a bitter experience for Frisch, the erstwhile "Fordham Flash," who had grown up in New York idolizing McGraw. McGraw fined Frisch $500, and the two men were not able to resolve their differences.

McGraw was sad and embittered. He realized that Frisch would have to go if he were to maintain control of his players. As a result, on December 20 the Giants traded Frisch and pitcher Jimmy Ring to the Cardinals. In exchange the Giants obtained the great Rogers Hornsby who wanted more money from the Cardinals after just having led the club to its first pennant and World Series win over the Yankees.

Ott wound up his rookie season hitting .383, the highest batting average of his career. McGraw's "boy wonder" played in 35 games, ten of them in the outfield. He had only two doubles among his 23 hits since he had yet to attain his full growth and adult strength. Yet he had fulfilled his early promise by improving in all phases of his game. His future, bright as the season began, was even brighter at its end.

Chapter 4

LEARNER
BECOMES REGULAR

As the Giants' training camp opened in Sarasota, the big story again was John McGraw's Pennant Park headache. The Florida land boom had collapsed completely and some of those he had freely advised to invest in the project were beginning to catch up with him. The project had been grossly oversold, and many of the investors insisted on dealing directly with McGraw.

McGraw escaped federal prosecution and managed to talk most of the aggrieved investors out of filing suits. He arranged out-of-court settlements in all cases, but it would prove to be an embarrassing, wearing, and costly process. By the time McGraw satisfied all of his obligations, he was estimated to have lost almost $100,000.

Rogers Hornsby provided much of the early training camp news after having signed a contract for a hefty $40,000 for the season. Then there was the matter of Hornsby's disposing of his stock in the Cardinals before he could play for the Giants. He was the second largest holder of Cardinals stock, not including Cardinals owner Sam Breadon. Hornsby demanded $116 per share for his stock while Breadon protested loudly that Rogers had paid only $45 a share a few years earlier. Hornsby's retort was that it was his efforts that were responsible for the increase in value. With both men refusing to budge, the other six National League clubs, fearing a disruption in the favorable (to them) structure of organized baseball, ponied up the money to pay off Hornsby and end the dispute.

Hornsby was named to replace the departed Frisch as team captain. He was a humorless individual whose credentials as a team leader had been firmly established in 1926 when he led the Cardinals to a World Series victory. His credentials as a world class hitter also were beyond question. He had led the National League in hitting seven times, had hit over .400 four times, and was en route to a .358 career batting average.

McGraw appointed Hornsby as acting manager on the frequent occasions when McGraw was not on hand because of personal or health problems. On these occasions Hornsby alienated his teammates by his brusque demeanor. Mild-mannered Travis Jackson recalled that "Hornsby had a good way of irritating us." And Fred Lindstrom openly defied Hornsby one day when Rogers bawled him out for the manner in which he made a play at third base.

Lindstrom protested, "That's the way McGraw wants the play made."

"I don't give a damn. When I'm in charge, make it the way I want it," shot back Hornsby.

Mel Ott (17 years old) in first spring training camp, Sarasota, Florida, 1926 (courtesy National Baseball Hall of Fame).

Lindstrom replied scornfully, "Who the hell do you think you are? After you put down that bat, you're no bargain."

Hornsby shouted, "I'm not going to argue with you. You do as I tell you to, and keep your mouth shut."

Predictably, the easy-going, respectful Ott had no problem with Hornsby. As a result, Rogers worked with Mel on his hitting, especially against lefthanders. For Ott, the 1927 season would continue where the last season had ended. He took endless batting practice and spent many hours working on his fielding. He became increasingly proficient at one of the most difficult outfield tasks, accurately and quickly judging the flight of a ball hit in his direction. Then, compensating for his merely average foot speed, Mel developed the knack of turning his back on a drive that appeared to be going over his head and digging for the spot where the ball would land. When he turned back towards the descending ball, he was able to make the catch easily.

There were a few lineup changes. Righthander Burleigh Grimes, a veteran spitballer with a menacing, stubble-bearded countenance, had come over from the Brooklyn Dodgers. Centerfielder deluxe Edd Roush was obtained from Cincinnati in a deal involving George Kelly. And a deeply depressed McGraw announced that his old favorite, Ross Youngs, had been diagnosed with Bright's Disease. This very serious kidney ailment would prevent Youngs from playing again. The Giants picked up rightfielder George Harper from the Phillies to replace Youngs.

The Giants opened the season with a flourish, winning three straight from the Phillies and holding on to first place through May 21 when a loss to the Pirates dropped them into second place. By mid–June, as their pitching faltered, the Giants had fallen into third place, four games out of the lead. They were playing .500 ball on July 19 when McGraw marked his twenty-fifth anniversary as the Giants' manager on a ceremony-filled day at the Polo Grounds.

The day before, Ott hit his first major league home run. With Chicago Cubs righthander Hal Carlson on the Polo Grounds mound, Mel cracked a low liner into center field, for which outfielder Hack Wilson made a futile shoestring catch attempt. The drive skidded by Wilson and rolled towards the distant clubhouse as Mel's stocky legs churned around the bases. This was one of the two inside-the-park homers hit by Ott during his career.

Mel's on-the-job training continued as it had in his rookie season. He played more frequently, and McGraw deployed him only in right field, obviously grooming him to replace Youngs on a regular basis when McGraw felt he was ready. On the occasions that Ott was in the lineup, he played with a stellar group of future Hall of Famers. This included the regular infield of Terry, Hornsby, Jackson, and Lindstrom. Edd Roush and Burleigh Grimes were the other future Hall of Fame players in the club.

In the early 1980s, I met an elderly lady who dated Mel Ott in the summer of 1927. She recalled that long-ago time:

> I lived in the Washington Heights area in uptown Manhattan at that time. I met Mel Ott through my dentist with whom Mel lived. I remember Mel as very sweet, shy, rather good-looking, and very polite. He spoke in a soft Southern drawl, and he rarely talked about himself or his experiences with the Giants. He did say that he was learning a lot and that he liked his teammates although they were much older. He didn't see much of them when the Giants were home because most of them were married.
>
> The Giants didn't play at night in those days, so Mel had his evenings free. We did the usual things that teenagers did in Washington Heights in those days. We went to movies, took long walks, and usually dropped in at a candy store on Broadway for an ice cream soda.
>
> My fondest recollection of Mel was the time I had a bad toothache, and the dentist worked on my tooth that night. Mel insisted on comforting me by holding my hand while the tooth was being drilled. I think it was wonderful that Mel had such a great career and that he was so well loved.

McGraw was sidelined with a severe sinus infection a few weeks after his anniversary celebration, and the heartily-disliked Hornsby managed in his place for several games of a western trip. Despite their dislike of Hornsby, the Giants won seven of nine games with the unsmiling second baseman leading them. McGraw returned and the Giants continued to win, returning home in mid–August only a game and a half behind the league-leading Pirates.

By Labor Day the Giants were in a three-way dogfight with the Pirates and the Cardinals which continued through the rest of the season. With McGraw ill again, Hornsby led the Giants through September as the team, beset by pitching problems, finished the season in third place, only two games behind the pennant-winning Pirates and a game and a half in back of the Cardinals.

Hornsby aspired to replace McGraw permanently if and when poor health forced McGraw to step down. But the outspoken Rajah ruined any chance he might have had when he got into a violent argument with traveling secretary Jim Tierney who had criticized a play made by Travis Jackson. Hornsby took very little guff from his fellow players and absolutely none from someone he considered to be a baseball illiterate. Hornsby ordered Tierney out of his office and team owner Charles Stoneham, a close friend of Tierney, became furious with Hornsby. From that time on, Stoneham became Hornsby's sworn enemy.

The Giants offense had performed well as Hornsby, Jackson, Lindstrom, Terry, George Harper, and Roush all hit over .300. Hornsby's managerial problems did not affect his play as he hit .361 and led the league in runs scored and slugging percentage. The pitching was decent with starters Burleigh Grimes (19-8), Freddy Fitzsimmons (17-10), Virgil Barnes (14-11), Larry Benton (13-5), and lefthander Dutch Henry (11-6). But the Giants fell just short.

It was another learning year for Ott. His batting average dropped to .282 and he had only 11 extra-base hits among his 46 hits. But the 18-year-old youngster continued to mature physically and to improve his hitting and fielding mechanics. McGraw felt it was only a matter of time before he was ready to become a regular player.

Many years later, Giants president Horace Stoneham revealed an interesting fact about Ott's apprenticeship with the Giants. He told *New Yorker* writer Roger Angell, "Ott didn't get to play much the first couple of years, and McGraw would sometimes let him go over to New Jersey on the weekends and pick up some extra cash by playing with a semi-pro team. He played with the Paterson Silk Sox."

Ross Youngs died a few weeks after the season ended. In eight full seasons with the Giants, the sturdy little outfielder was consistently among the National League leaders in several offensive categories. The Texas native was an extremely spirited player with a superb throwing arm and good speed. He was especially adept at playing the difficult right field position at the Polo Grounds, a skill he passed on to Ott. McGraw was so taken with Youngs that photographs of Youngs and Christy Mathewson were the only pictures of his players which hung behind McGraw's Polo Grounds desk.

On January 10, 1928, Jim Tierney called in the New York writers and handed out copies of a statement signed by Charles Stoneham, with McGraw's name conspicuously absent. Rogers Hornsby had been traded to the Boston Braves in "the best interests" of the club. The Giants received in return two relative unknowns, outfielder Jim Welsh and catcher Frank (Shanty) Hogan. McGraw was not enthusiastic about the trade, but he was unable to resist Stoneham's decision as effectively as he might have done when his teams were winning pennants. Still, McGraw gamely told the writers that Andy Cohen, a minor leaguer, would be a worthy replacement for Hornsby. Of course, he fooled no one.

After a poor start, Burleigh Grimes had 13 straight wins in the second half of the season. Nevertheless, in February he was traded to the Pirates for righthander Vic Aldridge. Both men were unhappy with the contracts offered them, and McGraw chose the dubious strategy of trading a discontented future Hall of Famer for a discontented journeyman.

In a deal that would prove very important to Ott, the Giants picked up Frank (Lefty) O'Doul from the Pacific Coast League. O'Doul had pitched with little success for the Yankees and Red Sox in the early twenties before switching to the outfield and becoming an extremely effective hitter on the West Coast. O'Doul would prove to be a high-average hitter and instructor, as well as a man who knew how to enjoy himself off the field, while with the Giants.

The Giants' pitchers and catchers reported to Hot Springs, Arkansas, in mid–February of 1928 for two weeks of light training, roadwork over the hills, and mineral baths for the overweight. Then the entire squad assembled at Augusta, Georgia, which McGraw had picked for the training site. McGraw stopped off in New Orleans to visit his prodigy before going to Hot Springs. "Come on along with me now, Mel, and you'll get a head start on the boys," McGraw told Ott. "The outfielders aren't supposed to report for a couple of weeks, but why don't you come along now? I want to try a little experiment with you."

Mel needed no persuasion. The regular season was not so long that the chance to play a couple of extra weeks failed to lure him. Besides, he

wondered what kind of experiment McGraw had in mind.
When Mel reached Hot Springs,
he discovered that he was the
only player there who was not a
pitcher or a catcher. He didn't
have long to wait to find out why
McGraw had brought him there.
He was going to learn to play
second base. "I'd fooled around
some in the infield," Ott recalled,
"but had never played it seriously. And I learned that there
was a lot to learn."

The Giants had a weakness
at second base, at least until
Andy Cohen proved himself. If
Cohen failed, McGraw wanted a
replacement, and the best man
he could think of was Master
Melvin, described by a writer as

Mel Ott at 19 (courtesy National Baseball
Hall of Fame).

"a steady, smart, nervy little fellow who seemed able to do everything
pretty well." Throughout spring training, Mel practiced at second. There
was no intention of making him the regular second baseman, but before
the season began McGraw proudly announced that Ott was being carried as a reserve infielder.

Mel had matured physically by early 1928. As he celebrated his nine-
teenth birthday on March 2, he looked broader in the shoulders, and he
appeared to be driving the ball for longer distances. That spring in Augusta
was a significant one for Mel in another way. He worked intensively with
O'Doul on his hitting, especially on his ability to pull drives sharply down
the right field line.

Ott always had lifted and lowered his front (right) leg slightly as he
waited for a pitch to come to him. But, working with the knowledgeable
O'Doul, Mel realized that lifting his front leg higher would have the
effect of moving his weight more forcefully into the pitch, thereby giving
his swing additional power. Mel felt that this was particularly important
considering his relatively small body (5 feet, 9 inches and 160 pounds).
He worked on the higher leg kick for hours on end until he felt completely comfortable with the innovation.

The astute McGraw had never tampered with Ott's batting stance

Ott works out at second base, Augusta, Georgia, 1928 (author's collection).

when the youngster first came to him. But, with the higher leg kick, McGraw wanted to make sure that Mel could handle pitches thrown at or near his feet. During spring training, Giants pitchers were instructed to feed Mel a steady diet of low, inside pitches, some aimed at his stationary left leg. After constant practice, he mastered the knack of hitting these pitches well and avoiding those too close to swing at.

Ott's stance was described by St. Louis sportswriter Bob Broeg as follows:

> He raised his right leg to knee height while the pitcher was preparing to deliver the ball. Then Ott planted the right foot on the ground again, just before the impact with the pitch. The stride was no more than a couple of inches.
>
> Put in other words, Ottie squared away to a pitch as though he was going to beat a rug. Crowding the plate with feet spread, he reared up his front leg, not unlike the family canine finding a favorite hydrant. At the same time he pulled back the bat, stepped lightly forward as the right foot descended, and then swung.

Many writers of the day wrote of Mel's stance as though it made it more difficult to be the hitter he proved to be. On the contrary, Branch Rickey, an expert in analyzing playing techniques, felt that Ott's lifting of his front leg was largely responsible for his powerful hitting. "You will notice," said the astute Rickey, "that he lifts that front leg just as the pitcher releases the ball and he puts it down after he sees what sort of pitch is coming and where it is coming from. That's why he never is caught off balance or out of position." Rickey concluded, "He puts that front foot down in the right place after he knows what is coming."

The Giants had a fine spring exhibition game record, winning 22 of 27 games. Mel hit .330, with a number of extra-base hits, in these games, but he started out the season on the bench. The Giants' infield included three bona fide stars, Terry, Jackson, and Lindstrom, and Cohen, an unknown quantity. The outfielders were George Harper in right, Roush in center, and O'Doul in left. Catcher Shanty Hogan was a powerful hitter and an adequate receiver but, at 21 years of age, he already had displayed an out-of-control weakness for food which would prevent him from reaching his full potential. Righthanders Larry Benton, Freddie Fitzsimmons, Virgil Barnes, and Vic Aldridge were the starting pitchers.

Andy Cohen had a Hornsby-like start for the first few weeks of the season, and many fans, including many of his Jewish rooters, suggested irrationally that he might be better than Hornsby. Rogers started slowly with the Braves, and one of the New York newspapers took to printing their statistics every day. Hornsby's only comment: "It's not fair to the kid. As soon as I get going, I'll lose him." Cohen was felled by a bad case of influenza in late April, and Ott replaced him very effectively over a five-game stretch. Then Mel filled in for Lindstrom at third base for a game.

Samuel J. Merin wrote a short, euphoric piece on Ott for *Baseball Magazine*. He wrote:

> This season Ottie has captivated the hearts of all Giant followers. Ott's versatility is phenomenal. When Andy Cohen was out, Mel filled in at second. He teamed up with Travis Jackson in three of the fastest twin-play killings ever seen at the Polo Grounds. Then Freddy Lindstrom developed a kink in his back, so Master Melvin took up the hot corner and melted the hearts of opposing right-hand hitters by plays frankly called freaks.
>
> This youngster certainly has seen his ball games from every available position on the field. And when he grows up—stop, Harlem, why are you grinning?

On May 10, the Giants traded a slumping George Harper to the Cardinals for veteran catcher Bob O'Farrell. McGraw explained, "We need a catcher and we're able to give up an outfielder because we have Ott. We can't keep him on the bench." McGraw continued, "From now on, he plays when righthanders are working against us."

As Mel told it: "One day we were playing against the Dodgers and (lefthander) Jess Petty was going to pitch. Mr. McGraw said to me, "You're playing right field today."

Ott responded, "I think they're going to pitch a lefthander, Mr. McGraw."

McGraw growled, "I don't care who pitches for them. You're the right fielder today, and from now on."

Mel was jubilant at his promotion. He had caught McGraw's eye at the start, and had slowly but surely justified the manager's confidence in him, keeping Ott on board rather than sending him out to the minors as everyone had expected. After this, there was no question of Ott's major league qualifications. The only doubt was just how far the quiet, unassuming youth would go. Certainly he had the skill, the ambition, and the courage. He lacked only color, or headline appeal.

Inexplicably, the Giants played little better than .500 ball into late July. The team was hitting well. And reinforced by Larry Benton, on his way to 25 wins, and Fitzsimmons, who would win 20 games, the pitching had improved even though Vic Aldridge had been a complete bust. Still the club was not playing up to its potential.

Early in July a Giants scout, Dick Kinsella, was a delegate to the Democratic National Convention in Houston. While there he saw a Beaumont lefthander pitch a masterful, extra-inning 1–0 win over Houston. The Beaumont pitcher was Carl Hubbell, a skinny, Oklahoma native. His special pitch was a screwball, a reverse curveball which broke away from righthand hitters. The Giants paid Beaumont $30,000 for Hubbell who reported to the Giants immediately. After a rocky start, he won his first game for the Giants on July 31. McGraw showed the same tolerance for Hubbell's unorthodox screwball pitch (which many baseball men felt would injure his arm prematurely) as he did for Ott's unusual hitting style. The gaunt Hubbell went on to win ten games over the last two months of the season.

Sparked by excellent pitching by Benton, Fitzsimmons, and Hubbell, the Giants mounted a drive that carried them into the league lead on August 19. The club had good hitting to go with their improved pitching as Lindstrom, Terry, O'Doul, Ott, and Hogan pounded the ball. But the Giants slumped a few days later and fell out of first place, with the situation worsened by McGraw's continual verbal abuse of his players.

Ott and Lindstrom had roomed together harmoniously since Mel's rookie season. McGraw, well aware of Lindstrom's zest for night life, had kept a close eye on the two young men, especially because McGraw still felt a particular need to look after Ott's youthful well-being. Years later, Lindstrom told a writer that McGraw could not relate to the newer generation of players.

Donald Honig, in his book *Baseball America*, discussed McGraw's rage at his inability to intimidate his players. With regard to the Ott-Lindstrom situation in 1928, Honig wrote:

> When he (McGraw) heard that his home run–hitting prodigy Mel Ott had taken a young woman up to Fred Lindstrom's hotel room, McGraw tore into Lindstrom for "immoral conduct." When Lindstrom angrily denied any involvement, McGraw refused to listen, and when his informant whispered to him that it had been Ott, the old man began screaming, "It wasn't Ott! It was Lindstrom!" Ott was his pet, his discovery, and he would not believe. "There were things, and that's a good example," Lindstrom said, "that he could not handle, that he refused to handle."

At about the same time as that incident, another training rule infraction occurred. Veteran writer John Drebinger wrote of it years later in *Baseball Magazine*:

> [Ott and Lindstrom] got along swell until one day came trouble. Seems there was something about a quart bottle [remember, this was during Prohibition] of something found in the Ott-Lindstrom abode by the eagle-eyed McGraw. To the Old Man this was always a mighty serious offense, for he simply would not stand for his players taking even an occasional light nip. The laugh to the other players came when McGraw, usually infallible in such matters, landed entirely on the wrong guy.
>
> The bottle, it seems, belonged to Ott, and vainly Mel tried to tell that to Mr. McGraw. But Mr. McGraw would have none of it. He was sure he knew the culprit, tersely told Master Melvin not to interrupt, and without further ado gave Lindstrom a terrific dressing down for "leading this little boy astray" and heaven knows committing no end of other heinous crimes. The upshot of it all was Ott and Lindy the next day found themselves teamed with new roomies." Mel was sent to room with newcomer Hubbell, the beginning of a lifelong, close friendship.

By September McGraw had calmed down, and the team reacted well to his more relaxed attitude. By September 27, the Giants were only half a game behind the league-leading Cardinals as McGraw's club began a crucial doubleheader at the Polo Grounds. With the Cubs leading 3–2 in the sixth inning, the Giants had men on second and third with one out. Shanty Hogan bounced back to the pitcher and reserve infielder Andy Reese, the runner at third, was hung up off the bag. Caught in a rundown,

Reese broke for the plate, smashing into Cubs catcher Gabby Hartnett who blocked him on the baseline. Hartnett, hurled back by the impact, grabbed Reese to keep from falling. While Reese wrestled to break loose, he was tagged out by the third baseman. Plate umpire Bill Klem called Reese out, and McGraw became almost apoplectic in claiming that Hartnett had interfered with Reese and that the tieing run should have been allowed.

The decision cost the Giants the game, and their protest was disallowed by league president John Heydler despite a photo which appeared to support McGraw's claim. The Giants won only one of their next three games and lost the pennant to the Cardinals by only two games.

McGraw's critics did not let him forget that the two major, preseason trades had hurt the Giants' chance to win. They had a point. Rogers Hornsby led the league with a resplendent .387 batting average for the Braves, and Burleigh Grimes won a league-leading 25 games for the Pirates.

There were some decent individual performances in a season when the Giants fell just short. Lindstrom and Terry were the leading Giants hitters. Lindstrom hit .358 and led the league with 231 hits. Terry duplicated his 1927 statistics with a .326 average. O'Doul hit .319 as a part-time outfielder, and Shanty Hogan hit .333 and performed capably behind the plate.

It had been a breakthrough year for Ott. He hit .322 and gave the first sign of his future home run exploits with 18 roundtrippers. Mel had fully developed the pull-hitting style which would make him a great home run hitter through the World War II era. Mel also began to show extra-base power with 26 doubles and 4 triples. And his outfielding skills continued to improve.

Ott was proud of other phases of his game which had developed during the season. He had shown his versatility in the field, especially the ability to play in the infield if he were needed. Another phase was his knack for hitting to the opposite field. Mel recalled near the end of his career:

> In 1928 I began to get the home run range and I was feeling pretty proud about that. Mr. McGraw thought I was getting a little cocky, and he ordered me to work harder in learning to hit to the opposite field for a change. I was disappointed because I was just a kid who wanted to clear the bases every time. But in the years that followed, I appreciated what Mr. McGraw had tried to do for me. He wanted to make me a better all-around hitter, and I think he wanted to teach me above all that there were eight other players on the team.

It was apparent that great things lay ahead for "John McGraw's boy."

Chapter 5

HITTING HIS STRIDE

Mel returned home to Gretna and relaxed for a few days, playing pickup basketball games when he was not hunting or fishing. His friends, relatives, and local fans had not seen him in a baseball uniform since 1925, and a special exhibition game between two local semi-pro teams was scheduled in his honor. He coached one of the teams and took a turn at bat as the crowd shouted its approval of the local youngster who had made good in the big leagues.

Mel obtained a job with a department store in New Orleans, the first time that he worked on a job which was unrelated to baseball. The salary was good, and the duties light. All he had to do was to be in the sports department for two or three hours a day and talk to customers. But Mel quit after one day, explaining, "There were a dozen people around me every minute, and all they wanted to talk about was me. It was worse than a doubleheader on a hot, humid day in St. Louis."

Mel went to many parties and, at one of them, he met Mildred Wattigny, a local girl. Mildred was slim, with curly hair and attractive features. They hit it off well from the start, and they saw each other frequently during the offseason. Many years later, Mildred described their first meeting in her gentle Southern drawl: "The first time I met Melvin, I was taken by his smile. It was at a party down home, and someone introduced us. He made a little bow, smiled, and after that I just had to like him."

The Giants made only one important trade during the offseason, sending Lefty O'Doul to the Phillies for another, less distinguished outfielder, Fred Leach. It was an unpopular trade among the fans and writers. O'Doul was a colorful, ever-smiling bon vivant who had been well-liked in New York while with the Giants and before that with the Yankees. And he had been extremely helpful to Ott as a hitting instructor.

The club, which trained in San Antonio, included an infield of Terry, Cohen, Jackson, and Lindstrom. The outfield regulars were Leach in left, Roush in center, and Ott in right. The catchers were Hogan and Bob

O'Farrell. And the starting pitching staff, which appeared to be the Giants' best in some time, included Hubbell, Fitzsimmons, Benton, and Bill Walker, a promising lefthander. McGraw had high hopes for the club. The Giants had been in the thick of the pennant races since Ott's rookie year, but had lacked the overall strength to go all the way. This club appeared to have better balance.

The Giants began the season on a cold, damp day in Philadelphia as Hubbell won on the strength of a six-run, ninth-inning Giants rally. O'Doul hit two home runs over Baker Bowl's nearby right field fence, an early sign that McGraw had made a mistake in trading him. Still the Giants did well in the first couple of weeks, sparked by Ott who had ten home runs with the season barely a month old. But there were signs of trouble ahead. Roush was hurt badly in a fall in the outfield, and he was out for a month. Andy Cohen was in and out of the lineup with spike wounds and other injuries. Leach was a flop, and he was traded to the Braves. And Benton was ineffective after his magnificent 1928 season.

An early bright spot came on May 8 when Hubbell pitched a no-hitter against the Pirates at the Polo Grounds. His only difficulty came in the ninth inning when two Giants errors left two men on with none out. But the calm screwballer struck out Lloyd Waner, then started a game-ending double play on Paul Waner's smash back to the box. Ott supported his roommate with two home runs.

Mel continued to pound the ball consistently and for distance. On May 16 he hit for the cycle in a game at Boston. His seventh-inning homer landed halfway up the right field bleacher section, the longest drive into that sector since spacious Braves Field opened in 1915. Mel's powerful hitting continued in June. On June 19, the sturdy little guy had six extra-base hits in a doubleheader win in Philadelphia, with two homers and two doubles in the first game and two doubles in the second game. The following day Mel batted in three runs, his eleventh consecutive game with at least one RBI.

The Giants dropped well off the pace by mid-season, and the club was effectively out of the race by the end of July. Solid hitting by Ott, Terry, and Lindstrom, and the effective pitching of Hubbell, Fitzsimmons, and Walker were wasted. Again, as in the past few years, the club lacked the pitching depth that McGraw believed he had at the start of the season.

A lineup shift in early August did not help the Giants, and it made all hands look foolish. On August 9 the Giants batted out of order in Cincinnati but got away with it. McGraw had switched the usual batting order, spotting Ott in the third slot ahead of Terry and moving Terry to

Ott's normal cleanup spot. In the Giants' half of the first inning, by force of habit, Terry batted before Ott and the Reds did not catch the error. In the third inning, the Giants got it straight and Ott stepped up to the plate before Terry, to the confusion of the fans and to the chagrin of Reds manager Jack Hendricks when he realized his earlier lack of alertness.

The final item of interest in a disappointing season was Ott's attempt to break the National League record for home runs in a season, held by Rogers Hornsby with 42 in 1922. On September 24, Mel hit his 41st and 42nd homers of the season to tie Hornsby. On October 5, Ott and the Phillies' Chuck Klein began the day's meaningless (the Cubs had clinched the pennant) doubleheader in Philadelphia on the next-to-last day of the season tied with 42 home runs. Klein homered in his first at-bat, breaking Hornsby's record. Mel singled and walked in the first game and singled in his first at-bat in the nightcap.

According to an account in the *New York American*, on Mel's next at-bat, Phillies pitcher Phil Collins threw the first three pitches "increasingly wide." The next pitch was described as "even wider," but the little slugger went after it, swinging and missing. The same thing happened on the following pitch. The next pitch was so far outside that "Ott couldn't have reached it with a pole." In a flagrant exhibition of poor sportsmanship by Phillies manager Burt Shotton (the Branch Rickey underling who would succeed Leo Durocher as Brooklyn Dodgers manager 20 years later), Ott was walked intentionally in his remaining five trips to the plate to protect Klein's lead. The last walk came with the bases loaded, forcing in a run, and Mel was so disgusted that, with the Giants having a lopsided lead, he deliberately stepped off first base and allowed himself to be tagged out. With today's greater emphasis on records, it would be inconceivable that a contender for a record would be so unfairly treated, especially if the game was being televised. Boston held Mel homerless the next day, and he finished the season one home run behind Klein.

In addition to his emergence as a great hitter in 1929, Ott gained recognition as a premier right fielder. In that year Mel participated in a remarkable 12 double plays, a record for outfielders which still stands 70 years later. During that season he had an impressive 26 outfield assists, a total he never exceeded. The reason is simple. Base runners learned to advance very cautiously on balls hit to Ott.

Mel also had great offensive statistics in his breakthrough year. He had career highs in doubles, homers, RBIs, runs scored, and slugging percentage. His 42 home runs and 151 RBIs are the most ever for players who were 20 or younger when the season began. Mel proved that he was a great hitter on the road as well as at the Polo Grounds; he set still-existing

National League away-from-home records for runs scored (79) and RBIs (87). Moreover, he hit more home runs on the road (22) than he had at the Polo Grounds.

Other Giants players had decent years as the club finished in third place with an 84-67 record. Bill Terry had an outstanding season with 226 hits and a splendid .372 average. Freddie Lindstrom hit .319, and Edd Roush hit .324, despite missing more than 40 games. Hubbell led the pitchers with an 18-11 record, Fitzsimmons won 15 games, and Bill Walker won 14 decisions with a league-leading 3.09 earned-run average.

McGraw's disappointment over his club's season was deepened by the sensational performances of players the Giants had traded for players who were no longer with the Giants. Rogers Hornsby hit .380 with 149 RBIs, while being voted league MVP for leading the Cubs to the pennant. And Lefty O'Doul led the league with a sparkling .398 average and a league-record 254 hits. The writers did not let McGraw forget what these performances could have meant to the Polo Grounders.

The season had indeed been a personal triumph for Mel, now being referred to euphoniously by some of the writers as the "boy bomber from the bayou." He had fulfilled the promise of his three years in training, years when almost every other player of his tender years would have been learning his trade in the minor leagues. Mel had shown that he was, and would likely continue to be, all that Harry Williams had predicted him to become, all that McGraw had worked for, and all that his family and hometown fans had hoped for. He was the brightest young star in the big leagues.

The stock market collapsed in late October, heralding the approach of the country's worst depression. What followed would linger on for the next decade. Yet its effect was not immediately felt in the baseball world. As a matter of fact, major league teams had a 33 percent increase in their profits in 1930 compared with 1929. Several of the Giants, most notably the tough-bargaining Terry, held out in anticipation of salary cuts which the club could attribute to the depressed economy. Terry signed his contract shortly before spring training, not unusually late for him. But Edd Roush refused to sign his sharply reduced contract, and he sat out the entire season.

As spring training got under way in early March, Mel came up to McGraw one day and said, "I found a man in my room this morning, Mr. McGraw." The Old man was taken aback until the warm young star added triumphantly, "I'm 21 today!"

There were early indications that 1930 would be even more of a hitter's year than 1929. The baseball had been modified with the stitches lowered, making it harder for pitchers to get a good grip on the ball. The resiliency of the ball had been increased since Babe Ruth's hitting exploits of the early twenties had shown that fans favored high scoring games. The 1930 baseball had even more bounce than those used in earlier years. Famed writer Ring Lardner described the 1930 ball as "a leather-covered sphere stuffed with dynamite."

The Giants started the 1930 season with rookie Eddie (Doc) Marshall at second base and Walter Roettger, obtained from the Cardinals to replace Roush, in center field. Otherwise, the lineup was the same as the one that finished the previous season. The only thing really new was that the Polo Grounds had been equipped with an amplified loudspeaker system, replacing the leather-lunged club employee who used a megaphone to announce the batteries from behind the plate.

The Giants started the season in good style as lefty Bill Walker defeated the Braves 3–2. McGraw's teams were noted for their fast starts, and this club was no exception as it reeled off six more wins before its first loss. But reality set in by mid–June. The Giants slipped back to third place, six games behind Brooklyn, now called "the Robins" in deference to their manager, Wilbert Robinson. The rotund Robinson had been one of McGraw's pre–1900 teammates with the famous Baltimore Orioles.

Terry led a potent Giants attack, hitting well over .400 in the first two months of the campaign. Ott, Lindstrom, Jackson, and Hogan also were hitting over .300 as batting averages exploded with the use of the new "rabbit ball." The Giants' pitching reliables, Fitzsimmons, Hubbell, and Walker coped with the enlivened new ball reasonably well, but the rest of the pitchers were ineffective.

Through July and August the Giants remained close to Brooklyn and Chicago as they took turns leading the league. As the season moved along, McGraw's health problems forced him off the bench, and coach Dave Bancroft filled in for him for a few games. As the Giants struggled to stay close to the leaders, McGraw's extreme irritability increased. All of the Giants were subjected to McGraw's vicious tirades since the portly manager played no favorites. Terry and Lindstrom were the Giants who were least willing to put up with the ailing manager's attacks. By the middle of the season, Lindstrom was shouting back at McGraw. Peter Williams, in his *When the Giants Were Giants*, wrote that Terry blew up at McGraw once, then did not talk to him for more than a year. There were no reports as to how the placid Mel Ott reacted to his mentor's frequent explosions. McGraw's treatment of his players is reminiscent of what Green Bay Packer lineman Jerry Kramer said of his tyrannical coach, Vince Lombardi. Said Kramer, "He treated us all the same, like dogs."

Catcher Shanty Hogan was a constant McGraw target, especially, because of Hogan's gargantuan tastes for food and beer. The good-natured Irishman had come to the Giants in 1928 as a 220-pounder. He continued to gain weight as McGraw constantly nagged him about his prodigious food consumption. As a result, Hogan tried every kind of subterfuge to conceal his eating excesses from McGraw. Best remembered were phony meal checks which he talked waitresses into giving him. The meal check submitted to McGraw showed that Shanty was eating fish, salad, and fresh fruit when, in reality, the big guy was eating multiple helpings of large steaks, fried potatoes, and Boston cream pie.

In later years, Ott enjoyed reminiscing about the old days with McGraw. He described a McGraw-Hogan encounter in a game in 1930 when the big catcher came back to the dugout after striking out with men on base.

"Hogan was burning," said Mel. "He threw his bat into the dirt in front of the dugout and said: 'Of all the ––– –––.'

"Mr. McGraw heard him and said: 'Don't call me a ––– –––.'

"And Hogan said, 'I didn't call you anything of the kind.'

"McGraw's beefy face reddened. He shouted, 'No, I guess not. I guess I'm deaf. Don't try to get out of it by lying.'"

Ott continued, "Well, as a matter of fact, Hogan had been calling himself names but when Mr. McGraw wouldn't let go of him, he got his back up and he yelled, 'All right, then! Have it your way! You are a ––– –––.'

"Now they really went at it. Everybody on the bench was dying to laugh, and not daring to, but fortunately, just about that time the side was retired, so we could leave the dugout. Of course, they took it up after the game, but the rest of us showered and left." Ott laughed and said, "I never did find out how it came out."

On August 31, Mel gave an impressive display of power in a game against the Braves at the Polo Grounds before more than 40,000 fans. He doubled and then homered twice into the upper right field stands. He followed these blasts with his third homer of the day, a tremendous drive which cleared the right field roof and disappeared completely out of the park. With the big crowd rooting him on in his last at-bat, Mel hit a long drive which was caught at the base of the right field wall, 380 feet from the plate.

The Cardinals came on with a rush in the last month of the season, taking over the league lead in mid–September. Meanwhile, the Pirates ended the Giants' pennant hopes by sweeping a doubleheader, leaving the Giants in fourth place, five and a half games off the pace with only 12 games left.

Bill Terry's effort to hit over .400 was the only remaining matter of interest as the Giants aimed for a third-place finish. On September 27, the next-to-last day of the season, the big first baseman tied Lefty O'Doul's National League record for hits in a season at 254 with a single off Phillies pitcher Phil Collins—he of the infamous intentional walk episode a year earlier when he robbed Ott of a chance for the home run title. Terry went hitless the following day as the Giants clinched third place with a win over the Phillies. Memphis Bill would up the season with a .401 mark and he remains the last National Leaguer to hit over .400.

It had been another good year for Mel. In a year when the overall league batting average was .303, he hit .349, his highest full-season batting average. He led the league in on-base-percentage and led the Giants with a surprisingly low 25 home runs, considering the liveliness of the baseball.

As soon as the season ended, Mel returned home to keep an important date with Mildred Wattigny. They married on October 2.

$\mathcal{E}$ND OF AN $\mathcal{E}$RA

The Giants made very few changes during the offseason. They had purchased third baseman Johnny Vergez from Oakland of the Pacific Coast League and McGraw proclaimed loudly that the deal would greatly strengthen the club. He planned to play Vergez at third base and move Lindstrom to the outfield. Some of the writers questioned his decision to move an established star third baseman to the outfield and replace him with an untried youngster. Time proved that Lindstrom would be a good outfielder, but Vergez was not an adequate replacement for Freddy, and the proud Lindstrom took McGraw's defense of the shift as unjustified criticism of his play at third.

Edd Roush, displeased at the contract offered him, and not too happy playing for McGraw, refused to report to the Giants' training camp at San Antonio. He was sold back to Cincinnati, and Lindstrom took his place in center field. Newlywed Ott, accompanied in camp by Mildred, would be in right field with Freddy Leach in left.

Terry held out as usual, but he signed eventually for $22,500. The other infielders were second baseman Hughie Critz, obtained from the Reds the previous season, Jackson, and Vergez. Hogan was the regular catcher; the starting pitchers were Hubbell, Fitzsimmons, Walker, and journeyman lefthand spitballer Clarence Mitchell, who came in a trade with the Cardinals.

The baseball played in 1931 was expected to resemble more closely the style that McGraw favored, with more emphasis on the defensive game. The covering of the ball was thickened and the stitches were raised. As a result, the ball was less resilient and easier for pitchers to grip, especially helpful in throwing curveballs. In addition, the scoring rules were changed to charge a batter with a time at bat after hitting a sacrifice fly. This had the effect of lowering batting averages. (The rule has since been changed back to its former status.)

The changes achieved the desired de-emphasis on offense. Compared with 1930, the National League's overall batting average declined a very significant 26 points, and home runs were reduced by 44 percent of the whopping 892 homers hit in 1930. The aggregate league earned-run-average also declined, from 4.97 to 3.86.

The season began well as the Giants won 14 of their first 20 games. The club sparred for the lead with the Cardinals and the Cubs until early June when it fell back after a poor western trip. Ott continued to produce runs in the early going although his batting average fell below .300. His popularity with the fans continued to grow, and the writers began to refer to the right field stands at the Polo Grounds as "Ottville." Many of Mel's fans abandoned expensive box seats near the plate for lower priced seats in order to be closer to their youthful favorite.

In June, to the disappointment of the denizens of "Ottville," Mel was moved to center and Lindstrom took over right field. A few days later, Lindstrom broke his ankle sliding into a base in Philadelphia, and he was out for the rest of the season. Smooth-fielding Hughie Critz injured his shoulder badly in a play at second base, and he was lost for the last two-thirds of the season.

By mid–July the Giants were eight and a half games behind the league-leading Cardinals, and McGraw appeared to have lost confidence in his club. He frequently began interviews with the complaint that "the men don't get out and fight for the games like they used to—that's what is wrong with baseball." A writer recalled how, in the old days, "everybody knew there'd be plenty of excitement to stir the blood when the Giants came to town. Now they were just another club."

In this atmosphere of falling spirits, Mel did not slack off. By early September he had hit a home run off Phillies righthander Frank Watt in every game Watt had pitched against the Giants during the season. As Ott stepped in to hit against Watt for the last time in the season, the pitcher shouted in to him sarcastically, "Here's your last chance to keep your record, Mel." On the first pitch, the stocky little slugger hit a line drive to deep right center in the cavernous Polo Grounds. As the ball ricocheted around the bullpen, Ott circled the bases. Watt cursed him out every inch of the way. This was the only inside-the-park homer of Mel's career other than his first major league home run in 1927.

The Cardinals clinched the pennant by the middle of September. A few days later the Giants played the Cards in a meaningless game in St. Louis. Burleigh Grimes hit Ott in the back of his head, and Mel dropped to the ground unconscious. Frank Graham wrote in the *Sun*:

> Grimes was a hard-bitten, hard-fighting ball player and would
> throw at batters to loosen them up. But everybody knew he didn't

throw at Ott. There was no occasion for it. And then, the hitter
was Ott and nobody ever threw at him. The ball struck Mel a fearful blow and, as he dropped, Grimes rushed in from the pitchers
box, almost in tears. While Ott was being carried to the clubhouse, Grimes sat in the dugout, and it was only on the insistence
of Cardinals manager Gabby Street that he continued in the game.
As soon as the game was over, he rushed to the hospital and was
much relieved to learn that the injury was only a concussion.

All this was natural enough. There have been few pitchers who,
no matter how much they might throw at the hitters, weren't upset
when they finally hit one. But the response of the fans was amaz-
ing. They telephoned, they sent wires, they wrote letters, they sent
fruit and flowers. To them he wasn't just a visiting ball player who
had been hit by a pitch. He was Mel Ott—as much of a hero to
them as any of the St. Louis players.

Mel spent a few days in the hospital and, with the pennant winner
decided, he was sent home. The Giants finished in second place, a full 13
games behind the powerful Cardinals. Terry had another fine year, hitting
.349, only .003 behind the Cardinals' Chick Hafey for the batting title.
Memphis Bill led the league in runs scored and in triples. Despite missing
the last two weeks of the season, Ott led the Giants with 29 home runs,
only two behind Chuck Klein's league-leading total. Mel also led the club
in RBIs, only six behind Klein who led the league. Fitzsimmons topped the
Giants' starters with 18 wins, and Hubbell won 14 decisions.

The Giants had a serious, long-standing front office problem which
had come to a head. Since 1920 the National Exhibition Company (the
Giants' corporate name) had been run by three ever-quarreling, rough-
and-ready men. Charles A. Stoneham, who had made his fortune in a
number of shady stock market ventures, was the principal stockholder.
Club treasurer Francis X. McQuade had been a judge in magistrate's court
and a prominent figure in Tammany Hall affairs. And McGraw had a relatively small amount of stock in the Giants, but he, of course, essentially
ran the club on and off the field.

In 1928 a bitter quarrel between Stoneham and McQuade led to
McQuade's dismissal as club treasurer. Two years later McQuade filed a
suit to recover his position and accompanying $10,000 a year in back sal-
ary. Stoneham and McGraw filed a countersuit for $250,000, charging
McQuade with "willfully and maliciously" trying to "wreck and destroy"
the National Exhibition Company. Eventually a New York State judge
threw out McQuade's suit, but an appellate court ruled that he was entitled to reinstatement as club treasurer. A subsequent appeal to a higher
court by the National Exhibition Company protesting the reinstatement
was upheld, and McQuade was left with nothing to show for his efforts.

The chaotic front office situation was a matter of interest to the players. But a more pressing concern was how the deepening Depression would affect contracts offered for the 1932 season. The players' concerns were justified. All of the Giants received sharply reduced contracts. Terry's contract called for a 20 percent cut of $5,000. Ott normally was easy for the club to sign, and he was not the type to negotiate through the press. But this time he did go public, telling John Drebinger of the *Times*, "In view of the fact that the Giants made money last season, I don't see how they expect a man to play ball for such low salaries. I hope I have mine adjusted, but I certainly don't feel I deserve such a cut." Eventually all of the players signed before spring training began, except Terry who did not sign until the players had been at the club's training camp in Los Angeles for two weeks.

When John McGraw began his thirtieth year as manager of the Giants in 1932, most baseball men rated him the greatest manager the game had known—10 pennants, only two seasons out of the first division, and a highly regarded baseball strategist and developer of talent. But as the training camp opened, he was a deeply troubled man. The club had not won a pennant since 1924.

Next to McGraw's vituperative attacks, his players most resented his never-ending signals from the bench, some of them given on each pitch of the game. Frank Graham, in his book, *McGraw of the Giants*, told a story, whether apocryphal or true, that typified Freddy Lindstrom's frame of mind and that of the other Giants as well. The Giants were playing a spring training exhibition game in Oakland. As Graham described it:

> McGraw, instead of sitting on the bench, sunned himself in the center field bleachers.... Mrs. Blanche McGraw, seated in a box near the dugout, was uncertain whether John was going to stay for the full game, so at the end of one inning she called to Lindstrom (who was playing center field) ... to have him ask her husband what he intended to do. Lindstrom didn't hear her and one of the reporters, seated nearby, yelled to him and, as he turned, indicated that Mrs. McGraw wanted to speak to him. He came over to the box and she said, in mock severity:
> "Freddy, why don't you pay attention?"
> His eyes widened.
> "Good God!" he exclaimed. "Are you giving signals, too?"

The Giants were rated the team to beat despite two straight pennants by the Cardinals. They started the season with the same lineup which had opened in 1931 except for Len Koenecke in left field. Koenecke, obtained from Indianapolis over the winter, was touted as a coming star. However, he fared poorly and was replaced by Joe (Jo-Jo) Moore, a bone-thin Texan who would be a Giants mainstay for the next ten years. The starting pitchers were Hubbell, Fitzsimmons, Walker, lefthander Jim Mooney, and veteran righthander Herman Bell. Hal (Prince Hal) Schumacher, a young righthand sinkerballer, became a starter during the season. Like Joe Moore, he would be a Polo Grounds favorite for the next decade.

The club started the season poorly and stumbled through April and May. The pitching was weak, only Ott and Terry were hitting, and Travis Jackson suffered from serious knee ailments that forced him to the bench. Eddie Marshall replaced Jackson with little success. (One writer was unkind enough to note that Marshall reminded him of the Ancient Mariner became he "stoppeth one of three.") McGraw's raw nerves tightened ever more under the strain of losing, and the players reacted by tightening up even more. They were afraid of missing one of McGraw's innumerable signs or of making a mistake and having to brave the tough little manager's ire. The net result was a team that was playing well below its capability. No one was surprised when the Giants began the month of June in last place.

On June 3 McGraw called Terry into his office off the Polo Grounds' clubhouse. Interestingly, the two men had not been on speaking terms for the last two years. McGraw told Terry to prop a chair against the door so they would not be interrupted.

"I thought he was going to tell me that I'd been traded," Terry told a writer later. Instead, McGraw said, "Bill, you don't have to answer this now. Wait a while, if you like, but would you like to manage the Giants?"

The composed, self-assured Terry answered without hesitation, "Mr. McGraw, there's no need for me to wait. I'll take it now."

That afternoon, although the Giants' doubleheader with the Phillies had been rained out, the press had not yet been notified of the managerial change. The *World Telegram*'s Tom Meany headed aimlessly for the Giants' clubhouse in search of a story or interview with no idea that he was falling into the biggest exclusive a New York sportswriter had obtained in years. As Meany neared the clubhouse steps, a hot dog vendor asked him, "Did you know McGraw is out, and Bill Terry is the new manager?" Meany then ran into a Giants coach who confirmed the story, pointing to a note on the clubhouse bulletin board. Meany read the full statement which described McGraw's lengthy consideration of the need to turn over the job to someone else because of his declining health. McGraw wanted a man "who was thoroughly familiar with my methods and who has learned baseball under me."

McGraw also expressed the belief that he was turning a good team over to Terry. That prompted Meany to write pointedly a few days later, "McGraw was right when he said he was turning over a good team to Terry. It's a good club all right but McGraw couldn't handle those fellows any more. A few years ago he would have made those guys produce or they would have been gone. But Mac isn't well and he knows it's best that he get out."

The secret was so well kept that Lindstrom was the only player who had known that McGraw was actively considering stepping down. Lindstrom complained angrily to his friends among the writers that the job had been promised to him. From that day on it was clear that Mel Ott's erstwhile roommate would not be with the Giants much after the 1932 season, if he lasted that long.

William Harold Terry had joined the Giants as a young lefthand pitcher in 1922. Even then he had no illusions about the glamor of big league baseball and, with a family to support, was interested only in bettering the salary he was receiving from an oil company in Memphis. He surprised McGraw with his matter-of-face reaction when offered a contract to play for the Giants. McGraw was not used to such independence in a young minor leaguer, and he probably admired Terry's attitude although he was never heard to admit it.

Terry took over with the clear understanding that he was the boss and not merely a frontman for McGraw. Assured of this, he stepped in and began to plan the moves he considered necessary to revitalize the Giants. He told the writers that he would make whatever changes he could but that the season was too far gone to make any significant personnel shifts. The players were pleased though by his first move. Terry fired the club trainer, whom the players considered to be McGraw's "stool pigeon." This move alone raised club morale considerably.

There were some memorable days for Giants fans to savor during the remainder of that lost season. The week after Terry took over the club, Ott moved the Giants out of the cellar with an impressive exhibition of clutch power hitting. On June 7 he brought down righthander Ray Kolp of the Reds with a ninth-inning home run for a 4–3 win. Two days later he beat the Reds again with a sixth-inning home run to give Giants lefty Jim Mooney a 3–2 victory. Two days after that Mel beat lefthander Larry French of the Pirates with a three-run homer.

McGraw, ever the traditionalist, had refused to follow the lead of other major league clubs that had begun to have identifying numbers sewn on the backs of their player uniforms. But Terry changed this, and the Giants players began wearing numbers in a home game against the Cardinals on June 23. Terry elected to wear number 4, and Ott was assigned number 5, and both players were those numbers for the rest of the season. Beginning with the 1933 season, Terry took over the number 3 uniform, and Mel wore number 4. Ott retained this number for the remainder of his Giants career. The Giants eventually retired the number in Ott's honor.

On August 13, Lindstrom and Terry joined Mel in another display of power hitting. Terry, Ott, and Lindstrom hit home runs on successive, fourth-inning pitches from Brooklyn righthander Hollis (Sloppy) Thurston. In the ninth inning the Giants' playing manager hit his third homer of the game, and Mel, still playing follow-the-leader, hit another blast into the upper right field seats. This was only the seventh time in baseball history that the same two players hit back-to-back home runs twice in the same game. Then, on September 20 at the Polo Grounds, Mel had four hits, including two homers, and six RBIs. In this game Memphis Bill had a monstrous inside-the-park home run that landed on the fly in the runway between the right and left center bleachers. The drive landed only a few feet in front of the Eddie Grant Memorial which stood 483 feet from the plate.

As usual, Terry and Ott dominated the club's hitting statistics. Terry was second in the league in hitting with a .350 average, and in runs scored, total bases, and base hits. Ott tied Chuck Klein in home runs with 38, and he led the league in bases on balls.

Even without any personnel changes, Terry succeeded in raising the club from last place to a sixth-place tie with the Cardinals, who also had flopped badly. Perhaps much of his success was inevitable. The Giants clearly had too much talent to remain in last place, and the easing of tensions after McGraw's departure was bound to improve the club's play. In 40 games under McGraw, the Giants won 17 and lost 23, a .425 pace. For the remainder of the season the club won 55 and lost 59, an improved .482 clip.

In light of the team's improvement, the Giants gave Terry a two-year, player-manager contract in September. It called for $30,000 a year, one of the highest salaries paid any player or manager in those depression-ridden times. But the real impact of Terry's leadership was not apparent until after the season. Recognizing the need for a competent catcher, Terry swung a major deal with the Cardinals, obtaining second-string catcher Gus Mancuso and righthander Ray Starr for pitchers Bill Walker and Jim Mooney, outfielder Ethan Allen and catcher Bob O'Farrell. The stocky, swarthy Mancuso would prove to be everything Terry wanted—a good handler of pitchers, durable, intelligent, and a key member of the Giants for several years.

Lindstrom had to go despite his great ability and long-time friend-ship with Terry because of his unconcealed disappointment at not get-ting the managerial spot. At the end of the season Terry traded him to the Pirates for outfielder George (Kiddo) Davis and righthander Glenn Spencer. Years later Lindstrom told Terry that he had made a mistake in asking to be traded because he missed out on a number of successful Giants seasons that followed his departure.

In other offseason transactions, pitchers Waite Hoyt and Clarence Mitchell were released, and Shanty Hogan was sold back to the Braves. Hoyt, well past his prime, had been a New York Yankee standout in the twenties. Tom Meany wrote of Hogan's departure, "Unfortunately, although Hogan eats like Babe Ruth, he plays like Hogan."

Although considerable attention had been paid to McGraw's curfew rules, bedchecks, continual signs from the bench, and other tactics, it was clear that these measures had not improved either team performance or esprit de corps. In his less flamboyant way, Terry set out to develop a more businesslike, no-nonsense approach to the game, a style more in keeping with his own personality. Typically, he had no immediate comment about off-the-field activities during McGraw's last managerial years, but his first statements to the press stressed his desire for stricter control of his play-ers' extracurricular pursuits and, unlike the free-wheeling McGraw, a close-mouthed attitude on the part of his players toward the press. It was clear that a new era had begun at the Polo Grounds for Mel Ott, his team-mates, and their fans.

A new era as parents would begin for Mel and Mildred. Their first child, Margaret Carolyn, was born on December 1.

Chapter 7

ᵂORLD CHAMPIONS

Franklin Delano Roosevelt was elected by an overwhelming margin in November. After he took office in March, his New Deal began to develop a stunning array of programs to deal with the nation's multitude of economic and social ills. It was in this grim environment that the Giants began spring training.

On paper the Giants club, which assembled in Los Angeles, was not a serious pennant contender. The consensus of players, managers, and sportswriters throughout the league was that the Giants were facing a long season with only four proven stars, a prayer, and a string of undistinguished or unproven players. The stars were Bill Terry, Mel Ott, Carl Hubbell, and Freddy Fitzsimmons. The prayer was that gimpy-kneed shortstop Travis Jackson, out of action for much of the 1932 season, could regain his old agility and play regularly.

Manager Terry was one of the ranking players of the day, a straight-away, line drive drive hitter who consistently hit for high average and with power. Memphis Bill also was one of the best-fielding first basemen ever to play the game. Moreover, his managerial duties did not seem to affect his playing.

Ott, beginning his eighth full year with the Giants at the age of 24, was one of the premier sluggers and outfielders in the game. Hubbell had pitched well since his first season with the Giants in 1928. The slender, frail-looking lefthander possessed an adequate fast ball, a good curve, and marvelous control to go with his famous screwball. The "scroogie" was simply a reverse curve which broke away from righthand hitters when thrown by the lefthanded Hubbell. Years of throwing the pitch with an outward reverse thrust of his elbow and wrist had caused King Carl's left palm and elbow to face out as his arm hung down at his side. The Meeker, Oklahoma, native was highly respected for his artful style and quiet concentration, his imperturbability, and his ability to win the big game.

Fitzsimmons, a stout and stouthearted knuckleballer, was an offseason chicken farmer in Arcadia, California. He had an unusual "turntable" pitching style, whirling with his back to the plate before wheeling back around to deliver the pitch. Despite his bulky frame, Fitzsimmons was an excellent fielder and noted for his fiercely competitive approach to the game.

Travis (Stonewall) Jackson had been the Giants' regular shortstop since the 1923 season until knee injuries limited his play in 1932. A steady hitter and fielder with a rifle arm, he was one of the most accomplished bunters in the game and was a great Polo Grounds favorite.

There were a number of other experienced players in camp. Round-faced Sam Leslie was a good-hit, mediocre-field first baseman. Second baseman Hughie Critz, the pride of Greenwood, Mississippi, had been around for some time but was still a good fielder. Third baseman Johnny Vergez was a steady fielder who had been hampered by injuries. George Davis was a competent outfielder but only a fair hitter. Outfielder Joe Moore, a gaunt, hollow-cheeked Texan with a great arm, had been a part-timer for the past two years. Gus Mancuso, obtained from the Cardinals in the big winter trade, was slated to be the first-string catcher.

The Giants had experienced pitchers as well. Terry was particularly high on Hal Schumacher, a sinkerball-throwing righthander from Dolgeville, New York, by way of St. Lawrence University. A grim competitor with a hard-throwing, arm-wrenching motion, Schumacher had pitched for the Giants for the last two seasons. Other pitchers included Ray Starr, obtained in the Mancuso trade; ex–Pirate Glenn Spencer; Leroy (Tarzan) Parmelee, whose nickname derived from his wildness; lefthander Al Smith; Herman Bell, a seasoned reliever; and Adolfo Luque, a wily 43-year-old Cuban whose National League career dated back to 1919 when he pitched for the Reds.

There were a number of promising youngsters in camp. The infielders included Smokey Joe Martin, a California product recruited by oldtime Giants star Fred Snodgrass; Blondy Ryan, a spirited Holy Cross graduate; and Byrnie James. Young outfielders included Hank Leiber, a blond youngster who had been brought to McGraw by ex–Giants pitcher Art Nehf; Homer Peel, up from the Texas League; and speedy Len Koenecke. Catcher Paul Richards, a Waxahachie, Texas, native later to gain wider fame as a manager and general manager, was Mancuso's backup man.

The exhibition season began in unpromising fashion. It became apparent very soon that Jackson's ailing knees had not recovered sufficiently to permit him to play regularly at shortstop. A disappointed Terry reluctantly installed the untried Ryan at shortstop.

Even the elements seemed to foreshadow a difficult year. On March 11, during an exhibition game against the Cubs at Wrigley Field in Los Angeles, a major earthquake struck. While the ground trembled and the steel stands swayed, the terrified players huddled around second base. The following day, as the earth tremors continued to shake buildings, Terry announced tentative plans to move the club to Phoenix, Arizona, to complete spring training if the tremors continued another day. But the upheavals subsided, and the club completed its stay in Los Angeles before breaking camp and beginning its long trek eastward.

Terry continued to experiment with different lineups. Always the realist, he recognized that the Giants' offense would depend primarily upon his and Ott's long-ball hitting and on the ability of the other players to come up with key hits. Baseball men predicted a low-scoring year after playing a few exhibition games with the deadened baseball which would be used during the regular season. Terry sought to develop the team's defense, and the big questions here were how well Ryan would fill in for Jackson and how much the veteran Critz had slowed down. Finally, there was the pitching staff. Hubbell and Fitzsimmons were established starters, but would Schumacher fulfill his promise and Parmelee control his wildness?

One casualty of the barnstorming tour east was coach Billy Southworth who suffered a minor knee injury in El Paso. Typical of the bland reporting style of that era, the *New York Times* account stated simply that Southworth's injury would force him to return to his home "for an indefinite period" and that he would be replaced by former Giants catcher Frank (Pancho) Snyder. There were rumors that Southworth's quick replacement was the result of a violent disagreement with Terry, his old comrade-in-arms in the McGraw era during the twenties. Memphis Bill turned up the next day with a black eye, which the *World-Telegram*'s Tom Meany attributed to Southworth. There was another theory that Terry's black eye was the result of a foul ball which hit the manager in the nose. Regardless, the story, which would have made headlines in today's papers, stuck despite denials by both Southworth and Terry.

When the regular season began, the Giants' stock as a pennant contender remained low. The Associated Press sportswriters' poll found 42 favoring the Pirates to win the pennant, 21 picking the Cubs, the Cardinals and the Phillies both collecting eight votes, and the Dodgers and the Braves both receiving one vote. Overall, the Giants ranked sixth, with only 18 voters picking them to finish in the first division. With this foreboding outlook the Terrymen began the season.

They did reasonably well through April only to lose Terry with a broken wrist at the end of the month. Still the team continued to win as

Sam Leslie filled in adequately for Memphis Bill. But the big story was Hubbell's brilliant pitching as he pitched 26 consecutive scoreless innings. The writers began to refer to Hubbell as "Meal Ticket," which Terry, for some reason, resented.

It soon became apparent that the Pirates, Braves, Cubs, and Cardinals would be the teams that the Giants would have to beat. The Pirates had powerful hitting but weak pitching. Manager Bill McKechnie's Braves were a weaker-hitting team, but they had three solid starting pitchers with righthanders Ben Cantwell and Fred Frankhouse, and lefthander Ed Brandt. Ex-Giant Shanty Hogan was the Braves' catcher, still fighting his twin enemies—a knife and a fork.

The Cubs were a potent club with established regulars such as manager–first baseman Charlie Grimm, Billy Herman, Billy Jurges, Gabby Hartnett, and Frank Demaree. Their pitching staff included Guy Bush, Charley Root, and Lon Warneke. The aggressive, up-and-coming Cardinals, an early version of the famous "Gas House Gang," were sparked by Frankie Frisch, Leo Durocher, Dizzy Dean, Joe Medwick, and Pepper Martin.

By Memorial Day the Giants had won 21 games and lost 16, nothing sensational, but enough to position them in third place, two and a half games behind the Pirates, and three games in back of the first place Cardinals. Finally jelling, the Giants began to win a series of low-scoring games. Hubbell, Fitzsimmons, Schumacher, and Parmelee rotated starting assignments, and Luque, Bell, Starr, and the all-purpose Hubbell excelled in relief. As Terry anticipated, Mancuso proved a steadying influence behind the plate. The veteran Critz and youthful Blondy Ryan worked well together around second base, and Johnny Vergez fielded competently at third base and contributed several key hits. In the outfield Ott led the attack as expected, and George Davis handled center field adequately. Joe Moore established himself solidly in left field and in the leadoff slot in spite of his tendency to swing at the first pitch thrown to him, usually considered an anathema in that position in the batting order.

A number of the Giants, including Ott, rented apartments in the Washington Heights area, a few miles north of the Polo Grounds. On their short trips to and from the ballpark, they were struck by the plight of the homeless and the hungry in that economically troubled time. Decades later Joe Moore recalled it vividly:

> Baseball was good to me because we played in a time when you couldn't hardly get a hold of a dollar. People can't believe that unless they lived in that era. In New York I saw street corner after street corner where they had soup kitchens, and the people waiting

would be four abreast and the lines would run for several blocks.

Terry returned to the lineup in early June, and the Giants took over the league lead on June 10 when Fitzsimmons defeated the Phillies. On June 15, satisfied that his wrist had recovered satisfactorily, Terry traded Sam Leslie to the Dodgers for lefthander Watson Clark and old friend Lefty O'Doul. The trade was hailed by Giants fans as pennant insurance because Hubbell was the only lefthand pitcher on the staff and O'Doul, while showing signs of wear and tear, had led the league in hitting again in 1932.

A few days later Terry took his club to Canton, in upstate New York, to watch Hal Schumacher receive his diploma from St. Lawrence University and then play the college team in an exhibition game. Peter Williams, in *When the Giants Were Giants*, wrote:

> Tough ballplayers though these guys were, they all put on jackets and ties for the pre-game ceremony. In the pictures, they looked good; one might have mistaken them for a group of insurance salesmen, even deans. Like Terry, the other players were fond of and respected Schumacher, who, at bottom, was probably as happy about being given the day as he was to get through it.

One of the season's high points came on July 2 when the Giants won a memorable doubleheader from the Cardinals at the Polo Grounds. Hubbell pitched an incredible 18 scoreless innings to win the first game 1–0 after Tex Carleton had pitched 16 scoreless innings and had been relieved by Jesse Haines. King Carl pitched perfect ball in 12 of the innings, allowing only six hits with no more than one coming in any inning. He struck out 12 batters and walked none. A single by Hughie Critz drove in the game's only run. In the second game, Parmelee, pitching in semi-darkness (the Polo Grounds did not yet have lights) and a steady drizzle, shut out the Cardinals, again by a 1–0 score. Presumably the Cardinals were not enthusiastic about facing the wild-throwing Parmelee with such poor visibility. The Giants' run came on a homer by Vergez. The one sobering note was a leg injury to Blondy Ryan, a spike wound which required 13 stitches. Stiff-legged Travis Jackson replaced him.

The Giants lost their next seven games as the crippled Jackson played poorly. After their seventh loss, the Giants received an unabashedly confident telegram from the injured Ryan. It read: "They cannot beat us. Am en route." The telegram was posted on the Giants' clubhouse bulletin board and remained the team's watchword for the rest of the season.

On July 13, with a football shinguard protecting his injured leg, Ryan replaced the faltering Jackson, and the Giants' fortunes again were on the upswing.

Hubbell continued his marvelous pitching, setting a record of 45 consecutive scoreless innings on August 1. Unfortunately, he lost the game to the Braves, and the Giants slipped back to a two-and-a-half-game lead over the second place Pirates. But by Labor Day the Giants had rebounded and increased their lead to seven and a half games.

There was another electrifying doubleheader against the Cardinals on August 27 at the Polo Grounds. The Cards won the first game 7–1 as Dizzy Dean defeated Schumacher. Following a tumultuous scene precipitated by the usually calm Terry, the second game was called because of darkness after eight innings. In the top of the eighth the Giants were leading 4–1, but the Cardinals threatened. With two men on, Frisch sent a high, bouncing "Baltimore chop" to Terry, who grabbed the ball and dashed for first base, arriving there almost simultaneously with the headlong-diving Frisch. Umpire Ted McGrew called Frisch safe, and the lid blew off.

White with rage, Terry charged McGrew. The umpire very emphatically waved Memphis Bill off the premises with the traditional jerk of the thumb. Uncharacteristically, Terry responded by firing his cap and glove to the ground and kicking both vigorously. In the meantime, fans in the upper deck took a hand in the affair, and pop bottles began raining down on the field. When order finally was restored after a riotous 15 minutes, McGrew caused even greater consternation by ordering peacemakers Mel Ott and coach Tom Clarke off the field, but permitting the infuriated Terry to remain in the game. After the game, Ott reported the following dialogue. McGrew: "Terry you're out of here!" Terry: "You can't throw me out; I'm the manager and our only first baseman." McGrew, turning to Ott and Clarke who were trying to placate the raging Terry, then boomed, "Okay, then you guys are out!"

Opening in Boston on their closing road drive to the pennant, the Giants dropped the first game, and at the same time they also lost third baseman Johnny Vergez for the season with appendicitis. Terry called on Hubbell the next day. With Travis Jackson replacing Vergez, the "Meal Ticket" turned in a masterpiece to win 2–0 in ten innings. Reformed baseball writer Heywood Broun, looking on from the press box, marveled at Hubbell's control as the great lefthander pitched his tenth shutout of the season. Hubbell not only did not walk a batter, but never was behind a hitter at any time in the ten innings, or even went to a three and two count in the game. "Such control in a lefthander is incredible," wrote Broun.

"There must be a skeleton in Hubbell's closet somewhere, perhaps a righthanded maternal grandmother."

Taking the next three games from the Braves, the Giants moved on to Pittsburgh where they won two games out of five. Then came Chicago and the final threat. The Giants lost the first two games but came back to win the next four and knock the Cubs out of the race. They clinched the pennant in St. Louis on September 19 when the Pirates lost to the Phillies. Simultaneous with the announcement of the Pirates' score, Ott celebrated in his own way by blasting his twenty-third homer of the year over the Sportsmans Park right field pavilion.

The exuberant Terry called the pennant win his greatest thrill in 18 years in the game, especially in view of the Giants' low rating at the start of the season. Terry's satisfaction was fueled also by the criticism he had received around the league. In Boston he had been described as being "too aloof." In Chicago, and he carried the clipping around in his wallet, a writer referred to him as "the most unpopular manager ever to win a pennant because of his surly disposition." In Pittsburgh they thought he "lacked color." Regardless, the Giants had won the pennant, winding up five games ahead of the Pirates, six and a half in front of the Cubs, and nine games ahead of the Braves.

In a year in which hitting performances were held down by the dead ball, commendable individual performances were turned in by Hubbell, Schumacher, Terry, and Ott. Hubbell, voted the league MVP, led the league with 23 wins, ten shutouts, and an astounding 1.66 ERA. And he was second to Dizzy Dean in strikeouts. Schumacher ranked in the top five in wins, ERA, and shutouts. Terry hit .322, the fourth highest batting average in the league. And despite his sub-par .283 batting average, Ott led the league in walks and ranked third in homers and RBIs.

New York roared a boisterous welcome to the Giants as their special train arrived at Grand Central Station from St. Louis. A crowd of more than 10,000, headed by two brass bands, put on a spontaneous demonstration that scarcely seemed possible in a city supposedly surfeited with pennant winners. Perhaps the city badly needed something to cheer about in that grim, economically-depressed time.

The Giants' official welcome was held the following morning at City Hall. The mayor welcomed the team, and congratulatory speeches followed from John McGraw and National League president John Heydler. Terry thanked the crowd and then asked, "Do you want to meet the boys?" Following the deafening response, each player stepped forward. The loudest cheers were heard for Ryan, Hubbell, and Ott, who could barely be seen as he stood shyly behind broad-shouldered Roy Parmelee.

Back at his desk in the Polo Grounds, Terry waded through a pile of congratulatory mail and telegrams from all sections of the country. He got a big chuckle every time he read one which began, "As one of the few who picked you to win...." Later in the day came the news that the Washington Senators had clinched the American League pennant, and Terry began planning for the upcoming World Series.

The Senators had won the pennant with relative ease, finishing seven games ahead of the heavily-favored Yankees. Managed by Joe Cronin, their 26-year-old shortstop, the Senators were a solid ball club with a stronger attack then the Giants, a sound defense, and an accomplished pitching staff.

Smooth-fielding Joe Kuhel was at first base. Buddy Myer, a fine all-around player was at second. Cronin at short was a better-than-average fielder and an exceptional hitter. Ossie Bluege, a defense wizard, was the third baseman. Heinie Manush, a lusty, high-average hitter was in left field. Centerfielder Fred Schulte was a steady if unsensational performer. And Leon (Goose) Goslin in right had been one of the American League's hardest hitters since joining the Senators 12 years before.

Workmanlike Luke Sewell was the catcher. The pitching staff, led by 20-game winners Alvin (General) Crowder and southpaw Earl White-hill, also included starters Wally Stewart, Monte Weaver, Jack Russell, and relief pitcher Al Thomas. Because of their superior strength, on paper at least, the Senators were rated 10 to 7 favorites to win the Series.

A crowd of 46,674 jammed the spruced-up, banner-bedecked Polo Grounds for the first game. The early birds were out in full force, many appearing at the chilly bleacher entrances by midnight, long hours before squads of police arrived to maintain order. When tickets for the 4,600 bleacher seats went on sale at 10 A.M., about 12,000 fans stood in line, an impressive testimony to the Giants' appeal.

The big attraction before the game was the standout comic routine of Al Schacht and Nick Altrock, baseball's foremost clowns of that time. The stands rocked with the crowd's laughter at their zany skits and antics—a hilarious tennis match featuring two incredibly inept but acrobatic players; a pepper game with skillful, sleight-of-hand tricks with a bat and ball; the inevitable game of catch with eggs that splattered the two deadpan participants; the well-timed pratfalls; and uncanny imitations of the players down to the last mannerism.

Tension began to build in the stands as the teams completed their warmups. Hubbell, as expected, was the Giants' starter. Cronin pulled a surprise by sending out lefthander Wally Stewart in an attempt to neutralize Terry and Ott, who represented much of the Giants' power. Hubbell began the game by striking out the side—Myer, Goslin, and Manush. All three were accomplished hitters, but no American League pitchers they had faced could throw a screwball comparable to Hubbell's.

Just as Hubbell dominated the top of the first inning, Ott took over the bottom half. Joe Moore led off with a sharp grounder that Myer bobbled for the first of his three errors. Stewart took care of Critz and Terry easily, but he still had Ott to face. Mel took the first pitch, then swung lustily at the next serve and sent it on a line into the right field seats about 400 feet away. In the third inning the Giants scored two more runs on hits by Critz, Terry, and Ott and a ground ball by Travis Jackson. That ended the Giants scoring for the day although Ott went on a "4 for 4" binge with two more hard singles, the second almost removing Jack Russell's pitching arm as the drive whistled through the box.

The first seven innings were vintage Hubbell as the Senators scored only once on some uncertain play by the Giants infield. The American Leaguers threatened in the eighth but were held scoreless as Goslin ended the inning with a scorching liner to Terry. Hubbell took a 4–1 lead in the ninth but ran into trouble as the Senators loaded the bases with none out.

The Giants huddled at the mound. A worried Terry looked down to the Giants bullpen as Dolph Luque pumped warmup throws furiously into Paul Richard's mitt. But Terry decided to stay with his meal ticket. Hub looked around calmly at the loaded bases, then went to work. He induced Kuhel to bounce out to Ryan as Manush scored to reduce the Giants lead to 4–2. The tying runs were at second and third. With the apprehensive home crowd roaring on every pitch, King Carl went to a full count before striking out Bluege with a crisp screwball. Luke Sewell worked Hubbell to a 2 and 2 count before topping a slow bounder down the third base line. Jackson hobbled in for the ball and threw a bullet to Terry to end the game. Giants fans let out a deafening shout as Terry trotted to the clubhouse with his arm around Hubbell's shoulders.

In the second game it was Crowder against Schumacher, with the Giants winning 6–1 before 35,461 fans. In the third inning Goslin drove a long homer into the right field seats for the Senators' only run. The rest of the scoring came in the Giants' sixth inning. Moore opened with a single, only the third hit off Crowder. Terry moved Moore to third by slicing a double to left. Ott was walked intentionally, and Lefty O'Doul was sent up as a pinchhitter. Lefty came through with a sharp single through the box to put the Giants ahead 2–1. The four additional runs were icing on the cake. Years later the impish Lefty confided to a writer, "You know, my hit was illegal. I wasn't going to let Crowder throw one by me so I crowded the plate closer with each pitch. On the pitch I got my hit on,

I actually stepped across the plate, and I was afraid the umpire would call me out. But fortunately he didn't see it, nor did anyone on the Senators."

The Series moved to Washington with the attendance held to 25,727 by a steady drizzle. President Franklin D. Roosevelt, then in the eighth month of his momentous first term in office, attended the game. He made an imposing entrance, entering Griffith Stadium by automobile through a runway as the players stood at attention. Onlookers not given either to ceremonial pomp or to FDR's policies nevertheless had to be impressed by the famous Roosevelt luck. As the president's limousine arrived, the drizzle stopped and the sun came out as if on cue. Senators owner Clark Griffith was overheard greeting FDR with, "We're glad you're here, Mr. President, and we hope to win this one for you." Always the consummate politician, the chief executive threw his head back in a characteristically jaunty gesture, smiled, and responded, "Wait a minute, Clark. I'm neutral. Don't forget, I may be living in Washington now, but I'm from New York."

The Senators beat Fitzsimmons 4–0 behind a masterful five-hitter by Earl Whitehill. The lefty handled Terry, Ott, and Moore with ease, holding the three lefthand hitters hitless. Fitzsimmons yielded three runs in the first two innings. He settled down after that, but the Giants were never in the game. But they were not down later in the clubhouse. As Terry put it, "I've said all along that pitching will dominate the Series. They got it today, and we didn't. I still think our pitching will pull us through. I expect Hub will put us back in the groove tomorrow."

Hubbell faced Monte Weaver the next day before a crowd of 27,762. The game was uneventful until the top of the fourth when, with the bases empty, Terry drove a towering blast into center field which just cleared a three-foot fence in front of the temporary bleachers. The Senators tied the game in the seventh when Kuhel reached base on Hubbell's error, was sacrificed to second, and scored on Sewell's hit. The tense game continued into the eleventh inning when the Giants took the lead on Jackson's bunt single, a sacrifice, and Ryan's hit.

In the home half, Washington loaded the bases with one out. Cronin sent up reserve catcher Cliff Bolton to pinchhit. The Giants infield gathered at the mound to decide how to defense Bolton, a hard-hitting lefthand batter but an extremely slow runner. Giants reserve infielder Chuck Dressen had managed Bolton at Nashville, and Terry called him out to join the confab. But the most active participant appeared to be Ryan who gestured vigorously as he talked to Terry. It was assumed that Terry would follow standard strategy for such a situation, that is, play the infield in to cut down the tying run at the plate.

Finally, with the crowd at fever pitch, the conference ended. The fans were surprised as Ryan and Critz played back for the double play, a risky maneuver. Bolton worked Hubbell to a full count. The next pitch came in low and outside and Bolton clubbed a deep bouncer to Ryan. Blondy glided to his right, scooped up the ball, and flipped it to Critz. Hughie pivoted neatly and fired to Terry for the game-ending double play.

In the clubhouse, an exhausted Terry heaped praise upon Hubbell but was ecstatic over Ryan and Critz. "It was Blondy and Hughie who convinced me to play Bolton the way we did," explained Terry. "With the bases loaded I wanted to play in and get the force at the plate. Blondy suggested that Jackson and I play in and he and Critz play back. Ryan promised me he'd get the double play if Bolton hit to him, and I went along with him. Am I glad I took his advice!"

The next day Schumacher faced Crowder again before 28,454 in what proved to be another thriller. Prince Hal himself drove in two runs in the third inning, and the Giants scored another in the sixth on Mancuso's double. But the Senators tied the game in the bottom of the inning on a home run by Fred Schulte. Luque relieved Schumacher and retired Sewell to end the inning.

The game settled down to a tense pitching duel between Luque and Jack Russell, who replaced Crowder in the sixth inning. Inning after inning went by without a serious threat until the top of the tenth. Critz and Terry were retired easily, and Ott stepped up. He had fanned his first two times up and had lifted soft fly balls on the last two. With the count at two and two, Mel cocked his right leg and smashed a long drive toward the center field bleachers. Schulte, moving back at top speed, got his glove on the ball just as it was about to drop into the low, temporary seats in front of the permanent stands. But the ball bounced out of Schulte's glove as he disappeared from sight after toppling over the low fence.

Second base umpire Cy Pfirman at first ruled the drive a double, undoubtedly influenced by Joe Cronin who kept shouting, "It's a double; it's got to be two bases on that one." The incredulous Giants carried their protest to umpires Moran and Moriarty. After a conference, Moran and Moriarty overruled Pfirman, and Ott was awarded the home run. That proved to be the game and Series as Luque retired the Senators in the bottom of the inning, striking out Kuhel with a flourish for the final out. The surprising Giants were the new World Champions.

Terry was almost too tired to talk after the game. "What can I say?" was his greeting to the writers who crowded into the clubhouse. Referring to the Yankees' dominance in preceding World Series, he continued,

"I guess we gave our league something to celebrate after all these years. Luque and Ottie did it. But still, the Series went as I expected." He concluded, "We had the pitching and good pitching will always do the job, particularly in a short series."

Cronin had little to say. Many years later, though, when he was president of the American League, he discussed Ott's winning home run with a writer. "Sure I knew it was a homer, but I just had to kick about it," he said. Cronin laughed. "I just didn't want to believe it, for one thing. And then, too, sometimes the umpire buys your argument and you get a break. After all, Pfirman held Ott on second before waving him around."

Owner Charles Stoneham was thrilled by the Giants' victory, and most especially by Ott, his favorite player. At the club's celebration party that night, a writer commented, "If the Giants had lost the game, the Series would have returned to New York for a Sunday game at the Polo Grounds. That gate would have netted the Giants more than $100,000." So there was a special meaning at the party when Stoneham told Ott, "Mel, that was the greatest thrill of my life. It would have been cheap at a million bucks."

McGraw, aging and in failing health, had been an inconspicuous figure since his retirement. Still, he was exhilarated by the Giants' success. He was proud of Hubbell's exploits and the heroics of Ott, still the apple of his eye. But he talked mostly of Terry, his handpicked successor. "Bill did a wonderful job for us," he chortled. "At times the Senators appeared in a fog and Cronin just couldn't bring them out of it. With our pitching, Mel's hitting, and Bill's handling the plays so well, I never doubted we'd win."

The players scattered on that triumphant note. Hubbell, Fitzsimmons, Schumacher, and Parmelee—the "Big Four"—remained in New York negotiating for vaudeville show appearances which were traditional for Series winners in those pre-television days. Luque left immediately for his native Cuba. Critz returned to his avid fans in Greenwood, Mississippi, to tell them all about that clutch double play on Cliff Bolton. Ryan departed for a big hometown welcome in Lynn, Massachusetts. And so it went.

Ott's sole concern was to get back to his family in Gretna and to spend time with his first child, daughter Margaret Carolyn, whom everyone called Lyn. Mel also received an unexpected surprise. He recalled:

> I had quit high school three months before my last term finished in the Spring of 1925. But I was sure I had enough credits to be entitled to get my diploma. I went to the school authorities a few years later, but they told me I was wrong. Well, anyway, when I

returned home after the Series the home folks gave me a big welcome home. And, lo and behold, there was my diploma all signed,
wrapped, and delivered.

Terry left New York a few days later, savoring a new $40,000-a-year,
five-year contract to go with his laurels as leader of the World Champions. To top it off, an Associated Press poll voted the Giants' Series triumph as the top team victory of 1933.

Chapter 8

$\mathcal{H}$EARTBREAK UNDER COOGAN'S BLUFF

The major leagues held their annual business meetings in New York in January, and several of the writers talked with Terry at the Hotel Roosevelt. Terry was high on his team's prospects, offering to "bet anybody in the room a hat we'll finish among the top three." (Hats apparently were a popular betting item at the time.) Finding no takers, the conversation moved to other matters, particularly the Giants' opponents and the livelier baseball the National League would use in 1934.

On the edge of the group stood the *New York Times*'s Roscoe McGowen, who covered the Dodgers. In the beginning he paid little attention to the discussion. But when Terry was questioned about the Giants' competitors, McGowen became more interested. He asked, "How about Brooklyn, Bill?" Terry smiled and asked, "Brooklyn, I haven't heard anything from them. Are they still in the league?" Everybody laughed, and everybody printed the comment. Memphis Bill, never known for his subtlety, had responded in jest, but it didn't come out that way in the writers' stories. Thousands of letters poured into the Giants' office from irate Dodger rooters. The Dodgers had left their fans cold since falling deep into the second division. But Terry's offhand comment had fired them up. Wait until the season started. Their team would show Terry whether Brooklyn was still in the league!

The Giants had moved their training camp to Miami Beach. In late February, 21 batterymen reported to Flamingo Park to be greeted by a broiling sun and an enthusiastic gathering of some 500 tourists and natives, many in bathing suits and other beach attire. Even then Miami Beach was a favorite winter spot for New Yorkers, and there were many ardent Giants fans in the crowd.

John McGraw died the next day, casting a pall over the camp. Terry was visibly shaken, commenting softly, "I owe everything I have to him.

He made me a first baseman and then he put me in as manager. At times he appeared to be pretty harsh and severe and I had my differences with him. But all he wanted was to get the best out of us." Henry Fabian, the veteran Polo Grounds groundskeeper had been a rookie with McGraw in 1891 in Cedar Rapids, Iowa. Coach Pancho Snyder said that McGraw would be remembered particularly by the older players for his loyalty and unpublicized handouts to them. Hubbell attributed his pitching success to McGraw's advice to keep throwing his screwball. Schumacher spoke of McGraw's support of the younger players despite his outbursts at their mistakes. A deeply saddened Ott, who with his wife had remained close to the McGraws, said, "He treated me as though I was his son and I've looked on him as a second father. I have lost the best friend I ever had."

In late March Terry surprised everyone by trading centerfielder George Davis to the Cardinals for the less agile but harder-hitting outfielder George Watkins. The trade made it clear that Terry had weakened in his conviction that a tight defense alone would be enough to win as had been the case in 1933. He was willing to exchange speed and better fielding for more punch.

After the Giants broke camp, they began the first of their annual series of exhibition games with the Cleveland Indians. This would prove to be the most financially successful of the preseason barnstorming series of that era. The Giants-Indians tour took them through a number of Southern cities in which major league baseball was rarely if ever seen— New Orleans, Baton Rouge, Meridian, Montgomery, Atlanta, Charlotte, Asheville, Nashville, and Louisville.

Favored to win the pennant in preseason polls, the Giants played well despite four changes in the lineup which had started in the World Series. Ryan was at second base, filling in for the injured Critz. The rejuvenated Jackson replaced Ryan at short. George Watkins was in center, and catcher Paul Richards replaced Mancuso who was still weak from a winter bout with typhoid fever.

Although the Giants continued to win through May, there were problems even with Mancuso back in the lineup. With increased emphasis on offense back in vogue, speed on the bases was at a higher premium, and the Giants' slowness afoot cost them several games. Watkins failed to hit, and Terry replaced him in center field with Ott, then widely considered the best right fielder in the game. Johnny Vergez fell into a slump, and Ryan replaced him. Fitzsimmons missed several starts after being hit by an errant fungo bat. And Parmelee was placed on the inactive list following an appendectomy, an ailment that in those days before antibiotics sidelined him for two months.

On Memorial Day the Giants beat the Dodgers in a doubleheader before the largest crowd ever to pack into Ebbetts Field. The insults and boos that accompanied Terry's every move were a reminder of Terry's offhand response to Roscoe McGowen back in January. Still, after the doubleheader win, the Giants were tied with the Cubs for second place and only one and a half games behind St. Louis.

On June 6 the Giants took over first place as Hubbell beat the Braves. Carried along by the timely hitting of Terry, Moore, and Ott, and the steady pitching of Hubbell, Schumacher, and Fitzsimmons, the Giants held the lead through June. After routing the Braves twice on July 4, they were in first place, three games ahead of the Cubs and four games in front of the Cards. Things continued to look up as Parmelee rejoined the club. Ott was reinstalled in right field, and burly Hank Leiber took over in center. The club appeared well-positioned to continue its march to a second straight pennant.

Terry, as manager of the 1933 pennant winners, piloted the National League All-Stars in the second classic at the Polo Grounds on July 10, with Hubbell, Ott, and Jackson joining him as the Giants' representatives. The National League's 9–7 loss was not the enduring story of the game. Hubbell's pitching to start the game was.

Charley Gehringer singled on Hubbell's first pitch in the first inning. Working too carefully, the Giants lefthander walked Heinie Manush. With two men on and none out, and the menacing trio of Babe Ruth, Lou Gehrig, and Jimmie Foxx up, Hubbell faced the ultimate pitcher's nightmare. Catcher Gabby Hartnett looked at Ruth walking to the plate with his characteristic mincing stride, scanned the array of powerful hitters in the American League dugout, then called time and lumbered out to the mound. "Come on, Hub," exhorted the red-faced catcher, "never mind going for the corners, just throw that 'thing' (the screwball). Hell, I can't hit it and they won't either."

King Carl's first pitch to Ruth was just off the plate, but he came back with three screwballs, each of which the Bambino swung at and missed. The piano-legged Gehrig stepped up, took a ball, and then swung futilely at three more biting screwballs. Moonfaced Jimmie Foxx distinguished himself by comparison, at least managing one foul tip in the process of missing three more screwballs. Hubbell had fanned three of the game's all-time great hitters with 12 pitches, and the Polo Grounds rocked with applause as the solemn-faced Oklahoman walked to the dugout.

With the fans buzzing, Hubbell, still throwing that "thing" to perfection, opened the second inning by striking out two more great hitters,

Al Simmons and Joe Cronin. As the fans marveled at Hubbell's artistry, Bill Dickey broke the spell with a clean single. Then Hubbell bore down on the weak-hitting, badly overmatched Lefty Gomez and struck him out to end the inning. (For years the wisecracking Gomez would brag about "being in such distinguished hitting company.") To this day, Hubbell's feat remains the most unforgettable pitching performance in All-Star game history.

By Labor Day, Terry's club was six games in the lead. But the Cards suddenly turned red hot. They were sparked by Dizzy Dean, who was having a remarkable year, and his younger brother Paul, who was a revelation after a slow start. The offensive load was carried by leftfielder Joe Medwick, first baseman Rip Collins, and manager–second baseman Frankie Frisch. Leo Durocher was a superb shortstop, and an inexperienced catcher, Bill DeLancey, had an excellent rookie year. By September 20, with ten games left, the Giants lead over the Cards had dwindled to three and a half games.

Fitzsimmons beat the Phillies on September 21. But this was a day when the Dean brothers led the Cards to a storied doubleheader win over the Dodgers at Ebbets Field. In the first game Dizzy toyed with Casey Stengel's club, allowing no hits for seven innings and only three hits altogether. Brother Paul pitched a no-hitter in the second game. After Paul's masterpiece, Diz was credited with the tongue-in-cheek line, "Shucks, if I knew Paul was gonna no-hit 'em, I'd a done the same."

By this time Terry had moved Jackson from short to third and replaced him with Blondy Ryan. But it did not prevent heartbreaking losses to the Braves and the Phillies, the last especially tough to take because Schumacher and Hubbell both were knocked out of the box. The Giants lost the game in the ninth when one of Luque's low-breaking curveballs bounced in the dirt and eluded Mancuso. After Dizzy Dean shut out the Reds on September 28, the Giants and the Cards were tied for first place with the last weekend of the season at hand.

The Giants entered the final two-game series with the Dodgers emotionally and physically exhausted. The hitters, Terry, Critz, and Jackson, were in fearful slumps. And Ott had not hit safely in the last four games. Hubbell, Schumacher, and Fitzsimmons were exhausted from starting games with insufficient rest and pitching in relief between starts.

Terry probably had given little thought to the Brooklyn fans during the season when the Giants were riding high and the Dodgers were floundering in the second division. But now, at the rain-swept Polo Grounds that final Saturday of the season, the Dodger fans were out in full force. They carried banners and signs aimed at Terry. Signs that read

"BILL WHO?" or "I WISH YOU WERE IN DIXIE." And the most prevalent, "YEAH, WE'RE STILL IN THE LEAGUE." They screamed and taunted all of the Giants, even the popular Ott and Jackson, who normally were treated with respect even at Ebbets Field. But they saved their choicest epithets for Terry, one of the gentlest beings: "Is Brooklyn still in the league, Terry? You'll find out, you cocky bastard. We'll show you."

Manager Casey Stengel started righthand fireballer Van Lingle Mungo against Parmelee. The Dodgers took a 2–0 lead after six innings and increased their lead to 5–0 in the ninth. The Giants' only run came on George Watkins' homer. Meanwhile, out in St. Louis, Paul Dean beat the Reds easily. The Giants were one game down.

With the Giants needing a win along with a Cardinals loss to stay alive, Sunday's game drew more than 45,000. Thousands of Dodger fans stampeded across the East River in a wild scramble to get into the Polo Grounds. Once inside, they raised a terrific din, augmented by whistles, horns, and bells. As the Giants took the field, it probably marked the first time a team making its last stand for the pennant on its home field was greeted by more jeers than shouts of encouragement.

Dodger righthander Ray Benge, opening against Fitzsimmons, was routed in a four-run Giants' first. After the Dodgers scored once, Fitzsimmons restored the four-run margin with a home run. But the fired-up Dodgers fought back to tie the game at five-all in the eighth, knocking out Fitzsimmons. As Schumacher, called in to relieve Fat Freddy, was taking his warmup throws, a loud cheer went up from the Dodger fans. The Polo Grounds scoreboards fronting the right and left field grandstands showed the Cardinals had taken a 3–0 lead over the Reds in the fourth inning.

With darkness settling over Coogan's Bluff, the game moved into the tenth inning still tied. After hits by Sam Leslie and Tony Cuccinello put Dodgers at first and third, Terry motioned Hubbell in to relieve Schumacher. King Carl struck out the next hitter, then passed the second to load the bases. But disaster struck when Ryan fumbled Al Lopez' grounder to permit Leslie to score to break the tie. Two more runs scored on a fly ball and another hit. The Giants went down meekly in their half of the inning, and that was the game and pennant. The exuberant Dodger fans streamed out of the Polo Grounds, their season a success despite another second division finish. With Dizzy Dean shutting out the Reds, the Giants wound up the season two games off the pace.

Leaving the Polo Grounds after the game, Stengel passed the crestfallen Terry. "I was going in to see you fellows after the game, Bill," Stengel said sympathetically. Terry, exhausted by the loss, the crowd, the long season, and the overwhelming disappointment, answered bitterly, "If you had, you would have been thrown out on your butt." The battle-scarred Stengel, stung by Terry's response, replied in kind. "I might have," he shot back, "but I would have taken a piece of your hide with me."

Hubbell again led the league with a 2.30 ERA, in fewest walks allowed per game, and in saves. He was second in complete games and innings pitched, and fourth in wins with 21. Schumacher was second in wins with 23, well behind Dizzy Dean's spectacular 30 victories. Terry was second in hits and batting average. And Ott, although hitless in his last 24 at-bats, tied Rip Collins for the home run lead with 35, led in RBIs with 135, and was second in total bases and in runs scored. Also, on August 4, he tied a major league record by scoring six runs in a game in Philadelphia.

Most of the Giants slipped quietly out of the town the next day, barely comprehending their loss. Terry had little to say. "No, I can't explain how it happened," he lamented. The slump came on us suddenly, and it was too late to do anything about it. But I'm not blaming anybody, and I have no alibis."

In November Terry made his first move to rehabilitate his club when he obtained shortstop Dick Bartell from the Phillies for $75,000 and four players, Ryan, Vergez, Watkins, and minor league pitcher John (Pretzels) Pezzullo. In Bartell the Giants were getting a fiery performer, a consistent hitter, and one of the better fielding shortstops in the game. He had earned the nickname "Rowdy Richard" for his peppery play and willingness to take on all comers despite his small stature. Bartell had been a participant in several spiking incidents, including two involving the Dodgers' Lonny Frey and Joe Judge. Terry, who had an interest in fueling the classic Giants-Dodgers rivalry, was well aware of these conflicts when he made the trade.

Bartell was a big hit in the spring training camp at Miami Beach. A fairly quiet little fellow off the field, his enthusiasm seemed to rejuvenate the other infielders. His wide range at short was particularly helpful to Jackson, who looked more assured at third base and was apparently free of injuries. The only other change in the starting lineup was in center field where big Hank Leiber began to show the form that McGraw had envisioned three years before.

Picked to finish second, the Giants opened in Boston before a freezing crowd that came out to see 41-year-old Babe Ruth, obtained from the Yankees over the winter, play his first National League game. The Babe rewarded their fortitude by leading the Braves to a 4–2 win over Hubbell. Ruth drove in the first run with a blistering single past Terry, and he blasted a 430-foot homer to drive in the other runs. To top off a great day, the Babe contributed the game's fielding gem when he raced in from deep left field to pick off a fly ball.

A week later the Giants returned the favor by beating the Braves in 11 innings before more than 47,000 fans, at that time the largest crowd ever to watch a National League opener in New York. Ott stole the big guy's thunder with a line single to drive in the winning run. Ruth went hitless, a forerunner of the career-end disappointment which would bring him to leave the Braves soon after.

The Giants went on to win their first eight home games and continued to do well in May. By Memorial Day, after a doubleheader win over the Braves, they had a comfortable first place lead. Ott, Terry, Moore, and Leiber were pounding the ball. Bartell had breathed life into his geriatric infield partners. Harry Danning, batting deep in the box à la Rogers Hornsby, was used more frequently to rest Mancuso. And young right-hander Clydell (Slick) Castleman pitched impressively enough to be promoted into the starting rotation.

By the All-Star game break, the Giants maintained a seven-game lead over the Cardinals with the Cubs and the Pirates filling out the first division. The Polo Grounders were well-positioned for a comeback pennant win despite the loss of Fitzsimmons for the season after elbow surgery.

The Giants began their third western trip with a good series in Pittsburgh and a split in Cincinnati. But they lost four straight to the revitalized Cubs. Terry's club finished the trip on a high note. They won four of six games from the Cards in four broiling, humid days and were three games ahead of the improving Cubs and three and a half games ahead of the Cards when they returned home. In the first game in St. Louis the Giants had a bad scare when Schumacher collapsed on the mound in the intense heat. But the Cards' team physician packed Prince Hal in ice and "brought him back from the dead," as Blondy Ryan dramatically described it.

Although the Giants' lead was reduced, Terry was not unduly concerned. His club had held off the Cardinals, the team Memphis Bill felt he had to beat. The Giants faced a long home stand in better shape than they had been for some time. But the Giants gained only a split against the weaker eastern teams and did poorly against the western teams. They would up the home stand one-half game behind the Cardinals.

As September began, the Cardinals were still in first place, two games ahead of the Giants. On their final trip west the Giants moved into St. Louis three and a half games behind the Cards. Dizzy Dean opened the important series by defeating Hubbell. But the Giants came back fighting.

Frank Gabler, a talkative rookie righthander, beat Paul Dean in an exciting, ten-inning, see-saw, slugging match. The following day Clydell
Castleman won 5–4 in 11 innings, and the Cubs moved past the Cardinals into first place. Then Hubbell beat Dizzy Dean in a game played
before an overflow crowd in Sportsmans Park with many onlookers sitting on the outskirts of the outfield separated from the players by only a
clothesline.

Mel Ott had a few fans among the largely hostile fans ringing the
outfield. Mel told of three young men who were rooting for the Giants:

> It took courage but they always had something to shout to me
> after I came out to right field each inning. If I'd batted in a run,
> or even hit a loud foul, they would give me a little cheer. The rest
> of the mob squatted out there on the grass and gave 'em plenty of
> dirty looks and muttered threats. But these three fellows just
> grinned and ignored them. Late in the game one of the Cardinals
> hit a long fly I had to backpedal for. Just as I got set to catch the
> ball I felt something tickle my ribs. I took my eye off the ball for
> a second and saw a pop bottle sail under my arm. It was the last
> out of the inning and naturally I turned around to see who had
> tossed the bottle. "Come on, Mel," one of my buddies shouted
> indignantly. "Let's get him." The three of them went cruising
> around that mob, doing everything but step on faces, and I went
> along. But we couldn't spot anyone with a guilty look and had to
> give it up.

The Giants were demolished in Chicago. Cubs pitchers Lon Warneke, Larry French, Charlie Root, and Bill Lee beat them with little difficulty. The Cubs were on their way to a 21-game winning streak, and the
Giants simply provided the thirteenth, fourteenth, fifteenth, and sixteenth
victories before the Wrigley Field steamroller. Terry's club ended the trip
seven and a half games behind the Cubs and five and a half games in back
of the Cards. They were a badly disappointed group although there was
some slight satisfaction in having retaliated against the Cards for the last-
ditch defeat Frisch's club had dealt them in the previous heartbreaking
season.

Terry, who hit well over .400 on the trip, and who had drawn grudg-
ing cheers from the rival fans for his brilliant play, held a press conference when the Giants returned home. He announced, "I'm retiring. The
problem is that we have too many old men, and that includes the first
baseman. From now on, we're out only for youth and speed."

The Cubs capped their incredible drive, clinching the pennant with
their twentieth consecutive win on September 27. Their twenty-first
straight win in the second game of the doubleheader was meaningless.

The Giants finished in third place, a whopping eight and a half games behind Charlie Grimm's Cubs.

Hubbell had another magnificent year, winning 23 and losing 12 and finishing second in the league in wins, strikeouts, innings pitched, and complete games. Schumacher was third in earned-run-average. Hank Leiber had what was to be his best year, hitting .331 and batting in 107 runs. Terry, retirement plans and all, tied for fifth in batting with a .341 average. And Ott had another solid year, finishing second in home runs and total bases, third in walks, and fourth in RBIs and runs scored. Mel again demonstrated his versatility, filling in effectively at third base in a number of games when Travis Jackson was unable to play. Mel left for home as soon as the season ended. His second child, Barbara Anne, was born on October 1.

On October 10 the Giants, who had long resisted broadcasting their games on radio, filed a suit to restrain "bootleg" broadcasts of all sporting events from the Polo Grounds. The suit was filed against several communication companies although the Giants admitted "the method of acquiring the simultaneous [the term 'real time' had not yet been invented] description of baseball games is unknown." And on that indeterminant note, another frustrating Giants season ended.

Chapter 9

*P*ENNANT *W*INNERS

At the winter meetings, Terry attended to one of his first priorities, a replacement for Hughie Critz who had retired. Terry's man was Burgess Whitehead, a utility infielder with the Cardinals. To get Whitehead, the Giants gave up a first-line starter, Parmelee, along with pitcher Allyn Stout, young infielder Al Cuccinello, and first baseman Phil Weintraub. Critics of the deal conceded that Whitehead was fast, an agile second baseman who could make the double play, an occasional hitter, and a good hit-and-run man, all of which the Giants needed. But they questioned whether the slim, frail-looking Whitehead had the stamina to play a full season. Even the doubters, though, were intrigued by the Tarboro, North Carolina, native who had graduated Phi Beta Kappa from the University of North Carolina, hardly a prerequisite to being a member of the rough-and-ready Gas House Gang.

Failing in attempts to trade for an established first baseman, Terry brought back Sam Leslie from the Dodgers just before spring training opened in Pensacola, Florida. The only other experienced players acquired were pitcher Dick Coffman from the St. Louis Browns, and ancient reliever Fred Marberry, who had labored for the Tigers after several big years with the Senators.

On January 6, 1936, President Charles Stoneham died. He was the only survivor of the triumvirate which had purchased the Giants in 1920, the others being John McGraw and Francis X. McQuade. Stoneham had been an unobtrusive club president with the aggressive McGraw running the club with an iron hand until June 1932, and the less flamboyant, but equally strong-willed, Terry calling the shots since then. A week later, 32-year-old Horace Stoneham replaced his father. Leo Bondy became the vice-president in addition to maintaining the position of treasurer. A few weeks later, popular Eddie Brannick, who had been associated with the Giants since he was a young boy, became the team secretary.

Whitehead made an unusual entrance at training camp, carrying a tennis racket along with his luggage. One of the case-hardened McGraw era coaches was heard to mutter, "What the hell does he think we're down here training for, a pennant race or Wimbledon?" But very soon White-head impressed everyone favorably, working smoothly with Bartell, han-dling the bat deftly, and moving with exceptional grace. Jimmy Ripple, a chunky young outfielder from Export, Pennsylvania, also looked good with his lefthand power and determination.

Just before the season opened, National League president Ford Frick announced a new "nonfraternization" rule. Under this edict, opposing team players were forbidden to talk to each other on the field. To make the rule even more ridiculous, if caught fraternizing (a term that would take on a more interesting meaning during World War II), both the players and managers involved were subject to fines.

Picked to finish behind the Cubs and the Cardinals, the Giants opened the season in fine style, reeling off five straight wins against the Dodgers and the renamed, but unimproved, Boston Bees. With Leslie at first and Jackson at third, the Giants won three action-packed games with the Dodgers at the Polo Grounds. In the second game, Dodger right-hander Van Lingle Mungo and Bartell became involved in a manner not to be confused with the fraternization that Frick had in mind. Bartell grounded to first baseman Buddy Hassett for what appeared to be a rou-tine, unassisted putout by Hassett. Mungo, coming over to cover the bag, appeared to give the much smaller Bartell a hard jolt with his hip as they met at the bag. Dick seemed to fly through the air as though shot out of a cannon. He turned a couple of somersaults and landed flat on his back.

Without stopping for a breather, the peppery Bartell scrambled to his feet. He screamed at Mungo, "You did that on purpose, you lousy son of a bitch." Almost simultaneously the two men charged each other and began flailing away, with the much larger Mungo falling on top of Bartell. The dugouts emptied quickly. Umpire Beans Reardon raced over from third base and, knee-deep in ballplayers, finally succeeded in prying apart the two battlers. Then he booted both men out of the game.

The next day both Bartell and Mungo were fined $25. Frick announced, almost apologetically, "The fines were the smallest for a fistfight in a good many years. I made them small because there are degrees of fights. This one was not premeditated. No one got hurt and no one even got a black eye." (Apparently a black eye was the acid test.)

But the fine was not the end of Mungo's problems that day. Pitch-ing in relief, he lost in the bottom of the ninth on a freak play which showed the Dodgers had not lost their flair for serio-comedy. Leading 6–5 with two out and no one on base, Mungo walked Whitehead and gave up a single to Ott. Leiber popped a fly into short left, apparently an easy game-ending out. Former Giants stalwart Freddy Lindstrom, just picked up by the Dodgers after a distinguished career with the Giants and the Pirates, trotted in easily to make the catch. Uncharacteristically, he crashed head-on into shortstop Jimmy Jordan as Jordan drifted back and reached up for the ball. The ball dropped out of Jordan's glove and both men tumbled to the ground dazed. Whitehead and Ott, running with two out, scored the tying and winning runs. Later in the clubhouse, Lindstrom said unbelievingly, "I've been in this league for 12 years and that never happened to me until I became a Dodger." The disillusioned Lindstrom retired several games later. Mungo's post-game comments were unprintable.

Before the Giants' first appearance of the year at Ebbets Field, Terry requested extra police protection, and 20 additional officers were assigned to the ballpark. There was some suspicion that the request was designed, in part at least, to exploit the traditional Giants-Dodgers rivalry as Bartell was ill and unable to play. All of the excitement was confined to the see-saw game which the Dodgers won in the tenth on a pinch hit by an obscure rookie catcher, one Sidney Gautreaux.

Ott had one of his best offensive days in a slugfest in Philadelphia on July 12. The little right fielder drove in five runs with a single and double over the first eight innings, but he saved his best for last. He came up in the ninth inning with two men on and two out with the Giants losing 12–10. Mel hit the first pitch over the right field wall for a three-run homer to pull out a 13–12 Giants win.

On Memorial Day the Giants surprisingly were only one and a half games behind the league-leading Cardinals as Terry maneuvered his troops masterfully. Leiber, in a bad slump after his fine 1935 season, was platooned in center field with Jimmy Ripple. Leslie also slumped, and Terry, still on the roster, took over at first base for a few games. Jackson, slowed up perceptibly, shared third base with Eddie Mayo, up from Baltimore. Only Whitehead and Bartell held the infield together with their consistent, sparkling play. Hubbell was superb, but the other pitchers were under par, and Castleman, in particular, was a bitter disappointment after his fine rookie year.

By the All-Star game break, the Giants had dropped to fifth place although they were only five and a half games behind the first-place Cubs. In the All-Star classic, the National League won 4–3 on Augie Galan's disputed home run at Braves Field in Boston. Hubbell, Ott, Moore, and Terry were picked to represent the Giants. Terry, however, had to bow out to visit his doctor in Memphis who told him that his ailing knee made further play inadvisable.

When Terry returned, it was widely believed that his playing days were over. The Giants' first base situation was up in the air. Sam Leslie had been erratic at bat, and his defensive play had not improved. One possibility that Terry considered briefly was to bring up Norman (Babe) Young, a recent Fordham University graduate, just beginning his minor league apprenticeship with the Giants' Greenwood, Mississippi, farm club. Another possibility was to try Leiber at first base, but Terry also discarded this idea. For better or worse, Leslie apparently would be the regular first baseman for the rest of the season.

After losing the first game of a doubleheader to the Pirates on July 15, the Giants' pennant hopes touched bottom. They were 11 games behind the league-leading Cubs and were lodged in fifth place, nearer to sixth than fourth. But they took the second game as Terry, playing on his crippled left knee, led his club with a single, double, and triple. The next day, Ott's eighth-inning home run brought about a come-from-behind win over the Pirates. Hubbell, helped by a record-tying four Giants triples in one inning, shut out the Pirates in the last game of the series. After taking two out of three from the Reds, the Giants returned home in fourth place, nine and a half games behind the Cubs.

The Giants continued their resurgence against the western clubs at the Polo Grounds and wound up the home stand only five and a half games out of first place. The high point of the home stand came on July 26 when the Giants came from behind with three runs in the bottom of the ninth to defeat Cincinnati. The game featured an unusual triple play. With men on first and second and none out, catcher Ernie Lombardi hit a 450-foot drive to the bleacher wall in left center. Hank Leiber made a remarkable catch on the drive. Then he flipped the ball to Joe Moore who had come over from left field. Moore dropped the ball but recovered it quickly and relayed it to Bartell.

The runners took off when they realized how far the ball had been hit, but started back to their bases when they saw Leiber make the catch. Third base coach Charlie Dressen saw Moore drop the ball and thought the runners were free to advance without tagging up, so he waved them around. But the runners still had their doubts, and the result was complete confusion. The runner on first rounded second, then headed back, then reversed himself and headed back to second. The runner who had been at second base originally went to third, then reversed himself and returned to second to tag up. Bartell tagged out both runners at second to complete the triple play as the excited home fans cheered.

The Giants stepped up the pace, winning 17 of their next 18 games. Their performances were marked by Hubbell's sensational pitching, Ott's clutch hitting, and the inspired play of their two crippled first basemen, the courageous Leslie who played with a severely pulled groin muscle, and Terry who played sporadically but effectively.

The final western trip began in Cincinnati with the Giants only half a game behind the league-leading Cardinals. The Polo Grounders moved into first place when Leiber beat the Reds with a late-inning hit. In Pittsburgh, Terry came off the coaching line to belt a pinch-hit single to beat the Pirates in 14 innings. The next day the Pirates' Red Lucas broke the Giants' 15-game winning streak. But the Giants came back to win a doubleheader from the Cubs, highlighted by Hubbell's twentieth victory (his seventh straight win) and Ott's dramatic ninth-inning home run, his seventh hit of the day. The trip ended successfully in St. Louis with Hubbell beating Dizzy Dean 2–1.

There was a play in the St. Louis series that Ott remembered for a long time. Years later Mel was talking with a group of writers, and he was asked about great outfield plays he had seen. Mel recalled:

> Terry Moore of the Cardinals made the greatest outfield play I ever saw back in 1936. He was playing in right center where he should have been, and the ball was hit on a line over the shortstop's head. It was a sure triple if I ever saw one, but Moore comes tearing over. He throws himself at the ball, hits the ground, skids along for about five yards, and sticks out his bare hand, and catches the ball.

A listener said, "Mel, it certainly must have made an impression on you, the way you remember the details so clearly."

"It should have," Mel said. "I hit the ball."

The Giants returned home triumphantly with a four-game lead over the second-place Cardinals. Since their comeback on July 15, they had won 39 of 47, a cool .830 pace. With their closest competitors finishing on the road, and the Giants home for most of the remainder of the season, Terry's club was in a strong position if the players could forget their shattering late-season experiences of the last two years.

The western clubs came in for the last time, and the Giants held their own against the Cubs and the Reds. The Cardinals were next, and the Giants also managed to hold them off, splitting a doubleheader before a full house at the Polo Grounds. There was a play in the second game that was strictly out of the old, daffy Dodgers' playbook.

Cardinals rookie pitcher Cotton Pippen was the runner at second base, and Terry Moore was on first when another rookie, Art Garibaldi, smashed a line drive to deep right center. It looked like a sure double or triple until the hard-to-understand, Cuban third base coach, Mike Gonzalez, got into the act. (Gonzalez had gained his share of baseball immortality with his memorable scouting report on a young prospect—"Good field, no hit.") As Pippen and Moore ran the bases, they became hopelessly confused by a series of staccato orders shrieked by Gonzalez in his best pidgin English, "Go, go! Hol' up, hol' up!" Pippen stopped uncertainly halfway between third and home. At the same time, Moore rounded second and raced for third until he saw the thoroughly confused Pippen becalmed between third and home. Meanwhile, Ott's rifle throw came in from deep right field and Pippen was tagged out between third and home, and Moore was caught between second and third. The Cardinals had succeeded in converting an apparent two-run double or triple with none out into a mere single and a double play with no runs in. Leo Durocher reported that after that loss manager Frankie Frisch berated the team in the locked clubhouse for nearly three hours, à la John McGraw.

The Giants won the rubber game of the Cardinals series to move four and a half games ahead of the Cards and six games in front of the Cubs. Both Hubbell and Dizzy Dean relieved the starting pitchers, and Hub wound up with his twenty-fourth win of the season. The Cardinals added their own brand of spice to the game with a free-swinging brawl on their bench between Joe Medwick and pitcher Ed Heusser. Since this was a private Gas House Gang fight, in the relative privacy of their dugout, although in clear public view, the umpires studiously ignored the brawl until the Cards themselves separated their battling teammates.

Terry's club clinched the pennant in Boston on September 24 when Schumacher won and drove in the winning run. The Giants finished the season with a 92 and 62 record, five games ahead of the Cards and Cubs who tied for second.

Hubbell had a remarkable year and was voted the Most Valuable Player award. He had 16 consecutive wins as the campaign ended, and led the league with 26 wins, in winning percentage, and in ERA. Over and above his imposing statistics, though, King Carl's true value was best reflected by his ability to win the important games and to give stability to the pitching staff when the older pitchers slumped and the younger pitchers floundered. Ott had one of his best years, leading the league in homers with 36 and in slugging percentage, and finishing near the top in RBIs, runs scored, and bases on balls. He, like his roommate and close friend Hubbell, was a blue chip performer all season, particularly in late inning, clutch situations.

Joe Moore had a great year, leading off effectively and playing a brilliant left field. Mancuso had a fine year and was given much of the credit for the pitching staff's late-season resurgence. And Bartell and Whitehead were the best shortstop–second baseman combination the Giants had had in many years. Their play was especially important for the kind of low score, defense-oriented style of play that was the Giants' hallmark. Whitehead, incidentally, played in every Giants game, an effective rebuttal to the doubters who thought he lacked the stamina to play regularly.

The Giants and their families luxuriated in the pennant win for a few days. Joe Moore told writer Walter M. Langford:

> Our ball club was a family back in those days. We all lived in the same neighborhood (Washington Heights) on Manhattan Island, with several families living in the same building. It was a cooperative-owned building, and we'd sub-lease. We all lived up there and we had good family relationships, the kids all played together, etc.

The Giants' harmonious teamwork on the field reflected the closeness of the players off the field. Mel and Mildred Ott were one of the more popular couples. The Otts were particularly close to Hubbell and later Cliff Melton and their families.

Ott posing in 1934 (courtesy Jay Gauthreaux).

The Giants' thoughts turned to the World Series with the powerful Yankees, as New York prepared for its first "nickel," subway World Series since 1923. The 1936 Yankees unquestionably were one of the all-time great ball clubs, compared favorably by many experts to the 1927 Yankees of "Murderers' Row" fame. Joe McCarthy's team had made a shambles of the American League race, clinching the pennant as early as September 9 and winning by an overwhelming 19½ games over the second-place Detroit Tigers. The Yanks had everything, a crushing offense, a great defense, and an excellent pitching staff.

Ott posing in 1939 (courtesy Jay Gauthreaux).

At first base Lou Gehrig was the greatest home run hitter of the day and a dependable fielder. Veteran second baseman Tony Lazzeri was a solid, baseball-wise player who could still hit the long ball. Frankie Crosetti was a spry shortstop and a good leadoff man. Third baseman Red Rolfe was a proficient number two hitter, a skilled bunter, and a sound fielder.

The outfield was dominated by young Joe DiMaggio. The graceful rookie's marvelous year had exceeded the rave notices he brought from the experts who had observed him in the Pacific Coast League. Right-fielder George (Twinkletoes) Selkirk, finally overcoming the burden he carried as Babe Ruth's successor, was a good hitter and outfielder although he was overshadowed by the superstars on the club. In the other outfield slot hot-tempered Jake Powell was an adequate performer. Lanky Bill Dickey, then in his prime, had long been recognized as one of the game's great catchers. He was an excellent receiver and thrower, a fine handler of pitchers, and one of the game's most consistent hitters with a classic, level swing.

The pitching staff was deep and well balanced. Big, rugged Charley (Red) Ruffing was the leading righthand starter. Lefty Gomez was an excellent pitcher, particularly effective in big games. Ex-Indians and Senators righthander Monte Pearson, Irving (Bump) Hadley, and Yale graduate Johnny Broaca were the other starters. Ex–Chicago Cub and world-class reveler Pat Malone did double duty as a spot starter and reliever, and Johnny (Grandma) Murphy, a Fordham University alumnus (and many years later general manager of the New York Mets), was one of the leading relief pitchers of the day.

The Yanks held a wide hitting edge over the Giants. They had set a new major league record for home runs with 182, including a league-leading 49 by Gehrig, 29 by DiMaggio, and 22 by Dickey. Even more remarkable was their feat of having five regulars—Gehrig, DiMaggio, Dickey, Lazzeri, and Selkirk—who had driven in more than 100 runs. By comparison, in the entire National League only six players had exceeded the 100 RBI mark, and Ott was the only Giants player who had done so. This unequal power distribution was expected to put a terrific strain upon the Giants staff.

The widespread interest in the Series was reflected in the heavy betting before the opener. Oddsmakers made the Yankees a prohibitive favorite to win the Series although the Giants were strong favorites in the first game with Hubbell pitching.

Hubbell faced Ruffing in the opener. It was played in a steady downpour at the rain-soaked Polo Grounds before 39,419 drenched onlookers. Selkirk and Bartell hit solo homers, then the Giants went ahead 2–1 in the sixth inning when Mancuso drove in Ott. Hubbell had no real trouble until the Yankee eighth. Crosetti doubled and Rolfe was safe on his sacrifice when Hubbell slipped on the wet grass fielding his bunt. With none out, DiMaggio lashed a screwball on a low line toward right field. Whitehead moved quickly to his left, speared the ball just off the ground, and doubled Rolfe off first base. Encouraged by that break, Hubbell retired Dickey to end the inning. In the bottom of the inning the Giants put the game away with a four-run burst on a bases-filled walk to Whitehead, Jackson's sacrifice fly, and a scratch hit by Hubbell. In the clubhouse there was unanimous agreement that Whitehead's play on DiMaggio's liner was the key play of the game. As Terry put it, "It meant the difference for them between at least having the tying run in, men on first and second or third and nobody out, compared with no runs, two out, and only a man on third."

Schumacher opposed Gomez in the second game before a crowd of 43,543, which included President Roosevelt who was in New York campaigning for his second term. The Yanks, unhampered by such obstacles as Hubbell's artistry, inclement weather, and poor field conditions, tore into Schumacher and four other Giants pitchers in a 17-hit, 18–4 slaughter in which every Yankee got at least one hit. Lazzeri hit a grand-slam homer in a seven-run, third-inning outburst, and Tony, along with Dickey, batted in five runs. The best-remembered play of the one-sided game was contributed by DiMaggio. The Californian made a stunning, game-ending catch on a prodigious blast by Leiber. Hank drove the ball to deepest center field almost to the base of the clubhouse. DiMag turned at the crack of the bat, looking first over one shoulder and then the other, and raced well beyond the bleacher screens. He made the catch half turned to the plate some 475 feet away. Then he casually trotted up the steps to the visiting team's clubhouse as the crowd looked on in amazement.

Moving to the Yankee Stadium for the third game, it was Fitzsimmons against Bump Hadley before 64,842, the largest crowd to attend a World Series game up to that time. Fitz was in good form, and the Yanks touched him for only four hits while the Giants collected eleven. Regardless, the power-packed Bronx Bombers eked out a 2–1 win on a deflected infield hit that the acrobatic Whitehead could not handle.

In the fourth game it was Hubbell against Pearson before 66,669, another attendance record. The Yanks scored one run in the second and three more in the third on Gehrig's majestic homer. The Giants came back with a run in the fourth when Ripple drove in Bartell. Hubbell held the Yanks at bay after that, but he left the game after the seventh inning, behind 4–1. The Giants could do little against Pearson and lost 5–2. After the game, Terry talked about his knee ailment. He said that he had been confined to his hotel room when he was not at the ballpark, sleeping at night with pillows under his left leg to reduce the swelling. He told the writers, "I'm playing out this string, but you can bet anything that I'll never play again after this is over."

Ott's classic batting style, batting practice in Wrigley Field, Chicago, 1938 (courtesy Brace Photo).

Schumacher next faced Ruffing before 50,024 on a warm, early fall day. Although loosely played, this was by far the most exciting game of the Series. The Giants went ahead with three runs in the first inning. The Yanks returned their fire by scoring two runs in the third inning and loading the bases with none out. But the gritty Schumacher struck out DiMaggio and Gehrig and then got Dickey to fly out to Ott. With the game tied at four–all, Moore opened the tenth with a double and moved to third on Bartell's sacrifice. With a count of 2 and 2, Pat Malone appeared to have struck out Terry with a sharp curve. But, as the Yankees claimed after the game, plate umpire Cy Pfirman missed the call in Terry's favor. Terry then lifted a towering fly to DiMaggio and Moore just managed to slide in under Dickey's tag. The tenacious Prince Hal held the Yankees in the bottom of the inning, and the Terrymen had reduced the Yanks' lead in games to 3 to 2 with the Series returning to the Polo Grounds. Many years later, Schumacher told writer Pete Williams that this was the best game he had ever pitched.

Ott in Wrigley Field, 1938 (courtesy Brace Photo).

In the sixth game Fitzsimmons faced Gomez on a gray, murky afternoon at the Polo Grounds with 38,427 on hand. Ott's ringing double drove in two runs in the first inning, but the Yankees chased Fitzsimmons in the fourth to take a 5–2 lead. The Giants fought back in the seventh inning, but Johnny Murphy relieved Gomez and struck out pinchhitter Mark Koenig to end the inning with the go-ahead Giants run on base. Homers by Ott and Moore brought the Giants to within one run of the Yanks after eight innings. All that followed was anticlimactic. Leading 6–5 in the ninth, the Yankees broke the game wide open, battering Giants relievers Dick Coffman and Harry Gumbert for seven runs, increasing their lead to 13–5. The Giants went down meekly in the ninth, and the Yankees were the World Champions.

In the victorious Yankee clubhouse, Joe McCarthy was magnanimous, telling writers, "The Giants are a much better ball club than people give them credit for. They gave us a whale of a battle." Terry could still smile. He knew his club had done well to carry the Series to six games. "That's the toughest club I ever faced," said Bill. "They have everything. They're just a great team." In a rare show of sentimentality, Terry talked about Travis Jackson who had shown his age during the season and particularly during the Series. "I wouldn't take him out of the Series," said Memphis Bill. "I thought he deserved to play after the kind of ball he has given this club for years. But next year? No, Jax can't go another season."

Pirates manager Pie Traynor lauded Terry who had played through the entire Series as a virtual cripple. Traynor added, "I don't think any other man in baseball could have finagled that team into a World Series. For that matter, he did well to win a game, let alone two games, against a powerhouse like the Yanks." There were few Giants players or fans who didn't agree with Traynor.

Mel Ott returned home to New Orleans with Mildred and Lyn. He was not unduly depressed over the loss to the Yankees. After all, the Giants had lost to one of the most powerful teams ever assembled. Moreover, Mel took home the loser's share of $4,655, enough to buy two automobiles in that economically-depressed time. And besides, Mel enjoyed being home in the offseason. He spent a lot of time with his family. He hunted and fished. He played basketball with fellow major leaguer Zeke Bonura and with Carl Lind and Eddie Morgan, both of whom had played with the Cleveland Indians after playing with Mel in 1925 on the Patterson Grays. And he loved the New Orleans scene in the fall and winter—the food, old local friends, baseball friends, and Tulane football. Then, before spring training began, there was the Mardi Gras. Mel was as happy a man in that relaxed offseason as he was in the less-than-relaxed regular season.

Chapter 10

TWO IN A ROW

For several years the Giants had relied upon trades to restaff the team. But now with Terry and Jackson retired, and the years taking their toll on some of the other McGraw-era holdovers, it was clear that the Giants had to build up their meager farm system to compete with such teams as the Cardinals and the Yankees with their extensive, flourishing farm club chains. With this in mind, the Giants purchased the Albany club of the Triple-A International League for $50,000. Then they transferred the franchise to nearby Jersey City and installed Travis Jackson as manager.

The new players of note obtained during the offseason were left-hander Cliff Melton, up from Baltimore, and utility infielders Lou Chiozza, from the Phillies, and Tommy Thevenow, from the Reds. With the Giants unable to secure an established first baseman, that position was up for grabs among fancy-fielding Johnny McCarthy, who had been brought up from Newark late in the 1936 season; old faithful, Sam Leslie; and Les Powers, purchased from Baltimore.

Spring training was split between Havana, Cuba, and Gulfport, Mississippi. On the barnstorming trip north, the main attraction was 18-year-old Bob Feller, who had been sensational since joining Cleveland during the 1936 season. Feller made believers out of the Giants in his first outing against them in Vicksburg, Mississippi, striking out a number of them handily with his blinding speed and sharp curve. Dick Bartell alone was unimpressed, commenting, "Heck, Van Mungo's definitely quicker and we've got several other guys in our league who can throw as fast."

Hank Leiber unfortunately became the Giants' foremost authority on the velocity of Feller's fastball when the Iowa youngster hit him in the back of the head in a game in New Orleans. Although batting helmets had not yet come into use, Leiber did not appear to be badly hurt. He remained conscious and simply bent over in pain, rubbed his head for a short time, and then walked toward first base before his teammates led him off the field. Although doctors could find no significant injury at the time, the injury was later diagnosed as a damaged optic nerve which affected the vision in his right eye. Hank suffered from dizziness for some time, and he was out of the lineup for two-thirds of the season.

The tour with the Indians took the two teams, traveling in style in eight Pullman cars and private dining and club cars, through the deep South, Texas, Oklahoma, and on into New York. Throughout, Feller continued to impress, and frighten, the Giants with his lightning speed, combined with his occasional wildness. As if in response to Bartell's putdown, Feller seemed to bear down especially hard on the little shortstop, fanning him 13 times in 18 at-bats. As Bill Corum, of the *Journal-American*, put it, "Bartell had to go all the way from Vicksburg to Charlotte before he got so much as a loud foul against the kid."

All of the players had rich memories of those barnstorming trips north. There was only one dining car on the train, so the two clubs ate together. They also shared post-game clubhouse facilities. Indian infielder Roy Hughes told a baseball fan group years later, "We got to know the Giants very well on those tours. Mel Ott was a great guy. He and I shared many a bottle of booze in those damp, chilly, bush league dressing rooms. Gosh, we needed something to fight off that chill."

The Giants and the Dodgers opened the season at Ebbets Field in typically explosive fashion. Bartell, leading off against Mungo, took the first pitch across the letters for a strike. As he turned around to protest the call by umpire Beans Reardon, he was hit squarely in the chest by an over-ripe tomato which came flying out of the stands behind first base. Rowdy Richard took this splattering with commendable aplomb, and the game continued after an extended toweling-off period.

A few days later at the Polo Grounds, hard feelings between the interborough rivals boiled over as Bartell tagged Dodger infielder Jimmy Bucher with more vigor than Bucher considered necessary. Both men bounced to their feet and squared off as both teams raced onto the field. But after the usual heated words and threatening gestures, the umpires restrained the would-be combatants and the game continued.

Harry Danning recalled that these encounters were par for the course when the Giants played the Dodgers. Danning saw the rivalry between the two teams as a continuing battle of wits as well as fisticuffs. This extended to the fans. Danning laughingly recounted the time that Ott, Leiber, and Moore drove over to Brooklyn from Manhattan for a game at Ebbets Field. It seems that the three players got lost in Brooklyn and asked a policeman for directions to the ballpark. The officer recognized the players and, in the best tradition of the ancient rivalry, misdirected them in an attempt to keep them out of the game against his beloved

Dodgers. Fortunately, they found their way to Ebbets Field in time for the game.

The Giants, without the headache-plagued Leiber, were in third place as they arrived in St. Louis to begin their first western swing. In the first encounter with the Cardinals, Hubbell defeated Dizzy Dean in a game marked by a monumental brawl involving almost all of the players. Trouble began brewing in the sixth inning when a balk, called by umpire George Barr against Dean, helped the Giants to three runs, wiping out a Cardinals lead. Facing Bartell with one out and Whitehead on second, Dean half turned toward second and then, without coming to the prescribed pause in his delivery, pitched to Bartell who lifted an easy fly ball for the apparent second out. But Barr disallowed the play and called the balk. Given another chance, Bartell lined to Pepper Martin in right field. The colorful Pepper, busy preparing a fresh chaw of tobacco with his glove tucked under one arm, could not get his guard up fast enough and he muffed the ball. Whitehead scored, and Dean fumed on the mound. The Giants scored two more runs during the inning as Dean's temper rose to the boiling point.

Dizzy took his anger out on the Giants. He began to throw bean balls, pitches thrown not so much to keep hitters loose at the plate, but rather to force them to hit the dirt to avoid being skulled. Batter after batter, the Giants went down like duckpins. An angry shouting match continued between Dean and the Giants. The climax came in the ninth when Dean sent Jimmy Ripple sprawling to avoid a pitch headed for his chin. Climbing to his feet, Ripple looked into the Giants dugout, nodded as if giving his teammates a signal, then shouted to Dean, "The next one is going down the line, you hillbilly bastard! Let's see if you have the guts to cover."

With that, Ripple bunted well inside the first base line. The ball, bunted harder than Ripple had intended, bounded to second baseman Jimmy Brown, who prepared to throw it to first baseman Johnny Mize. But Brown held the ball as Dean, who no longer had any business in the play, raced over to first base determined to block the stocky Ripple's path to the bag. The two men crashed right on the base. Almost simultaneously, the Giants raced out to the mound where they were joined by the entire Cardinals team. Fists flew wildly, and for a time it was difficult to tell the fighters from the peacemakers. Off to one side, near the backstop, Gus Mancuso and Mickey Owen became embroiled in their own private slugfest.

Eventually, umpires Barr, Dolly Stark, and Bill Stewart and a squad of policemen managed to separate the battlers. Surprisingly, the umpires evicted only Mancuso and Owen, presumably because they had started a private fight. The ruffled, but otherwise uninjured, Dean and Ripple were allowed to remain in the game. Ripple was credited with a single as, in all the excitement, he had not been put out at first base. Equally surprising, considering the number of players involved, the only reported injury was a magnificent black eye administered to Cardinals rookie third baseman Don Gutteridge by doughty Dolph Luque. Through it all, a serene Carl Hubbell, the only player who remained quietly on the sidelines, moved along imperturbably to win his sixth straight victory of the campaign and his twenty-second in a row, not counting his World Series loss to the Yanks.

The next day Ford Frick fined Dean and Ripple for starting the brawl. Frick did not fine Mancuso or Owen despite their ejections from the game. Manager Frankie Frisch would not answer Frick directly when asked if Dean had thrown bean balls. And Terry's only comment was a solicitous, "We all feel sorry about little Gutteridge's black eye."

In Chicago Terry benched Ott, who was battling a dismal .167, and replaced Mel with Ripple. (Ott had tried everything to shake a season-long slump, including switching back to his old familiar number 4 uniform after having been assigned the retired Terry's number 3). This was the first time Ott had been benched for not hitting since he became a regular in 1928. It was not the immediate solution since the Giants lost to the Cubs the next day. But on the following day Ott's brief rest cure ended, and he responded by supplying all of the power in a victory over the Cubs with a three-run homer off lefthander Larry French, one of his favorite "cousins." Mel also hit homers to provide the winning margins in succeeding series as Hubbell beat the Pirates and the Reds to run his consecutive game-winning streak to 24. Sparked by their two leaders, the Giants continued to win and returned home in second place, only one and a half games behind the Pirates.

Hubbell's winning streak came to an end at the hands of the Dodgers, his career-long nemesis, in the first game of the Memorial Day doubleheader. The second largest crowd in Polo Grounds history, 61,756, watched as King Carl was routed in the fourth inning after retiring only one batter. But it was not Hub's last appearance of the day. Between games of the doubleheader he stood at home plate to receive the 1936 National League Most Valuable Player award. It was presented to him by a portly, snappily-dressed Babe Ruth, a man still waiting for an offer to manage a major league team.

Towering Cliff Melton, who had been a pleasant surprise all season, relieved Clydell Castleman in the second game and took a fearful riding from the Dodgers. Brooklyn shortstop Woody English in particular gave the toothy, guileless southpaw from North Carolina a rough time. Batting against the elephant-eared Melton, English yelled out to him, "You ought to paint those ears green." Melton drawled back, "What for?" English rasped in reply, "To give us a good hitting background, you busher!" The good-natured lefty grinned sheepishly. But he had the last laugh. He was the winning pitcher when first baseman Johnny McCarthy singled in the winning run in the bottom of the ninth to give the Giants an even split on the day.

The club held its own in June as Hubbell, Schumacher, Melton, and Castleman pitched steady ball. Mancuso, Bartell, and Whitehead anchored the defense. And Ott regained his hitting form and continued to play the best right field in the league.

Ott was so accomplished an outfielder that he worked on plays designed specifically to trap baserunners. Mel and Bartell developed a variation of the time-honored cutoff play. On a hit to right field with a runner on first, they reasoned that the man on first in most instances would go to third base. In such cases Bartell would signal Ott to throw directly to him. Dick would then throw to second base and on occasion nail the hitter who had made up his mind to take second in anticipation of a throw over the cutoff man to third base. Mel also had set plays with the first baseman and catcher. On a hit past first base into right field, the first baseman might return immediately to the bag in anticipation of a quick throw from Ott to catch an unsuspecting runner rounding the bag. In a variation of this play, the first baseman would stray from the bag deliberately to decoy the runner rounding the bag, and Ott would throw to catcher Harry Danning who had sneaked up to take the throw at first base.

Terry made two trades before the June 15 trading deadline. One deal brought outfielder Wally Berger to replace the ailing Hank Leiber. The second trade was a shocker as Fitzsimmons was traded to the Dodgers for Tom Baker, a young righthander. This proved to be one of the worst deals in Giants history. Baker, sent to Jersey City for more seasoning, came back to win a total of two games for the Giants before they released him in 1938. Fitzsimmons, who had done little for the Giants all season, found a new home at Ebbets Field and helped the Dodgers for several years. At the time of the trade, though, Freddy thought it was the worst day of his life. He told a writer years later, "I'll never forget riding across the bridge to Brooklyn in a taxi that afternoon. More than once I almost told the driver to turn around and go back. What was I going to Brooklyn for? I was a Giant, and for years I had hated the Dodgers. It almost made me feel sick. But it all turned out well."

The last of the epic Hubbell–Dizzy Dean pitching battles came on June 27. This one was won by King Carl in St. Louis as Ott supported him with two home runs. Hubbell won eight of the 11 head-to-head games between the two future Hall of Famers.

The Giants were a game behind the league-leading Cubs by the All-Star game break. Terry managed the National League squad which included Hubbell, Ott, Moore, Bartell, Whitehead, and Mancuso. The game, which was played in Washington, was won by the Yankee-dominated American league, 8–3.

The Giants slumped in July. In a loss to the lowly Phillies on July 12, Terry was ejected from the game for the first time in his 15 years with the Giants. In that same game, the Giants pulled off a triple play, courtesy of Ott. With the bases loaded, Phillies outfielder Morrie Arnovich hit a low liner into short right field which appeared to be a sure hit. But Mel raced in and snared the ball just off the grass, juggled it, and finally brought it under control. Ott gunned a throw to Mancuso to cut down the runner coming in from third base, and Gus nailed the runner who had been on second base trying to take third.

By early August the Giants had fallen seven games back of the league-leading Cubs, and Terry shook up the lineup in the middle of a western trip. He replaced the weak-hitting Chiozza at third with the versatile Ott. Leiber took over in right field with Ripple going to center field, and Sam Leslie took McCarthy's place at first base. The lineup changes helped, and the Giants picked up three games on the Cubs by the time they returned home. Terry's club won nine of 11 games against the western clubs to move into first place with a one-game lead over Chicago. Ott led the attack, clouting six home runs and hitting safely in each of the 11 games. Mel was not a polished third baseman, but he played a sound, dependable game, and the Giants lineup had more punch with Ripple playing every day.

Amidst all the excitement during the home stand, there were rumors that Terry had been approached by the Cleveland club about managing the Indians. But club president Horace Stoneham ended all speculation by signing Terry to a five-year contract as general manager. In announcing the contract in early September, Stoneham explained, "We felt it was much better to take this action now and end all of the rumors rather than wait until the end of the season. Bill will continue as manager, and he also will be responsible for directing our farm system, making deals, and signing players." The last-named duty was greeted with little enthusiasm by several of the players, especially Leiber, Danning, and Bartell, who had experienced difficulties in negotiating contracts with Terry who was a tough bargainer, whether representing himself as a player or representing the Giants in dealing with a player. Many years later, both Moore and Hubbell expressed the view that Terry lost rapport with the players after he took on these larger responsibilities.

The Giants held a two and a half game lead over Chicago when they arrived in town for their final three-game series with the Cubs. Charlie Root won the first game for the home club, but Melton evened the series with a sparkling shutout. Schumacher started against righthander Curt Davis in the pivotal third game before a large midweek crowd.

The Giants had a 3–0 lead after three innings, but the Cubs knocked out Schumacher and tied the game against Hubbell, who relieved Prince Hal. The Giants moved ahead 8–3, but the Cubs drove out Hubbell, and Harry Gumbert came in and lasted until the bottom of the ninth when the Cubs, behind 8–6, loaded the bases with one out. Terry, sparing none of his horses, brought in Melton who retired outfielder Carl Reynolds on a fly ball as another run came in. With the winning run on base, Augie Galan stepped in to hit. The fleet outfielder worked Melton to a full count and then tapped a slow bouncer to the right of the straining Melton. Ott raced in, shouted Melton off the ball, and gunned out Galan to end the game. The Giants returned home triumphantly with a three-and-a-half-game lead.

The Giants kept up the pace after returning to the Polo Grounds, taking four in a row from the Dodgers and the Bees as the pitching staff got some much-needed help from two new members, righthanders Walter (Jumbo) Brown and Bill Lohrman. Then, on September 30 in Philadelphia, the Giants clinched the pennant on Hubbell's 2–1 win over righthander Claude Passeau. It was a typical 1937 Giants win—Hubbell's airtight pitching, good defense, and a one-run victory.

Coach Pancho Snyder managed the team in the clincher with Terry back in New York nursing a heavy cold. In their clubhouse the Giants were their usual undemonstrative selves, except for the ebullient Bartell. The little shortstop held up the ball he had caught for the final out and loudly proclaimed, "Now bring on those Yanks."

Hubbell had another brilliant year, leading the league with 22 wins and 159 strikeouts, and extending his winning streak to 24. Melton had an outstanding rookie year with 20 wins, ranking second in the league in saves and ERA, and fourth in strikeouts. Bartell and Whitehead again held the infield together with their adroit, steady play, and Bartell's consistent hitting in the early months kept the offense going when Ott was laboring through his early-season slump. Mel came back with a great second half, tying Joe Medwick for the home run lead with 31, leading the league in walks, and finishing fifth in RBIs. Most experts considered the successful switch of Ott to third base and Melton's strong season as the keys to the Giants' pennant win.

The Yankees had won the American League pennant again, and they were heavily favored as the teams prepared for the World Series. After all, the Bronx Bombers had beaten the Giants decisively the previous fall and had dominated the American League a second time, while the Giants again had to struggle to win the pennant. Still, there were some who thought the Giants had a better chance than in 1936. DiMaggio, Gehrig, and Dickey were as devastating as they were in 1936, but the other Yanks had not done as well. Moreover, the Giants had a much more balanced pitching staff than in 1936 when they were almost completely dependent on Hubbell. This time the general feeling was that even if Hubbell should fail, it would not necessarily finish off the Terrymen.

The opener was played at Yankee Stadium before 60,573, with Gomez opposing Hubbell. Behind 1–0 in the sixth inning, the Yanks came back with a vengeance when Gomez walked and moved to second on Crosetti's hit. With Rolfe up, Mancuso whipped a bulls-eye peg down to second that appeared to have picked off Gomez. But Bartell dropped the throw as Lefty dove back to the bag. DiMaggio, Dickey, and Selkirk drove in five runs and that was enough for Terry. He took out Hubbell and motioned in Dick Coffman.

As Coffman began the long walk in from the bullpen, the perplexing announcement boomed out over the loudspeaker, "Gumbert, Number 10, now pitching for the Giants." This astonished the crowd as Harry Gumbert was sitting quietly in the Giants dugout, hardly ready to face the murderous Yankees. As it turned out, the mistake was not the announcer's but rather that of captain Gus Mancuso, who had notified plate umpire Red Ormsby erroneously that Gumbert was the reliever. The rules required Gumbert to pitch to at least one batter, so the cold righthander rose resignedly from the bench, peeled off his jacket, and replaced the warmed-up Coffman on the mound. Gumbert took his allotted eight warm-up throws, added a few extra tosses to first base for good measure, then bent to the task of retiring Lazzeri. He did his job as Tony bounced to Whitehead, but Burgess let the ball roll through his legs for an error and the Yanks had their sixth run. Coffman immediately took the mound and allowed another run before retiring the side. That was the story of the game as Gomez won easily, his fourth World Series victory without a loss. After the game, Terry, ignoring the shellacking absorbed by Hubbell, said, "That throw that Bartell dropped with Gomez six feet off the bag was the break of the game."

In the second game it was Ruffing against Melton before 57,675. The game was almost a carbon copy of the opener. The Giants scored in the first inning when Ott drove in Bartell. Helped along by Bartell's defensive heroics, Melton held the Yanks scoreless until the fifth when Selkirk drove in Myril Hoag. Two more hits brought in Selkirk, and Gumbert relieved Melton. This time Harry's entrance was made uneventfully, and he retired the Yanks, holding the score at 2–1. But the Bronx Bombers moved well ahead in the sixth and went on to win 8–1 as Ruffing polished off the Giants effortlessly.

"What is there to say? Those guys just beat the hell out of us," croaked Terry hoarsely. He still felt the effects of the heavy cold which had plagued him for two weeks. Fans and writers recalled that the Yankees had crushed their National League opponents in four straight in the 1927, 1928, and 1932 World Series, and there was considerable speculation that the machine-like Yanks were headed for another grand slam Series victory. With this a looming possibility, the classic moved across the Harlem River to the Polo Grounds.

In the third game it was Pearson against Schumacher before 37,395. It was the same unhappy story as the Giants lost 5–1. The Yanks chopped away methodically at Schumacher, and the Giants were helpless offensively. After the game, Terry said grimly, "Who would have thought that we would have been held to only three runs in three games?" Unaware that Joe McCarthy had announced that Bump Hadley would pitch the following day, Terry added, "I'll be surprised if they don't start Gomez tomorrow. Hub will pitch for us."

A Saturday afternoon crowd of 44,293 was on hand for the fourth game, fully expecting that it would be the last game of the Series. For some reason, the Yanks were annoyed at Terry's offhand prediction that Gomez would start. Apparently they considered it an affront to Hadley. As a result, the usual needling between the teams had a special edge from the start of the game. The Yanks scored in the first inning when Rolfe tripled and DiMaggio drove him in. The Giants fought back to tie the game and then moved ahead 6–1 after two innings on hits by Moore, Bartell, and Leiber. As the game continued, the jockeying between the clubs intensified. The Giants became particularly incensed at some of Art Fletcher's antics in the third base coaching box. The lantern-jawed Fletcher was noted for his ability to steal signs and pick up telltale mannerisms of opposing players.

Fletcher tried to stir up Hubbell by going through motions indicating he was stealing signs and tipping off the hitters. At one point the normally easy-going Ott begged his roommate, "Come on, Hub, dust a couple of them off just to shut Fletcher up." The unruffled Hubbell replied, "What for?" Mel answered, "He's trying to get your goat by making you think he's stealing our signs." The great lefthander shrugged and responded, "Don't worry, Mel. Fletcher's not fooling anyone. He isn't bothering me at all, and besides, I'm not going to start throwing dusters at this stage of the game.

Hubbell continued to handle the dynamic Yanks with ease, yielding only a harmless bases-empty home run to Gehrig in the ninth. The final score was 7–3 and the redoubtable "meal ticket" had at least averted another Yankees sweep. After the game, the Bombers were snappish despite their still-imposing lead in the Series. "So Terry was surprised that I didn't pitch Gomez today?" growled McCarthy. "Well, let him run his club and I'll run mine!" The belligerent Fletcher added, "Terry's the guy that's down. Let him crawl out of it."

And so the Series moved into its fifth game with Gomez facing Melton before 38,216 fans. The Yanks took the lead in the second inning when Hoag homered. DiMaggio increased the lead to 2–0 in the top of the third with a tremendous blast over the left field roof. The Giants tied the score in the bottom of the inning as the overdue Ott, who had been held to three singles in the first four games, clouted a two-run homer deep into the upper right field stands. Gomez and Gehrig drove in two more runs to end the scoring.

Gomez's performance was distinguished not only by his pitching mastery and a rare base hit, but also for his nonchalance on the mound. In a late inning, with a Giants runner on first and the dangerous Ott at bat, Lefty stepped off the mound to stare up at a passing airplane. The crowd buzzed in amusement while Joe McCarthy fidgeted uneasily in the dugout. After the plane passed out of sight, the casual Gomez stepped back on the mound and proceeded to rub the Giants out with ease on the way to a 4–2 win, and another Yankees Series victory.

McCarthy and Fletcher were jubilant in the clubhouse. Fletcher told the writers, "Why don't you guys go back and tell Terry—well, what the hell," he interrupted himself in midsentence. "He's all right, everything's all right. Just tell Terry that I hope he gets over his cold soon and that we meet him in the Series again next year." The acrimony of the day before had disappeared with the Yankees triumph.

Interviewed after the game, Terry at first complained about the umpiring in the Series. But after a while Memphis Bill gained his composure and talked candidly about the Series, his disappointment, and his admiration for the Yankees. After all, the Giants had been beaten soundly and, as the *World Telegram*'s Joe Williams put it, "The turning point of the Series was when the Yanks suited up for the first game."

Chapter 11

THE RANKS ARE DECIMATED

After training for the 1938 season at Baton Rouge, Louisiana, and completing their annual barnstorming tour with the Indians, the Giants were ready to go after their third straight pennant. Johnny McCarthy was set at first base, with Sam Leslie backing him up. Lou Chiozza replaced the high-strung Whitehead who would be out for the season following an emergency appendectomy which brought on a nervous breakdown. Bartell was primed for another strong year, and Ott was playing third base with more assurance after a full preseason at the bag. Blondy Ryan and journeyman Mickey Haslin were the utility infielders.

Ripple started the season in right, with Leiber in center, Moore in left, and Wally Berger in reserve. Heavier hitting had won Harry Danning the starting catcher's job over Mancuso. The pitching staff looked solid enough with Hubbell, Melton, Schumacher, and Gumbert in the starting rotation and Castleman scheduled to join them after he recuperated from back surgery. Two young righthanders, Bill Lohrman and Hy Vandenberg, showed promise, and Dick Coffman and Jumbo Brown were the relief pitchers.

Favored to win again, the Giants started beautifully, winning 18 of their first 21 games to move out ahead of the second-place Cubs. John Drebinger, of the *Times*, described their start as "one of the most impressive breaks from the barrier a serious contender has been able to effect in years." Second base was the only problem in sight with Whitehead gone and replacement Chiozza not hitting.

The Giants remained in first place on Memorial Day, two and a half games ahead of the Cubs. With neither Chiozza nor Haslin adequate at second base, Terry traded Wally Berger to the Reds for second baseman Alex Kampouris. The Giants replaced Berger by purchasing outfielder Bob Seeds from Newark, where he had been burning up the International

League. There were other changes as Terry maneuvered to keep his club on top. An injury to Moore forced Ott's return to the outfield with Blondy Ryan taking over at third. And Leslie replaced the slumping McCarthy for a number of games. Despite these changes, the Giants held their own through June, and on July 4 they were still in first place, three and a half games ahead of the Pirates and six games up on the Cubs.

The Giants' representatives on the All-Star team were Hubbell, Ott, Moore, Leiber, Danning, and Terry, who managed the National League squad. He had the satisfaction of seeing the National League regain some prestige as it defeated Joe McCarthy's American Leaguers 4–1 in Cincinnati's Crosley Field. Ott played the entire game in center field and whacked a triple, the longest hit of the day.

The Giants slipped after the mid-season break and relinquished the league lead to the Pirates just before arriving in Chicago to complete their third western trip. Gabby Hartnett replaced Charley Grimm as Cubs manager the day before the Giants arrived, and capacity crowds watched as Bill Lee and Dizzy Dean won the first two games.

Dean had been sidelined with a sore arm most of the time since joining the Cubs just before Opening Day. Dizzy showed no sign of his former speed, but he exhibited a remarkable display of sheer pitching wizardry as he kept the Giants off balance all through the game. A violent brawl between Bartell and Billy Jurges enlivened the game. It started when Jurges crashed hard into Bartell on a rundown play. The two shortstops rolled around second base kicking and punching, and it took a number of players to pry them apart. As the Giants returned to their dugout, Jimmy Ripple was heard to comment, "Well, the season is official now, Bartell finally got into a scrap."

The Giants returned home four games behind the Pirates, having won only four of 13 decisions on the trip. Things continued to deteriorate. Chiozza broke his collarbone and was finished for the season. Schumacher developed bone chips in his pitching arm which hampered him for the rest of the season and required post-season surgery. Kampouris was a flop at second base. The final blow came on August 18 when Hubbell sustained a serious elbow injury while pitching against the Dodgers. After the game, he said ruefully, "My elbow felt as though knives were cutting through it every time I tried to put anything on the ball." Carl continued, "I've had some pains going back to 1934, but they always worked themselves out before long. But I'm afraid this is a different story." A few days later Hubbell had bone chips removed, and he was finished for the year.

Ott, who was carrying the club offensively, received a fine tribute from Pirates manager Pie Traynor in an interview with Garry Schumacher, a writer for the *New York Journal-American* and later a Giants official. Traynor said, "You newspaper fellows write a great deal about ballplayers and love to compare them. But when you talk about National League players, Ottie has got to be the best in all the years I've been with the Pirates. My logic is simple. The best players are those who win the most games, and I can't name a player who has exerted as strong an influence upon so many games as Mel. I know that he personally has beaten the Pirates more often than any other player, and on the other teams the players I talk to express the same thought."

A short time after this professional testimony to his ability, Mel received tangible evidence of his personal appeal to the fans. A cereal company ran a contest to determine the most popular major league player at each position. Mel received most votes given both the third basemen and the right fielders. He was presented with a resplendent, blue sedan for winning the right fielder vote, and popular Chicago Cubs third baseman Stan Hack, who was second to Ott in the third baseman vote, was also awarded a car.

New York Daily News writer Dick McCann wrote of Ott's concern for the vote for his close friend Hubbell. McCann was in charge of publicity for the award, and he dropped in to the Giants dugout to inform Mel of his winning the vote. Mel said, "Thanks a lot. How about the pitchers? Does Hub have a chance?" When McCann told Mel that Hubbell also had been selected, Ott responded, "Gee, that's swell. Excuse me." McCann wrote, "He ran all the way to the clubhouse to tell Hubbell. Believe me, he was more pleased over Hubbell's winning than he was over himself."

Ott also was a favorite of the Dodgers' groundskeeper Buddy Schwab. Years later Schwab told sports editor Jimmy Powers of the *Daily News*:

> I remember when I first got the job in '38, the Dodgers were returning from a western trip to play the Giants. I had had a tough time with the turf. The infield was in horrible condition and the Giants made four errors in the first inning, two by third baseman Ott. When the Giants returned to their dugout they were cussing furiously. Ott merely said, "I guess that's the worst infield in the league." I happened to be sitting nearby and I told Mel I had had tough luck, rain, poor fertilizer, etc. in my first try. Mel immediately said, "Oh, I didn't know that. Don't feel too bad." On the next Giant trip to Ebbets Field, Ottie came over to me and complimented me on having the best field in the league. He lied like a gentleman, but I appreciated his kindness.

One of the most enduring stories in sports in years concerned baseball heroes who cheered sick or dying youngsters by paying them a well-publicized visit. Dick McCann wrote about such a visit by Mel:

> There was the time we asked Ott to drop in and see a dying boy who, in his delirium, kept talking about the Giants. Doctors said it might help if one of the players could see him. Ott agreed to meet us in his hotel lobby the next morning. As usual, we were late. We figured Mel had gone off in a huff, so we rushed over to the hospital to apologize to the boy's mother.
>
>   Yes, you guessed it. Mel was already there, sitting on the edge of the bed. And the boy, his eyes bright and not completely with fever, was fingering an autographed baseball and a Polo Grounds pass Mel had thoughtfully brought along. The doctor said, "It's amazing. He's been here ten minutes and he's done more for the boy than I did in ten days." And, now, here's the Ott touch: When we asked Mel to pose for a picture with the boy, Mel said, "No, it would look like I did this just to get my picture in the paper."

Considering their injuries, the Giants did well to finish in third place, clinching that spot on the last day of the season when Gumbert beat Boston. Individually, only Ott, Danning, and Moore had good years. Mel led the league in homers with 36 and in runs scored, was second in walks, and third in total bases. Defensively, his willingness and ability to shift back and forth between right field and third base gave Bill Terry at least some of the defensive flexibility he needed. Danning, despite personal difficulties with Terry, established himself as the regular catcher with his solid hitting and improved handling of the pitchers. Moore, although handicapped by injuries, hit .302.

Meanwhile the Cubs, after falling well behind the Pirates, came back in a manner highly reminiscent of their great 1935 stretch drive. They won 20 of 23 games to pull even with Pie Traynor's club and moved ahead on Gabby Hartnett's dramatic, tie-breaking homer in the gathering darkness of Wrigley Field. They went on to clinch the pennant a few days later leaving the Pirates with broken dreams of their first title since 1925, and thousands of unusable World Series tickets. None of the Giants or their fans were surprised by the outcome of the World Series. The Yankees polished off the Cubs in four straight.

The Giants pulled off a major trade with the Cubs in early December. Bartell, Leiber, and Mancuso were traded for their opposite numbers; shortstop Billy Jurges, outfielder Frank Demaree, and catcher Ken O'Dea. After the deal was announced, a writer asked Terry, "What do you think of the trade?" Never one to suffer fools or foolish questions gladly, Terry snapped, "What the hell do you think I think of it? I just made the trade!"

The following week the Giants obtained Ott's old basketball companion, first baseman Henry (Zeke) Bonura from the Washington Senators. A New Orleans native, the powerful Bonura had been one of the

American League's hardest hitters in four years with the Chicago White Sox and in 1938 with the Senators. His fielding was another matter. One of the Washington writers, having observed Bonura's still-life, wooden Indian style at first base for a full season, commented, "I hope Mel Ott hasn't signed yet. The extra chasing he'll be doing in back of Zeke ought to be worth a few extra thousand dollars." But Terry was pleased at bolstering his club's attack. "I know all about Zeke's fielding," he said, "but we're prepared to work on that. What counts most is that we've finally got a first baseman who can powder the ball."

Brooklyn Dodgers president Larry MacPhail, having opened up the New York City area to night baseball in 1938, announced that the Dodgers planned to broadcast all of their home and away games in 1939. In January the Giants and the Yankees, bowing to the inevitable, made arrangements to broadcast all home games over station WABC. Mel Allen handled these early broadcasts along with Arch McDonald.

There were a number of question marks as the Giants regrouped for spring training. Hubbell, Schumacher, and Castleman were recuperating from surgery. Among the other pitchers in camp were Gumbert, Melton, Lohrman, Johnny Wittig, Dick Coffman, Jumbo Brown, Hy Vandenberg, and Pacific Coast League righthander Manuel Salvo. Danning, with Mancuso gone, began a season for the first time as the uncontested first-string catcher. Ken O'Dea and Tommy Padden were the backup receivers.

The infield was unsettled except at shortstop where Jurges was unchallenged. Bonura, of course, had to be considered the regular first baseman although Johnny McCarthy was still on hand. Second base presented an unclear picture with Whitehead having missed the entire 1938 season and Chiozza, Kampouris, Bill Cissell, and ex–Reds player Alban Glossop also in camp. At third base, two youngsters, George Myatt and Tom Hafey, up from the Giants' Knoxville affiliate, competed for the starting job. The regular outfield appeared set with Ott (newly installed as captain, replacing Mancuso) back in right field, Frank Demaree in center, and Moore in left. Jimmy Ripple and Bob Seeds backed up the starting trio.

Picked to finish second behind Cincinnati, the Giants had their poorest start since Terry took over the club. The first New York World's Fair had just opened, and Terry, Hubbell, and Ott participated in a baseball clinic at the fair. At that time the Giants were in seventh place while the Dodgers, under new manager Leo Durocher, roosted in second place. Terry found himself surrounded by young hecklers from Brooklyn. A group of them shouted a number of pointed questions at the Giants manager, questions like, "Is Brooklyn still in the league?" and "Do you think you'll make it out of the second division?" Terry brought a round of appreciative laughter with the sly response, "I realize the Giants are only in seventh and the Dodgers are in second. But I'm sure Durocher and his gang feel just as much out of place as we do."

After splitting a Memorial Day doubleheader with the Dodgers, the Giants were in fifth place, half a game behind Durocher's club. Only Gumbert and Lohrman were pitching well. Hubbell, Schumacher, and Castleman were having post-surgery problems, and Melton and Salvo were completely uneffective. The only bright spots were the hitting of Bonura, Ott, and Danning and the superior defensive play of Whitehead and Jurges.

Bonura had become a Polo Grounds favorite despite his atrocious fielding. The fans loved to watch big Zeke hit, and they were intrigued by some of his fielding mannerisms as well, particularly his manner of handling unassisted putouts. After snaring a ground ball, Bonura would charge to the bag with his right arm outstretched and his palm down, looking for all the world like a fullback straight-arming a would-be attacker.

By July 2 the Giants had moved up to second place, four games behind the Reds, after a tempestuous doubleheader with the Dodgers at the Polo Grounds. Leo Durocher's club won the opener 3–2 before more than 51,000 highly excited fans by routing Bill Lohrman and weathering a Giants threat in the eighth on Ott's two-run homer off Luke Hamlin.

With Schumacher facing Whitlow Wyatt in the second game, the Giants moved out to an early 4–0 lead. The Dodgers came back in the fourth with three runs, driving out Schumacher. Durocher, in his last season as a regular player, ended the inning by banging into a double play. As Lippy Leo crossed first base and ran down the baseline, there was an astonishing sight. Bonura, after taking the third out throw, wheeled and chased Durocher. On the way Zeke fired the ball at Leo's head, barely missing, and then threw his glove at Durocher. Bonura closed in on the Dodgers manager and with his left arm clamped a hammerlock around Leo's head, meanwhile delivering a series of uppercuts. The smaller Durocher returned fire with an assortment of body blows. For a moment it looked as if the fight would extend to other players as both dugouts emptied onto the field. But the umpires managed to avert a free-for-all, and the two belligerents were separated and ejected as the fans showered the field with pop bottles and assorted fruits and vegetables.

After the Giants tied the game at four–all, Danning broke the tie with a home run, and the Giants won 6–4. The large crowd left, still highly excited by the fight and the two tight games. Later in the Giants clubhouse Bonura was still furious. "That little bastard spiked me deliberately," Zeke fumed. Durocher told the writers, "If that big clown hadn't got his foot in the way, I wouldn't have been close to him." Actually, Leo felt that Schumacher had pitched him too close after the Dodgers scored three runs off Prince Hal and, with Hal taken out of the game, Bonura became the fall guy for Leo's retaliation. The teams met again a few days later in Brooklyn, but the games were surprisingly peaceful.

At the All-Star game break, the Giants were in second place, five and a half games behind the Reds. Ott, Jurges, and Danning were voted to the National League All-Star squad, which lost 3–1 at Yankee Stadium. Ott, the only Giants participant, played the entire game in center field and contributed two hits.

The resurgent Giants began the second half of the season by taking on the western teams at the Polo Grounds. They split two uneventful games with the Reds. The third game would be remembered for many years. Harry Gumbert held a 4–3 lead as the Reds came to bat in the eighth inning. With a runner on, Reds outfielder Harry Craft lined a low, curving drive into the lower left field stands near the foul pole. Plate umpire Lee Ballanfant ruled it a fair ball, giving the Reds a 5–4 lead. Danning stormed around Ballanfant, shoving the official and shouting his protest of the call. Harry the Horse was immediately thumbed out of the game.

But the protest was still building as the Giants took their case to Ziggy Sears, the second base umpire. After a long harangue with Sears, easy-going Joe Moore, who presumably had the best view of the ball when it passed the foul pole, was thrown out of the game. The Giants had plenty of manpower left, and they continued the verbal abuse until big George Magerkurth, the first base umpire, moved up to home plate to end the argument. He began to talk animatedly to Jurges. Suddenly, according to Magerkurth, Jurges shouted at him, "Don't you spit in my face." Magerkurth, a confirmed tobacco chewer, bellowed back, "Don't get your face so near mine and it won't get spit on." Jurges spat on the umpire, and the two men exchanged blows.

The fisticuffs brought the protest to an abrupt halt as Ballanfant ordered Jurges off the field. The Giants put a patchwork team on the field when the game resumed several minutes later. Chiozza moved from third to short, and Ott came in to play third. With Ripple already used as a pinchhitter, Johnny McCarthy went to right field and Hal Schumacher took over in center field. Not surprisingly, the Giants lost 8–4. In addition to the unusual player-umpire fight on the field, the incident is of special interest to baseball historians. It led to the installation of a net along the length of each Polo Grounds foul pole to aid umpires in judging whether a drive was fair or foul. All major league ballparks have been equipped with foul pole nets since that incident.

The next day league president Ford Frick suspended both Jurges and Magerkurth for ten days and fined each man $150. Danning, Moore, and Terry were fined $50 each. Terry's fine was "for failing to cooperate in handling the situation." The Giants took the field against the Cardinals with Chiozza at shortstop and Ott at third. To add to their problems, Danning reported a leg infection and was hospitalized. With the Giants losing 4–3 in the top of the ninth, the hitter lifted a fly into short left field. Chiozza, inexperienced at short, and Moore both raced for it. Chiozza caught the ball just before Moore crashed into him with terrific force. Both players were knocked sprawling, writhing in pain on the outfield grass as the players of both teams rushed to help them. Moore was lifted to his feet in a few minutes and was able to continue in the game. But Chiozza suffered a compound leg fracture and was taken off the field moaning in pain. His season was over.

Years later Harry Danning recalled the two disastrous events. He remained acutely aware of the damage it had done to the Giants' pennant chances, both the suspension and Chiozza's injury, which was a direct result of Jurges's enforced absence. Danning said, "Ballanfant was the only person in the ballpark who thought it was a fair ball. The Reds were laughing in their dugout. But it kicked us out of the pennant." With the Giants' season crumbling before their eyes, Horace Stoneham appealed to Ford Frick to permit Jurges to return to action, but he was turned down. The Giants lost all nine remaining games of the home stand and fell ignominiously into sixth place, 12½ games behind the Reds.

During the last 1930s and early 1940s, Toots Shor's restaurant in midtown Manhattan was the Giants' unofficial headquarters as it was for much of the New York show business and sporting crowd. Jack White's Club 21 was another favorite haunt. White was famous for his method of signaling Giants victories and defeats. A Giants win was indicated by a large sign at the club entrance giving the score with embellished details. Defeats called for a curt "No Game Today" message. Comedians Olsen and Johnson provided the shy Ott with one of his most embarrassing moments during an intermission of their famous extravaganza, "Hellza-poppin." They turned the spotlight on Mel and presented him with a softball autographed by the cast.

Effervescent actress Tallulah Bankhead was perhaps the most baseball-happy stage figure of that time. She discovered the Giants in the late 1930s and immediately embraced them with characteristic all-out enthusiasm. She even took the blame for their disastrous home stand. In a breezy *Sunday New York Times* article in 1947, she wrote:

> Back in the summer of 1939 I thought I had voodooed the Giants. I'd seen them play a dozen games in a row, save for matinee days, and they were doing fine until I invited the entire club to see a performance of "The Little Foxes." After the performance, I gave them a buffet supper—canapes and caviar and some of the minor beverages. First, Hubbell couldn't come because he was going to pitch the next day. Harry Danning didn't show up because he had a poisoned foot. Jurges had spit in an umpire's eye and had just escaped from Alcatraz. But Ott and Jo-Jo Moore and most of the rest of them came and said they had enjoyed the show.
>
> And what happened after that? The Giants lost eight in a row. Sure that I'd hexed them, I stayed away from the park. I even barred my maid from the Polo Grounds.

According to some Bankhead-watchers, her enthusiasm for the game far outstripped her knowledge of it. Ott, who wore No. 4, was her favorite Giants player. It was reported that her mind nearly cracked at the 1939 All-Star game when there seemed to be four Mel Otts playing. Her most frustrating experience came when she ventured over to Ebbets Field and spent the afternoon rooting for the Dodgers' Dolph Camilli, also No. 4. How was she to know that the Dodgers, and not the visiting Giants, would be wearing the white uniforms that afternoon? Tallulah hotly contested this story with the indignant response, "I'm no kin of Abner Doubleday's, and I have no desire to have my ashes cast in a silver urn at Cooperstown, but I know a hawk from a handsaw. I can tell Ott from Camilli on a clear day, even if I am nearsighted and color-blind."

On Labor Day the Giants were in fourth place, half a game ahead of the Dodgers but 13 games behind the league-leading Reds. A few days later there was a bizarre affair involving Burgess Whitehead. After not playing in 1938, the sensitive second baseman had gone through a poor season, compounded by the team's misfortunes in July. In mid–August he was suspended indefinitely for what Terry blandly described as an "infraction of club rules." It developed that Whitey had shown up just a few minutes before a game with the Dodgers. The following day he was not at Ebbets Field for a game, and this led to his suspension. It seems that Whitehead had appeared instead at Yankee Stadium in full uniform and sought permission to work out with the Yanks. Joe McCarthy, of course, vetoed the idea. Two days later Whitehead rejoined the Giants. The club had rescinded the suspension although Burgess hardly was back in Terry's good graces. In mid–September, Whitehead left the team again, and this time he was suspended for the rest of the season.

In spite of Bonura's team-leading .321 average, Terry lost all patience with Zeke because of his fielding shortcomings. Memphis Bill told the writers that Bonura would not be his first baseman in 1940. First baseman Norman (Babe) Young was brought up from Knoxville, and he played the rest of the season, impressing with his relaxed, lefthand, pull-hitting style and his smooth fielding. In other moves, Terry released pitcher Dick Coffman, sold Jimmy Ripple to the Dodgers, and purchased young, highly-regarded outfielder Johnny Rucker from the Atlanta club.

As the season wound down, the Giants sank unhappily into fifth place, finishing 18½ games behind the pennant-winning Reds and a humiliating six games behind the third-place Dodgers. Only Hubbell, Gumbert, and Ott had fairly decent seasons. King Carl was second in the league with a respectable 2.75 ERA, despite a modest 11 and 9 record. Harry Gumbert was fourth in the league in winning percentage with 18 wins and 11 losses. Although Ott missed the last month of play with severe charley horses, he was second in home runs, only one behind Johnny Mize, and second to Dolph Camilli in bases on balls.

There were the usual post-season rumors that Terry would be replaced as manager. Frankie Frisch's name bobbed up as the most likely successor. But Stoneham reaffirmed his confidence in Terry and announced that Memphis Bill would be back in 1940.

Chapter 12

THE DOLDRUMS

Through the fall of 1939, Horace Stoneham and Bill Terry pondered their next moves. The club had slipped from first to third in 1938, and now it had finished in fifth place. Attendance was down. To make matters worse, the Giants' downfall was accompanied by the rise of the Dodgers, who had climbed to third under the aggressive leadership of Larry MacPhail and Leo Durocher. New York fans other than the Flatbush Faithful began to realize that the Giants were no longer the only National League club in New York.

Stoneham and Terry considered building the Giants' farm system as the most logical means of revitalizing the team. MacPhail, on the other hand, picked up and discarded players like so many chewing gum wrappers. When Terry took over the club in 1932, the Giants had only 27 players in their organization, all of them on the Giants' roster. By midseason of 1939, the Giants owned or controlled the contracts of well over 100 players. This included 82 minor league players either directly owned by the Giants or on teams with which the Giants had a working agreement. The club now owned franchises in Jersey City; Clinton, Iowa; and in Forth Smith, Arkansas, and had working agreements with five other minor league teams. Supervision of the farm system had become a full-time job, and Terry was relieved of this responsibility.

The farm system talent was not ready for the majors, so the Giants were forced to buy promising minor league players. Johnny Rucker had been obtained from Atlanta before the 1939 season ended. In December, infielder Mickey Witek was acquired from the Yankees' prime breeding franchise at Newark. The Giants parted with Alex Kampouris, catcher Tommy Padden, and $40,000 for Witek, who had been named the most valuable player in the International League in 1939.

The easy-going Ott had sent his contract back unsigned for only the third time in his career. The Giants were concerned about the condition of his legs which had caused him to miss the last month of the season.

As a result, they wanted to cut his salary from the $20,000 he had been paid in 1939. Unlike many other players, including Terry in his playing days, Mel refused to adopt an attitude of wounded pride or to wail publicly about ungrateful owners. Rather, he considered salary negotiations as a private matter between himself and the club. Mel settled for a $19,500 salary and he reported to the club's Winter Haven, Florida, training camp on time.

The Giants had other question marks. The catching appeared to be solid enough with Danning at his peak and Ken O'Dea backing him up. But the pitching staff was something else. Gumbert had become the leading starter. Hubbell and Schumacher clearly could no longer be expected to match their heroics of past years. Melton had gone through two mediocre seasons since his outstanding rookie year in 1937.

The infield had potential, but the only settled position was at shortstop with the accomplished Jurges. Babe Young appeared ready to replace the disqualified Bonura. Witek showed promise at second. Whitehead, more or less back in the manager's good graces, had been shifted to third. In the outfield, Demaree was a sound player, but Moore had slowed down perceptibly. Ott had a terrible spring, hitting infrequently and with little of his customary power. Most of the attention was focused on handsome Johnny Rucker, dubbed the "Crabapple (Georgia) Comet," who became the camp sensation after a few unsteady weeks. He gained almost instant celebrity when *Life* magazine published a feature story on his life and times as an up-and-coming rookie in his first training camp.

Bonura, protesting a big cut in his $15,000 salary, reported unsigned at Stoneham's request. He was permitted to stay in camp at the club's expense, much to the disgust of Terry who never coddled signed regulars much less an unsigned ex-regular who no longer fit into his plans. Zeke was given permission to make a deal for himself. Eventually, he was traded back to the Senators for $10,000 and a young lefthander, Rene Monteagudo, who did not pan out.

For the first time since 1933, Terry's first full managerial year, the pollsters forecast a second division finish for the Giants. Despite these predictions, the club started off surprisingly well as Danning and Young hit with power, Jurges and Whitehead steadied the infield, and Gumbert, Hubbell, Melton, and Lohrman pitched well.

During the winter Stoneham and Terry had decided to equip the Polo Grounds for night baseball, and $125,000 worth of lights and auxiliary equipment was installed. The Giants' first night game at the Polo Grounds on May 24 was a big success as Gumbert won an 8–1 decision over Casey Stengel's inept Bees before a good-sized crowd.

The Terrymen had a big Memorial Day. They won a doubleheader from the Dodgers at Ebbets Field and in the bargain knocked Durocher's club out of the lead. Hubbell pitched a masterpiece in the first game as he held the Dodgers to one hit and faced only 27 batters. Johnny Hudson got the Dodger hit in the third inning, but he was promptly erased in a double play. The Giants wound up the day in third place, only four games behind the first-place Reds and two behind the Dodgers.

In early June Terry replaced the slumping Ott in the cleanup spot with Babe Young. This was the first time since Ott became a regular in 1928 that he was not batting cleanup. In another surprise, Mel showed up before a game in St. Louis wearing glasses. As he explained it, "I suppose I've always been nearsighted, but it's only been the last few years that I've noticed it, and it got worse this season." He laughed and said, "Before this it was tough in the outfield, too. If something stayed up in the sky, I knew it was a bird, and if it came down, it was a fly ball."

On June 23, the Giants suffered a crippling blow. Billy Jurges came up to bat to face the Reds' Bucky Walters. Bucky lost control of a pitch which struck the Giants shortstop squarely in the back of his head. There was a crack that sounded like bat meeting ball, and the ball caromed off Jurges' head and bounced beyond the mound. Walters was one of the first to reach Jurges, with fear in his eyes and a tremor in his voice. "I'm sorry, Billy," he said over and over again. Although there was no fracture, Jurges suffered a severe concussion and he would be out indefinitely.

Despite the loss of Jurges, July 4 found the Giants still in third place, only five games behind the league-leading Dodgers. Durocher's club was sparked by the addition of rookie shortstop Pee Wee Reese, the sterling play of Dixie (Peoples' Cherce) Walker, and a solid pitching staff of Whitlow Wyatt, Luke Hamlin, Vito Tamulis, Hugh Casey, Tex Carleton, Curt Davis, and the not-quite-washed-up Freddy Fitzsimmons.

The Giants faltered after the All-Star game, won by the National League 4–0. The hitting and pitching were spotty, and the defense had slipped badly with Jurges out. As July ended, the Giants had fallen 12 games behind the Reds and eight behind the Dodgers.

Ott's drastically reduced home run and run production totals had convinced many of the writers and fans that his days of stardom, if not his career, were coming to an end. In their desire to express their fondness for him, and their appreciation of his 15-year contribution to the New York baseball scene, a "Mel Ott Night" was held on August 7. A crowd of almost 54,000 filled the Polo Grounds to honor the Giants captain as the Giants took on the Dodgers. Ott, usually the focal point of horseplay and friendly needling among his teammates, sat alone in a corner of the dugout nervously twisting a piece of twine and dreading the thought of making a speech before such a large crowd.

A gift-laden table was brought out for the ceremonies. Covered with a Giants banner embroidered with Mel's familiar number 4, the table was unveiled to reveal a sterling silver set of 208 pieces and a sterling silver tea service. This was the fans' gift, derived from thousands of small contributions. It was presented to Mel by New York sports commentator Paul Douglas, who attained greater fame years later as a movie and stage actor. Hubbell, on behalf of the Giants, gave Ott a set of matched golf clubs. Then John Drebinger presented the little slugger with the first solid gold life membership card of the New York Baseball Writers Association to be given to a ballplayer. Brushing back tears, Mel thanked his admirers briefly but sincerely with the words, "I shall always remember these gifts as an expression of you fans and wish to thank you sincerely for all your loyalty and support over the years."

The game had an Auld Lang Syne quality as Hubbell started for the Giants and Fitzsimmons and Mancuso formed the Dodgers battery. But unfortunately for the Giants, the final score reflected the current reality. Hubbell was knocked out of the box, and Ott was held to a single although he made a great running catch on a Dolph Camilli drive. Dixie Walker belted out four hits in leading the Dodgers to an 8–4 win.

When Mel and Mildred returned to the Riverdale apartment they were renting, he found a special delivery letter from the widow of Ott's benefactor, Harry Williams. He had been killed in a plane crash years before. "Do you mind if I add a little something to your gifts?" wrote Mrs. Williams before sending the Otts a matching salad set. She added, "If Harry were alive, he would want me to, I know. It would have made him very happy."

Joe Williams, the *World Telegram*'s rather cynical sports editor, had nothing but praise for the tribute to Mel. He wrote:

> As a rule we do not get too enthusiastic about testimonials to well-paid ballplayers, but we felt a real pleasure in participating in the Ott affair. We sensed that there was solid sincerity on the part of Gus H. Fan, and we knew, too, that if Mr. Ott could have had his way the rituals would have been held under the grandstand in almost complete privacy. There was a decency to this expression that is not always present. They tied up the Ott tribute with a ball game that would have come close to packing the stands anyway. The Giants vs. the Dodgers at night is almost sure-fire.

By Labor Day, the Giants had dropped to fifth place, 17½ games behind the Reds. The club's difficulties on the field were matched by its deteriorating relations with the press. Stoneham was popular enough with the writers, and secretary Eddie Brannick had long been one of their favorites. But Terry came across as a cold, rather unfriendly, man, and he reinforced this notion by closing the clubhouse to the media and discouraging his players from talking to writers. Ott was an exception to this rule. Two highly-respected writers, Joe Williams and Dan Daniel, wrote years later that Mel was not afraid to talk to the writers although no one ever accused him of undermining his good friend Terry.

Terry's practice was to receive reporters in an annex of his Polo Grounds office. Writers had to climb a flight of stairs, descend another flight, pass a special policeman, then remain in a waiting room until Terry got around to coming out. Interviewing a player was comparable to visiting a relative in jail, as Tom Meany described it. Meany wrote:

> If a writer wanted to talk to any particular Giant player, he had two alternatives. He could wait until the player showered and dressed after a game and pounce upon him like an autograph hound. Or the writer could send in word through the policeman that he wanted to speak to a player. Then he could interview the player through a crack in the door with the same privacy you would find in a prison.

This presented a severe problem to the writers, and it was reflected in the increasingly poor press the team received. Of course, the club's poorest showing since 1937 stimulated press criticism and demand for a change, but much of it also stemmed from Terry's long-standing difficulties with the press.

The Giants fell apart completely in September, and on September 19 they lost their eleventh consecutive game, a new low for the years Terry managed the Giants. The club finished in sixth place, 27½ games behind Cincinnati. The pennant-winning Reds did not have to contend with the Yankees in the World Series. They beat the Detroit Tigers in seven games.

Despite the Giants' dismal year, there were some noteworthy individual performances. Schumacher was fourth in the league in strikeouts, Lohrman tied for the lead in shutouts with five, and Jumbo Brown shared the lead in saves. Babe Young's first full season was a success as he ranked fifth in RBIs. Danning was among the batting leaders until the last six weeks of the campaign when he tired and his hitting tailed off. And Ott, who had given up wearing glasses while playing, ranked second in walks and led the Giants in home runs with a late-season surge.

The Otts moved into a handsome, ten-room house in Metairie, a New Orleans suburb, over the winter. Mel signed his 1941 contact after meeting with Stoneham at the National League's winter meeting in

Atlanta. He had no complaint about being cut to $18,000 after his difficult season. Mel told the writers: "I only wear glasses occasionally off the field. I just needed an excuse for my slump last season. That's why I resorted to glasses for a few games. But I'm not too old at 31 to come back and have a good season."

Over the winter the Giants picked up Gabby Hartnett as a player-coach. There was much speculation that the move was a prelude to Gabby's eventual succession of Terry. But Memphis Bill played it straight, stating that "Gabby will make a good coach, and I think he can catch enough games to give Danning and O'Dea some rest."

When the full Giants squad reported to Miami, there were fewer new faces than the fans expected. Outfielder Morrie Arnovich had been purchased from the Reds. Infielder Joe Orengo and righthander Bob Bowman had been obtained from the Cardinals. Stocky righthander Ace Adams was brought up from the minors. But Giants fans who expected a major team overhaul were keenly disappointed.

The tentative regular infield included Young, Whitehead back at second, the headache-plagued Jurges at short, and Orengo at third. The infield reserves were McCarthy, Chiozza, and Mickey Witek, who concerned Terry because of his difficulty in pivoting on double plays. The outfield starters were expected to be Arnovich in left, Rucker in center, and either Ott or Demaree in right, depending upon how Mel looked after his sub-par season. Joe Moore and Buster Maynard were the reserve outfielders. Danning, O'Dea, and Hartnett were the catchers, and Hubbell, Schumacher, Melton, Gumbert, Lohrman, and Bowman were the likely starters.

Danning signed after a stubborn holdout. Terry surprised everyone by assigning Harry to left field, a position that the slow-footed Danning had never played before. Terry told the skeptical press, "Don't worry about our catching. O'Dea can handle it for most of the games, and Hartnett should be able to start 40 or 50 games." Reports coming out of Miami reflected the writers' doubts about Danning's shift, and their concerns proved justified as the experiment was abandoned after a few weeks.

There were some bright spots. Johnny Rucker seemed more relaxed and improved. Babe Young was hitting and fielding well. Ott, without benefit of glasses, was hitting solidly and giving every indication of having regained his old form, and Terry announced that Mel would start the season in right field. Hartnett had slimmed down considerably and was in his best condition in years.

The Reds were favored to win the pennant again with the Giants relegated to sixth place. As the 1941 season began, Terry claimed unconvincingly that his team "had improved in every department and would give a good account of itself." But the season proved almost a carbon copy of the 1940 campaign. Although the Giants were in third place by Memorial Day, they were eight and a half games behind the league-leading Cardinals. The hitting had improved with Ott back in form, but the pitching was poor, and the infield erratic with Jurges still suffering from his head injury.

In mid–May Terry traded Harry Gumbert to the Cardinals for pitcher Bill McGee. A big, apple-cheeked righthander, McGee had been a winning pitcher for the Cards in 1939 and 1940 after bouncing around the Cards' farm system, but he had been ineffective early in the 1941 season. The quiet Gumbert had been the Giants' biggest winner over the past three years, and writers and Giants fans were unhappy with the trade. A few days later Terry bolstered his infield by obtaining Dick Bartell from the Detroit Tigers. The players were amused as Bartell was assigned the locker next to Jurges, one of his long-standing adversaries.

For the first time the effects of the stepped-up war in Europe began to be felt at the ballparks. The draft had begun in late 1940, and several major leaguers, notably Hank Greenberg and Phillies pitcher Hugh Mulcahy, either were in the service or would be in uniform before long. The serious nature of the war was brought home to the fans dramatically during a night game at the Polo Grounds on May 27. That night President Roosevelt delivered one of his famous fireside chats, proclaiming an "unlimited emergency" and the U.S. intention of resisting further Nazi attempts to stop or destroy Allied vessels. With Schumacher facing the newly-renamed Boston Braves in a 1–1 tie in the third inning, umpire Jocko Conlan shouted "Time!" For 45 minutes the crowd sat in absorbed silence, listening to the president's solemn voice booming out of the loudspeakers atop the center field clubhouse. The players sat on the stairs leading up to the clubhouse or leaned out of the clubhouse windows overlooking the field, the game ignored as the national emergency commanded attention.

A few weeks later, a night game in Pittsburgh was halted temporarily in the fourth inning so that the fans could listen to a championship fight between Joe Louis and native son Billy Conn. The delay caused the game to be called after 11 innings, tied 1–1, because of a league ruling prohibiting the start of an inning after 11:30 P.M. Terry was furious, telling reporters that he could see halting a game to hear an important presidential address, "But hell," he complained, "not for a prize fight. They might as well hold up a game to listen to a Jack Benny or Bob Hope radio show."

Ott passed a career milestone on June 1. Mel helped Schumacher with a 3–2 victory over the Reds at the Polo Grounds by hitting his 400th home run and driving in his 1500th run. He had long since passed Rogers Hornsby's National League home run total of 298.

Mel took seriously his responsibilities as team captain. His teammates had teased him when he took over the captaincy after Gus Mancuso was traded following the 1938 season. They told him he would have to learn the rule book line by line. And they warned him that he could no longer go to his right field position directly from the Polo Grounds clubhouse at the start of each game as he had done for years. Instead, he would have to be in the dugout in order to bring the Giants' lineup to home plate before the start of a game. Terry told the writers, "Mel took over as captain as solemnly as though he was taking over control of the U.S. Army."

John Drebinger described Ott's unexpected firmness in an article in *Baseball Magazine*:

> One day (in 1941) Ott, as captain of the club, was assigned to take full charge for a day or so while Terry went off on some other business. Just before leaving, Bill instructed Mel that there was to be no beer drinking that evening on the train. Terry usually was never strict about such matters, but he felt that the boys were feeling a trifle too logy and so banned the beverage. The boss gone, a couple of players immediately ordered their bottle with the evening meal. But to the consternation of one and all, Ott stepped up, instructed the waiter that under no circumstances was beer to be served, and so help us, that order stuck.

The Giants were in third place on July 4, nine games behind the first-place Dodgers. After the All-Star game, won by the American League on Ted Williams' dramatic home run, the Giants began to lose ground to the Dodgers and Cardinals. The still-ailing Jurges returned to the lineup, and Bartell moved to third base replacing Joe Orengo. Hubbell, now a spot starter, won his seventh straight game. But it was clear that the Giants could not overtake the leaders, and Terry was the first to admit it, and he took his first housecleaning steps. Frank Demaree was sold to the Braves, and the Giants purchased outfielder Babe Barna from the Minneapolis club.

The team collapsed completely on its third western trip, winning only two of 13 games and returning home in fifth place, 16 games off the pace. During the trip, Terry told the writers that he would have a "sensational" announcement the following day. The writers speculated all night over their drinks about the announcement. Several were sure that Gabby

Hartnett would replace Terry. Whatever Memphis Bill had in mind fell through, though, because he told the reporters that he had reconsidered and no announcement would be made.

It was learned later that Terry had planned to announce his resignation in Pittsburgh. He had called Stoneham in New York and told him of his intended announcement. The owner flew out to Pittsburgh immediately and talked Terry into remaining. Stoneham told the writers that there would have to be a general housecleaning in 1942. He added that only Hubbell, Ott, Young, and Rucker were sure of their jobs, and that Terry would remain as manager "as long as he wants."

Will Wedge, a reporter for the *New York Sun*, wrote:

> Mel Ott, like Hubbell, could, and probably will, be kept around for old times' sake. Long since has passed the time when Ott might have been raffled off for a good price. Owner Horace Stoneham never wanted to part with Ott and still holds that view. While Ott has looked like a museum piece the past month, no one who knows him, or who has merely watched him during his spells of pumping homers into the bleachers, would like to see him leave the New York baseball scene. Considering how the loyal Stoneham feels about the matter, Ott should hang on for indefinite additional seasons as an extra outfielder and pinch hitter.

Terry still sought respectability for his club even as they slipped out of contention. He employed an old McGraw stratagem in an attempt to loosen up his shellshocked troops. Pitcher Johnny Wittig described it:

> We traveled to Boston and lost both ends of a doubleheader. After the second game, Bill jumped on a trunk in the clubhouse and hollered, "If I catch anybody out of the hotel after twelve o'clock tonight, it'll cost you $500." Well, everyone got in early that night because we knew he and Pancho Snyder would be up waiting for us in the lobby. We made another swing around the league, wound up in Boston on a Sunday, and got thumped again in a twin bill. After this one, Bill was back up on that trunk yelling, "If I catch anybody back in the hotel before two o'clock and sober, it'll cost you $1000."

Several new Giants received their baptism of fire in the fading weeks of the season. Babe Barna joined the club in September and homered on his first trip to the plate. Sid Gordon, a stocky Brooklyn native, played his first game, singled in his first at-bat, and was promptly picked off first. Several young pitchers also made their major league debuts.

The Giants completed the season in fifth place, a whopping 25½ games behind the Dodgers, who outfought the Cards for the pennant.

Individually, Ott, Young, and Rucker were among the offensive league leaders. Mel was second in home runs and third in bases on balls. Young was fourth in homers, second in RBIs, and fifth in total bases. And Rucker, despite a few hitting slumps, was third in doubles.

Just before the season ended, Hartnett was released. Terry said, "Gabby was a big help to us and we turned him loose so that he would be free to negotiate for a manager's job. If he doesn't land what he wants, he's welcome to come back with us as a coach." One writer commented wryly, "What a hell of a way to treat a guy after *we* appointed him manager. Where does that leave us?" Giants fans wondered the same thing as they watched the Dodgers lose to the Yankees in a new, less satisfactory, version of a subway series.

Chapter 13

ℳANAGER MEL

Horace Stoneham and treasurer Leo Bondy arrived in Jacksonville, Florida, on December 1 for the annual minor league convention determined to force a showdown with Bill Terry. Jerry Mitchell, of the *New York Post*, reported that both men were set to ask Terry what he would take "to leave quietly and let them name somebody else as manager for the next season, possibly either Dick Bartell or Billy Jurges." As Mitchell saw it, Terry was equally determined to make one final effort, either to get into the front office, to obtain a new contract as manager for three seasons or more, or to stay on to complete the last year of his contract as manager. After considerable discussion, Stoneham and Terry worked out what appeared to be a happy solution.

Also on December 1, Mel Ott left for the convention from his home in Metairie. He enjoyed the company of baseball people and had attended these meetings several times in past years just for a social break in the long offseason. But this time Mel had some things on his mind. He faced a heavy pay cut and the bitter gall of seeing a younger man, Babe Barna, coming along fast after his job as the Giants' regular right fielder. Worried about the size of the cut he might be offered, Mel went to Jacksonville with a view to putting up an argument. But he was so humble about his mission that at first he hesitated about barging in on Stoneham and Terry. Apparently bent on stalling for time, so he could frame some pointed arguments, he was lunching by himself down the street from the hotel when Stoneham and Terry decided to offer him the job as manager. They put in a call for Ott at his home and were completely surprised when Mildred Ott told them that Mel was in Jacksonville.

"Hi, ya, manager! I have a new job for you, at more money," Stoneham told Ott as Mel entered the Giants' suite. Stoneham smiled at Terry and told Ott what the job was. Dumbfounded, Mel looked from Terry to Stoneham and then said, "You aren't kidding, are you?" Thinking of the man he was being asked to replace, he looked at Terry again. "Go on, son, take it," Terry said. Ott thought a minute, then said soberly, "I guess a fellow couldn't refuse a chance like this, could he? The men shook hands all around and Mel said, "I've got to call Mickey (his nickname for Mildred)." With that done, he returned to the suite and sat down weakly in a chair, shaking his head in disbelief.

Ott had long been Stoneham's favorite player. Now Horace had to spread the good news. He called Toots Shor at Shor's midtown restaurant in New York shortly after. "Hello, kid, I've got swell news for you," shouted the jubilant Stoneham. "Ottie is my new manager. Yeah, Ott. I need a drink. Wait a minute, here's Mel." Ott told his old friend, "I can't believe it. That's right. I'm the man." The two men talked excitedly and Mel finally hung up. Back at the restaurant, someone asked, "What's going to be done with Terry?" Toots answered, "Jeez, I forgot to ask." He hesitated a moment, then shouted, "Who cares, anyway? Ottie's the new manager now."

At 3 P.M. on December 2, the news was released to the press. Ott had been named the new manager, and Terry was now the general manager in charge of farm and scouting operations. Reporters agreed that the sudden change amounted to a victory for Terry and a big break for Ott as well as for the ball club and its fans. Memphis Bill finally was rid of the manager's role which had irked him for the last few seasons. He was now in the front office with a two-year contract at $30,000 a year, instead of the one year remaining on his old contract of $42,500. Mel had been rewarded with a job he hoped to have some day, but never as soon or as sudden as this. His new contract called for $25,000 a year for two years, a $7,000 increase over his 1941 salary of $18,000.

That night Mel went out celebrating with Stoneham, Terry, and Bondy. Before he left the hotel, he called Mrs. John McGraw to share the glad tidings. Later Mrs. McGraw told Jimmy Powers, of the *Daily News*, "The club officials did themselves proud." She recalled, "I'll never forget the first time I saw Mel. His father brought him to training camp. He was a fat-legged little boy, and I didn't think he was a player at all. I thought he was just a hero-worshipper who wanted to meet my husband. I know Mel will be a popular manager, and I'm sure he'll make good."

Reaction to Ott's appointment was largely favorable. Some veteran baseball men questioned whether the easy-going, gentlemanly Ott was sufficiently tough for the job. But most thought that the Giants had made a wise move. Larry McPhail said, "They moved Terry up to the front office where he ought to do them a lot of good, and they made a smart choice in picking Ott. The only thing is that being a player-manager from the outfield is a difficult job. Ty Cobb and Tris Speaker, the last ones to do so, found that out." Leo Durocher added, "Yeah, I'll bet he winds up as a bench-manager long before the season is over." Yankee president Ed Barrow said, "Ott is a grand man, and I'm sure he'll be a big success. We across the Harlem River will be rooting for him."

The writers were pleased. They were happy to see one of their favorite baseball figures move up. They also anticipated that covering the Giants would be fun again as it was during the McGraw days and in the earlier years under Terry. Ott cheered them further with the promise: "No longer will writers be discouraged from sitting on the bench. No longer will players be told not to talk to newspapermen. Nor will it be necessary to get a pass from the manager to see a player in the clubhouse after a game. As for myself, you'll find me available every day, at all times."

The Giants players were happy at the news. Several sent Mel congratulatory telegrams or called him to tell him that they were looking forward to playing for him. Many fans expressed their pleasure. A group of Mel's hometown friends wrote an open letter to him in a three-quarter page advertisement in a New Orleans paper. They told of their appreciation of his qualities as an athlete and sportsman and their gratification at his promotion.

Even some Dodger fans expressed their fondness for Ott, many also bemoaning the fact that Terry would no longer be on the field as a ready target for their boos. Brooklyn newsdealer Roy Richards said, "Ott oughta make a pretty good manager, but he ain't got no players. I don't like Terry being out of there because you gotta have someone to razz. It helped to sell papers while I was yelling, "Terry, the bum, is wrong again." And Flatbush fruit dealer Domenico Pagnotta said, "Not good for business. Dodger fans bought fruit to toss at Terry, but they like this Ott."

Before leaving Jacksonville for New York, and then on to Chicago for the major league meetings, Ott dispelled all thoughts that he simply would be Terry's lieutenant on the field. He immediately countermanded three of Terry's policies. First was the removal of Harry Danning from the trading block. Terry had long admitted that he had not hit it off with the catcher, but Ott said he knew Danning well enough to be confident that under his regime Harry would have his best year. Then there was the acquisition of Hank Leiber from the Cubs. Terry had not gotten along with Leiber either and had no interest in getting the big slugger back from Chicago. And then there was Ott's dismissal of coach Pancho Snyder. Memphis Bill originally had intended to retain Snyder, but Ott asked Terry to take Snyder (who even looked like Terry) back into his own department as a scout or minor league manager. Terry took good care of his long-time coach, elevating Snyder to the manager's slot with the Jersey City Giants.

John Kieran, the renowned sports editor of the *New York Times*, wrote an amusing column about Ott's exhausting first few days in his new job. Kieran wrote:

> Master Melvin is a truly rural gent and if anything ever happened after 10 P.M. Mel wouldn't know about it except reading or listening the next morning. Ignorant of the changed life that lay ahead, Mel joined the league gathering at Jacksonville. After he accepted the nomination, he didn't know what was coming.

Kieran went on to write humorously of the partying and the exhaustingly late hours Mel faced. Most tiring was the night of the Leiber deal when terms of the deal that Ott proposed before sundown were accepted by the Cubs at 2 A.M., at which time, Kieran wrote, "Mel was practically in a coma."

On December 7, as the Giants party was getting settled in its hotel suite in Chicago, the Japanese bombed Pearl Harbor. All bets were off. Prospective player deals were almost forgotten as baseball officials waited for some indication of the government's policy on baseball's future status. As Ott put it: "We just can't be concerned with who will be drafted. Baseball will be glad and proud to see its men, just like the rest of the youth in the land, called up. We'll carry on our game as best we can, but everything else but the war effort is secondary."

Convinced that they could not obtain Cookie Lavagetto from the Dodgers because of the tightened manpower situation, the Giants purchased third baseman Bill Werber from Cincinnati. The trim Duke University graduate had batted only .239 in 1941, but he was an accomplished third baseman, something the Giants had lacked for years. Ott regretfully sold his old friend Joe Moore, along with outfielder Morrie Arnovich, to Indianapolis. A few days later Burgess Whitehead also was sent to the minors as Ott continued to clean house.

The most important deal came in mid-winter when the Giants obtained Johnny Mize from the Cardinals for Bill Lohrman, Ken O'Dea, Johnny McCarthy and a bundle of cash. This trade made a big impression on writers and fans alike because of its underlying meaning, as well as the power Mize brought to the Giants. The Dodgers at the time were hot on the trail of Mize, and MacPhail had seldom failed to land a player he wanted. But Ott had firmly informed Stoneham that he wanted Mize at almost any cost, and Stoneham, perhaps as amazed as anyone at Mel's forcefulness and persistence, parted with $50,000 (a lot of money in those days) for "The Big Cat," the players' nickname for the big Georgian with the smooth swing.

Peter Williams, in his 1994 biography of Terry, entitled *When the Giants Were Giants*, expressed the view that these deals were made in an attempt to show that Ott was his own man. John Drebinger, who was thought originally to have held that view, had changed it as indicated in an article he wrote for *Baseball Magazine* a few months later. Drebinger wrote:

> Let it be made clear ... that under no circumstances is Ott to "front" for Terry and that the old Colonel in his new post will not continue to pull strings in directing the affairs for the Giants. That such an arrangement was distinctly out was made clear from the very beginning by both Terry and Stoneham. He (Ott) was told that if he took over the job, the responsibility of running the club would be strictly his and no one else would share it with him. No ballplayers would be taken off the roster, none would be added, without his full consent.

The uncertainty as to baseball's position was clarified during the winter. Baseball commissioner Kenesaw M. Landis wrote President Roosevelt, not seeking any preferential treatment for the game, but to ask what its role should be with the nation at war. FDR wrote Landis that there would be no "work or fight" edict as there had been during World War I. The president stressed the importance of the game as a public morale-builder and urged its continuance so long as the clubs could field teams.

In the remaining few weeks before spring training, Ott was honored at two big dinners. The New York chapter of the Baseball Writers of America presented him with an award for "outstanding service to baseball over a period of years." In accepting the award, the new Giants manager first praised his predecessors, McGraw and Terry. He concluded with, "I know the kind of baseball New Yorkers want and I promise to give it to them." Ten days later the New Orleans Quarterbacks Club, several hundred strong, gave Ott a testimonial dinner at which they praised their fellow townsman to the skies. Mel responded simply: "A few years ago I left for spring training as a rookie with the good wishes of all of you. It looks like I'm still a rookie and it's wonderful to know that I still have your good wishes."

As spring training began, the writers detected a more upbeat, enthusiastic attitude among the players than had been apparent over the last few years. The writers themselves also seemed more enthused. Frank Graham wrote in the *New York Sun*:

The most engaging news on the sports pages these days has to do with the beginnings of Melvin Thomas Ott as manager of the Giants. Now he is actually at work. The league meetings, the dinners, the mass interviews, these are all behind him. Now he is at Miami and the advance guard of the Giants is in uniform, hitting, jogging around the bases, trotting around the field, limbering up in bunting games. And Melvin Thomas Ott is in uniform, too, telling the young men what to do and, whenever he gets a chance, running up to the plate to take a swing in batting practice himself.

It is a great opportunity for him and, also, a great responsibility. The majesty of the Yankees ... the upswing of the Dodgers ... these have not dimmed, in the eyes of countless thousands of New York fans, the glory of the Giants. To these fans the Giants always will be the No. 1 team in New York and they have stuck loyally to the Polo Grounds entry through all the miseries of the last few years. It is Ott that they are looking to bring the Giants back and nobody knows it better than he does or could try any harder than he is trying.

As the training season moved along, the team started to take shape. Mize, after taking it easy in the spring favoring an old shoulder injury, began to round into his old slugging form. Second base was still up for grabs between rookie Connie Ryan and Mickey Witek. Billy Jurges, now the team captain replacing Ott, was set at shortstop. Bill Werber looked sharp at third. Babe Young's draft status was indefinite, and he, Joe Orengo, and Bartell were the backup infielders.

In the outfield, Mel was hammering the ball and appeared ready for a good season. Leiber replaced Rucker in center since Johnny had a poor spring. Willard Marshall, an unsung, rangy youngster up from the Southern Association, had become the apple of Ott's eye with his hard hitting and willingness to learn. He was picked to start in left field. Babe Barna, Sid Gordon, and Rucker were the reserve outfielders. Danning, of course, was set behind the plate with Ray Berres his backup man.

The pitchers included the two elder statesmen, Hubbell and Schumacher; Melton, still seeking to regain his old form, and Bob Carpenter, who hoped to improve on his 11 wins in 1941. Two new lefthanders, Tom Sunkel and Dave Koslo, and righthanders Hugh East, Harry Feldman, and Rube Fischer were other potential starters. Ace Adams was the unchallenged king of the bullpen.

None of the writers expected the Giants to do more than perhaps challenge for a spot in the first division. Ott's major plan was to develop a potent offense which the club had lacked for years. Several reporters wrote that Mel had very definitely changed the team's emphasis on defense which had been the hallmark of Bill Terry's teams.

The Giants were picked to finish fifth by the 74 reporters polled by the Associated Press. The reporters favored the Cardinals to win the pennant, with the Dodgers, Reds, and Pirates predicted to finish in that order. Unconcerned about expert opinion, Giants fans eagerly awaited the start of the season to see how their favorites would fare under Mel Ott's leadership.

Chapter 14

A GOOD START

Mel Ott picked Carl Hubbell to pitch the opener against the Dodgers at the Polo Grounds. He was teased by reporters for choosing his old roommate and closest baseball friend to help inaugurate his managerial career. Ott responded, "Sure, you could call it a sentimental choice. But it's downright common sense, too. Hub's the best pitcher on the staff right now. His arm is all right, he feels strong, and I'm convinced he's our best bet." If this told something about Mel's sense of loyalty, it also told something about the weakness of his pitching staff. Great as Hubbell had been, he had not won more than 13 games in any year since 1937.

The Opening Day ceremonies were led by fiery New York City mayor Fiorello H. LaGuardia who presented managers Ott and Durocher with war bonds, representing ten percent of their first salary checks. Leading off in the first inning, the Dodgers loaded the bases. Joe Medwick sliced a double to right for two runs, and the Dodgers scored two more runs before the inning was over. Pee Wee Reese gave the Dodgers a 6–0 lead with a two-run homer in the fourth inning, and that was the end for Hubbell and the Giants for the day. Ott called time, walked in from right field, and took the ball from King Carl without a word.

As Bob Considine of the *New York Mirror* dramatically described it:

> So Hub turned away from the mound ... and he started that eternity of steps toward the center field locker room. And the great crowd ... sensing the rather brave thing Hub had tried and failed at, stood up and cheered the old guy as he trudged along. Eager hands reached down over the barriers as Hub went past the bleacher section and tried to touch him. He shied away, with his head down, and walked up the steps. He was the picture of Defeat, the symbol of a man who had tried to do something for a friend of many years, and had failed. It was too much to ask of an old arm. (But) to us, it was as overwhelming a scene in sports as some of Hub's miraculous deeds of bygone years, when he had it."

The next day Melton beat righthander Kirby Higbe on young Willard Marshall's grand slam, but Dave Koslo lost to Ed Head in the third game. Ott's club had lost its first series under his leadership, and to their traditional interborough rivals at that. There was another managerial first for Mel the next day in Boston. He was ejected from the game, along with Schumacher and captain Billy Jurges, by umpire Ziggy Sears in a tough loss to the Braves. Schumacher was fined and suspended for five days for pushing the umpire after Sears' delayed call in ruling a Boston runner safe. Mel was still sizzling the next morning. He complained that he had not said a word to Sears before Schumacher's ejection and that all of his remarks before that had been intended to calm down Prince Hal. The next day found Stoneham at the Braves' park in a box seat behind the Giants dugout to see for himself whether his players received any more "pushing around."

The Giants bounced back to slug out six wins in their next nine games. The pitching was unsteady, but Giants rooters enjoyed the team's explosive attack. After years of watching the club struggle for each run, the fans particularly appreciated the Giants' newly-created "Dynamite Division," comprising Ott, Mize, Marshall, Leiber, and Danning batting in the third through seventh batting order positions.

With Ott now responsible for running the club, "Ottville" in the right field stands became even more densely populated as closer proximity to the manager apparently gave the fans more of a feeling of being part of the game. As Larry MacPhail had predicted, Ott found the job of managing from the outfield exhausting. The added mental and nervous strain was difficult enough, but to this was added the physical burden of trudging into the infield several times a game on his stumpy legs. It seemed as though half of each game found Mel either at the mound cajoling, encouraging, advising, or removing a pitcher, or elsewhere in the infield registering a complaint on an adverse call by an umpire.

Master Mel, still a player at heart, had a tendency to give a pitcher every opportunity to work himself out of trouble. It was a long way in from right field to the mound, frequently long enough to permit his empathy for the pitcher to override his better judgment. He came in one day presumably to remove Schumacher from a game with the Dodgers with two men on and the dangerous Dolph Camilli at bat. Prince Hal figured he was gone as soon as he saw Mel start in from the outfield. But by the time Ott reached the mound, he had changed his mind. "You've been pretty lucky getting Camilli out," he told Schumacher. "I'm gonna let you pitch to him." Hal then walked Camilli, filling the bases and bringing Ott in again. (This was long before the current rule which requires the pitcher's automatic removal after two trips to the mound in the same inning by a manager or coach.) This time, to prevent another change of mind, Ott wigwagged Harry Feldman in from the bullpen before he went to the mound to remove Schumacher.

After one of the early-season games, Ott talked to a writer about the problems of managing and playing at the same time. He admitted, "I'm really getting an education even after all my years in the game. Sometimes the decision as to when to pull a pitcher can be murder. My instinct tells me to take him out, but my desire to give him another chance to build up his confidence tells me to leave him in." Mel continued, "Another problem is to anticipate plays and circumstances and make the right move in time. Every manager faces these problems, but they must be more difficult when you also have to concentrate on the game as a player. The other day Pete Reiser hit a fly ball out to me when I was thinking about something else and it actually startled me until my normal reflexes took over."

There was another, more visible, sign of the stress of managing. Ott had always been in the habit of tapping the outfield sod with his right foot as he played his position. After a few games the small bare spot in right field began to grow in diameter under the pressure of his nervous foot-tapping. One of the fans teased Ott about ruining the velvety sod. Mel grinned and drawled, "You're kidding me about it, but the grounds-keeper is threatening to ask Stoneham to bill me for the resodding cost if I don't cut it out."

One day a reporter asked Ott, "Mel, has being the manager made any difference in your hitting?"

"No, I hit the same way."

The reporter said, "I mean psychologically. For instance, when you go up there now do you think about the effect on the team if you, the manager, strike out in the clutch or hit into a double play?"

"Oh, no," Mel answered. "Say, if I went up there thinking about things like that, I would never get a base hit."

Comments and questions from nearby Polo Grounds stands were easily heard by the players. Ott told about an amusing exchange with one of his more intense rooters in the heat of a close game. The fan leaned over the right field wall to ask Mel whether one of the Giants runs in the previous inning was earned or unearned. The preoccupied manager answered the question with an arms-spread gesture indicating he did not know. The fan, not satisfied by Ott's response, asked in wonderment, "What have you been doing here for 17 years, anyway?"

The writers were welcomed to the clubhouse after home games, a complete reversal from the Terry era. Ott, still in uniform, sat and chatted with them, candidly discussing his strategies, players, and problems. He even poured a drink for those who desired one. The writers were free to talk to the players as they showered and dressed. The men covering the Giants were pleased at the easy accessibility of the boyish Ott and his players, and the favorable press the club received reflected their appreciation.

The Giants closed out their first round of games with the eastern teams by losing a doubleheader to the Braves at the Polo Grounds before almost 50,000. Still the club had won nine of its first 15 games, and more than a thousand fans jammed Eighth Avenue outside the Giants clubhouse to wish the team well. When Ott came out, they let loose a resounding cheer and then dispersed. As Joe King, of the *World-Telegram*, wrote the next day, "It couldn't be clearer that Mel has resuscitated the old Giant fan who appreciates that Ott is trying hard to give him renewed hope and a run for his money."

The Giants had their problems on their first western trip, losing six games out of ten. Four of the losses were by one-run margins. There were injury problems too. Jurges' dizzy spells returned, and Bartell replaced him at short. Leiber pulled a leg muscle, and Rucker took his place. After a few games, when it became apparent that Rucker would not fill the bill, he was optioned to Jersey City, and Buster Maynard was inserted in center. Ott himself went into a slump. The only bright spots were the powerful hitting of Mize and Marshall and the steady relief pitching of Ace Adams. Desperate for pitching help, the Giants reacquired Bill Lohrman from the Cardinals where he had been sent as part of the winter deal for Mize.

The Giants returned home and lost their first game of the season at Ebbets Field as Camilli's homer beat Melton in another one-run game. The only consolation was that almost $60,000 was raised from the paid attendance for the Navy Relief Society. John Drebinger wrote: "It was probably the best-natured gathering in years when the Giants played in Brooklyn. Gone were the jeers that met Terry—only cheers greeted Manager Ott."

The western teams came in for the first time, and the Giants continued to struggle, again winning only four of ten games and slipping down to sixth place. Jurges and Leiber returned to the lineup, but Danning and Werber replaced them on the injured list. Ott continued to experiment, substituting Connie Ryan for Mickey Witek and shuffling his pitchers in and out of the starting rotation.

During the home stand, New York City civil defense officials prohibited all evening activities which required outside lighting after one hour following sunset. German submarines were operating close enough to the East Coast to be aided in targeting shipping by the glow which silhouetted Allied vessels. In effect, there would be no more night games for the duration of the war. The New York clubs began to play twilight games, starting at 7:00 P.M. and continuing through the curfew if necessary.

As the western clubs left, the Giants' weaknesses were all too apparent. The offensive power was there, but the defense, speed, and above all the pitching were seriously inadequate. It was clear that the team did not have the horses to compete seriously for the pennant with the Dodgers and the Cardinals. The team needed some kind of spark if it had any chance to finish in the first division.

Ott, the player rather than the manager, supplied a good portion of the spark in a game against the Dodgers as Melton outpitched Ed Head. In the first inning Mel had started his club off on the right foot with a two-run homer. But it was his base running that threw some concern and respect into the Dodgers and gave the Giants the lift they needed. In the third inning, with one out and men on second and third, Head walked Ott intentionally to set up a double play. Mize slashed a sharp grounder to the sure-handed Camilli at first base, and a double play appeared inevitable. Camilli threw to Pee Wee Reese for a force on Ott, but Pee Wee, streaking across the bag offered a perfect target. Instead of sliding, Mel threw his body into Reese and bowled him over. As a result, Reese's relay to first base was wild, and two more Giants runs scored.

The Dodgers did not take kindly to Ott's rough but clean base running. They retaliated by running the bases with special aggressiveness and also resorted to the customary dusting-off pitching tactics which were standard under Durocher's leadership. Twice after his rugged base running, Ott came to bat, and both times, once with righthander Hugh Casey, and then with lefthander Larry French, the first pitch was aimed at his head. Ott, hopeful that he had lit a fire under his club, was impassive through it all. In the clubhouse after the game he commented straight-faced, "French and Casey were a little wild out there today, don't you think?"

The Giants wound up their eastern swing in fourth place. With Danning injured and weak-hitting Ray Berres the only able-bodied catcher, the Giants acquired old reliable Gus Mancuso from the Cardinals. Ironically, with this acquisition the Giants had regained the three players involved in the big trade with the Cubs after the 1938 season. Bartell, Leiber, and now Mancuso were all back.

The Giants were in a cheerful mood as they arrived in Chicago to start their second western tour. Although Ott had no illusions about finishing ahead of the Dodgers or the Cardinals, he was pleased on several counts. The Giants had taken two straight series from the Dodgers. Mize was hitting the ball lustily and leading the league in RBIs. Ott's faith in Willard Marshall had been rewarded, and the young Virginian was close behind Mize for the RBI lead. Mel felt that the pitching had stabilized, after much painful experimentation, with Lohrman, Carpenter, Melton, Sunkel, and Schumacher in the starting rotation. All had pitched well except Schumacher, but Ott was confident that his good friend, Prince Hal, would regain something of his old form. Hubbell was being used as a spot starter. Bill McGee had a bad back and was of little use. Ace Adams as always was a one-man relief staff.

Mel had the personal satisfaction of tying Rogers Hornsby's then-existing National League Record of 1,582 RBIs in a game in Chicago. The little manager was not hitting for average, but he was getting timely hits and home runs and a lot of walks. He was on base frequently to be driven in by Mize and Marshall. And he was still regarded as the best defensive right fielder in the game.

The Giants split 12 decisions in the West and returned home in third place. Mize, Marshall, and Ott continued to carry the offensive load, and Mel broke Hornsby's RBI record against the Cubs on June 4. But the pitching was just fair, and the fielding was uncertain as Jurges and Werber had slowed up considerably. Barna and Leiber were being platooned in center field, but neither man was hitting with any consistency.

The Giants played .500 ball over the next three weeks, and at the All-Star break they were in fourth place, 14 games behind the league-leading Dodgers. Ott, Mize, Marshall, and Melton represented the Giants on the National League All-Star squad. The game was played at the Polo Grounds with the American League winning 3–1. Ott was the only Giants player to start, and he went hitless. By mid-season about 60 major league players were in the military as the country continued to gear up to fight the war. Still, there were ready replacements from the higher minor leagues, and most baseball men agreed that the overall quality of play was not yet unduly affected despite the loss of several top-notch players.

The Giants opened the second half of the season in St. Louis. Koslo was beaten soundly in the first game, and Ace Adams lost a ten-inning heartbreaker on his own wild throw. These losses convinced Ott that the club needed another shot in the arm. His solution was to start Hubbell who had won only one game in the first half of the season. Hub pitched the next day against Cardinals lefthander Howard Pollet, who normally was poison to the Giants. With only a trace of his former stuff, but with plenty of savvy, Hubbell beat Pollet 8–3 and gave the Giants a breather. After the Giants lost three of their next four games, King Carl came back and defeated the Pirates 3–1 with the support of a revamped lineup. Ott benched Werber and replaced him with the peppery Bartell. Even more significant, Babe Young replaced the slumping Marshall in a move reminiscent of 1937 when Terry brought in Ott from the outfield to replace Lou Chiozza at third base. With the help of Young's potent hitting, the Giants rebounded and returned home only half a game behind the third-place Reds.

Back at the Polo Grounds, the club held its own against the western teams to remain in fourth place just one game behind Cincinnati. The home stand began on a surprising note as the Giants picked up ex–Dodger Van Lingle Mungo from Minneapolis. The writers, recalling the Mungo-Bartell fisticuffs of the past, chuckled as Mungo was assigned a locker next to Bartell's. One scribe, noting that Bartell's locker was sandwiched in between those of Mungo and Jurges, Rowdy Richard's other old sparring partner, cracked, "Bartell is like Jimmy Durante—he's surrounded by assassins." Mungo pitched creditably in his first effort but provided little help in alleviating the Giants' pitching shortcomings.

The biggest disappointment of the home stand came on July 26 when the Reds took a doubleheader from the Giants. Ott's club had moved into third place ahead of the Reds by half a game, and there was a near-capacity crowd on hand to see what promised to be an exciting two games. In the bottom of the first inning of the first game Ott came to bat. He was on a home run hitting tear, and the crowd buzzed with anticipation. With a one-strike count, Mel took a low, outside pitch from righthander Elmer Riddle which umpire Jocko Conlan called a strike. The Giants manager stepped out of the batters box and argued the call vigorously. Riddle's 0 and 2 pitch was a curve which appeared to shave Ott's chin. Conlan surprised everyone with a booming "Stee-rike, you're out!" Ott immediately turned on Conlan, shouting his disapproval and emphasizing his complaints by pounding his bat on the plate in an uncharacteristic display of temper. Suddenly, Conlan turned on Ott and ejected Master Mel from the game with an unmistakable, sweeping motion of his arm.

After a few more minutes of impassioned protest, Ott slammed his bat down and began the long walk to the clubhouse, banished for the second game as well as the first under the rules then in effect. As the stocky little manager walked past second base, the fans began to shower home plate with a barrage of fruits and vegetables. A tomato intended for Conlan struck Babe Young, the next hitter, squarely in the back. As Ott stomped up the steps to the clubhouse and slammed the door, a cascade of beer bottles descended upon the field, the fans realizing belatedly that he was out of the second game as well. It was the first game that Mel had missed all season. After that violent episode, the loss of two important games was almost an anti-climax to the disappointed throng.

After the doubleheader, Conlan told reporters, "After what he called me, I had to put him out. I know there were a lot of people who wanted to see him play, but we don't take that from anyone and he can't get away with it just because of the crowd." Ott, still fuming in the clubhouse, said, "It was a terrible call, but it doesn't even matter who was right. Just because I questioned his call and punctuated it with a cuss word is no reason for throwing me out of a game at the beginning of a doubleheader. Durocher throws towels in an umpire's face and little is done about it. I open my mouth once and I'm out."

As the western invasion ended, Frank Graham wrote about changes in Ott since he had taken over the Giants:

> Someone was remarking the other night that a change has come over Mel Ott since he has been manager of the Giants. "Mel used to be such a mild-mannered little fellow," he said, "and now every time I see him he is arguing with the umpire or snapping at the opposing players. And I never will forget the day he put a savage body block on Pee Wee Reese to break up a double play. What has come over the young man, anyhow?"
>
> The answer to that question comes in two parts. The first is that Ott, feeling that he assumed a heavy responsibility when he took over, is trying in every way he knows to win. The second is that he felt he had to do something drastic to shake up the Giant players. There is no record that he has had to put the blast on any of his own players. But no one walking into the Giant clubhouse can have the faintest doubt as to who is boss. He is, as the players show in every move they make and every word they say. Some must ask themselves if this is the same quiet little guy who used to dress over in the corner of the room and seldom had anything to say. And the umpires do not like Mel as well now as they did before. He knows that, but it doesn't bother him in his attempt to give New York the best and most exciting Giant team since McGraw.

Ott had a few disciplinary problems, and these came early in the season when a few players took advantage of his good nature and easy manner and broke training rules. One day before a game Mel called the Giants writers together in the dugout. He told them, "Some of you are bound to notice that two of my players have not suited up for today's game. These are young fellows who broke training but who never pulled anything like this before." He added, "For their good I'd appreciate it if you would pass up the story." All of the writers honored Ott's request.

Mel did not believe in delivering pep talks to the entire team. His policy was to talk over matters with his players individually and privately, although he met with the pitchers and catchers before games to go over pitching strategies. He told a writer, "I simply don't believe in mass oratory. Most of my players have been in the game long enough to know their business. And there are no cliques on the club, no prima donnas. The team spirit is good." Mel's view was supported by a veteran Giants player who put it simply: "He's a human being—he knows guys, understands them, and treats us accordingly."

The Giants played well over the next two weeks and moved up securely into third place, five games ahead of the Reds. With Mize and Marshall out of the lineup because of injuries, Young, Ott, and Barna carried the offensive load. The defense picked up as Mickey Witek improved at second, and Jurges returned to his old form. And the 39-year-old Hubbell led the pitching staff with eight straight wins.

By early August it had become clear that twilight games at the Polo Grounds would have to be abandoned as two games with the Dodgers wound up in utter confusion. In the first game umpire George Magerkurth halted play in the last half of the ninth with the Giants losing by three runs but rallying with two on and none out. Magerkurth called the game at 9:10 P.M. and walked off the suddenly darkened field to the boos of 57,305 onlookers, the largest crowd ever to see a single game at the Polo Grounds. The uproar continued until it was quieted by the opening bars of "The Star Spangled Banner" echoing across the field while a solitary spotlight focused on the flag atop the center field clubhouse. After the game, Horace Stoneham announced, "We'll play the twilight game scheduled for tomorrow night, but that will be the last one. Playing against the clock this way is too tough." As if to emphasize his point, the next night's game ended in a 1–1 tie as Pee Wee Reese's grand slam homer in the top of the tenth was wiped out by the time deadline.

An amusing story accompanied a Giants win over the Phils. The Giants won in the tenth inning when Ott deftly squeezed in Bill Lohrman who was the runner at third. A few days later at Toots Shor's, comedian Jay C. Flippen and several other habitues were sitting around when Mel and Mildred walked in for dinner. Flippen greeted Ott with: "Congratulations on that beautiful squeeze play, Mel." Ott gave him a sheepish look and replied, "Thanks, Jay, but it's not something I'm bragging about. Remember when Dolph Luque came in from third base coaching box? It was one out with the bases loaded. Dolph suggested that it would be a good spot for a squeeze play but I told him no, that I would hit away." Mel continued, "So I tap my bat on the plate like I always do and get ready for the first pitch. But just as the pitcher delivers the ball, to my complete surprise here comes Lohrman in from third. I made a last-minute stab at the ball and luckily it was a good bunt and he scored. I had forgotten that by tapping the plate I had given the squeeze bunt sign. And yet everybody's been congratulating me ever since on the play."

The Giants retained their firm grip on third place by winning seven of ten games on their final western trip. The pitching was solid. Mize was back in the lineup and pounding the ball. Young, back in center field, continued to hit well. Ott moved into the league lead in home runs and belted out his 2500th career hit against the Cubs. And Witek hit safely in every game on the trip.

There were several items of interest during the last three weeks of the season. Bill Voiselle, a strapping righthander from Ninety Six, South Carolina, joined the club from Oklahoma City and pitched well in his major league debut against the Phillies although he lost the game. The Giants brought up a young catcher from the Appalachian League, Charley Fox, who one day would manage the Giants. Willard Marshall, who had the bearing and look of a Marine, enlisted in that branch of the service, and Babe Young joined the Coast Guard. With the Giants firmly entrenched in third place, Ott acceded to Hank Leiber's request to pitch a game, and Hank threw a complete game against the Phillies, but lost it convincingly. And the next day, the Giants, leading Boston 5–2 in the eighth inning, lost a game by forfeit when overenthusiastic fans overflowed the Polo Grounds field.

The powerful Dodgers and Cardinals fought it out again for the pennant. Leo Durocher's lineup was almost identical to that of the 1941 club which beat out the Cards by two and a half games. This time it was Billy Southworth's team which won by a mere two games. St. Louis was strengthened by the addition of young righthander Johnny Beazley, who won 21 games, great seasons by pitcher Mort Cooper and his batterymate brother, Walker; and the first full campaign of a young player, Stan Musial, whose future greatness was readily apparent. The Cardinals went on to beat the Yankees in the World Series, winning four straight after losing the first game.

The contributions of Ott and Mize to the Giants' surprise showing were reflected in the individual statistics. Despite his managerial burdens and 17 major league seasons, Mel missed playing in only two of the club's games, and one of them was attributable to Jocko Conlan's heave-ho. The little manager led the league with 30 home runs and in walks and runs scored. He also ranked in the top five in RBIs, slugging percentage, and total bases. Mize was the league leader in RBIs and slugging percentage and in the top five in total bases, runs scored, home runs, and batting average. Ace Adams broke the then-existing record for pitchers by appearing in 61 games, and he was second in saves. Bill Lohrman ranked fifth with a 2.47 ERA.

A number of writers in New York and around the league campaigned unsuccessfully during the last month of the season for Ott's selection as manager of the Year and Most Valuable Player in the National League. But Giants fans were not particularly concerned when the pennant-winning Southworth received the first award and Mort Cooper the second. Polo Grounds rooters were more than happy with the Giants' resurgence in Mel Ott's first year at the helm.

Chapter 15

*D*ISASTER

The impact of the war effort, relatively light in 1942, changed major league baseball completely during the next three seasons. Through 1942 club owners pursued the usual goals of healthy profits and success on the field. For the remainder of the war, club survival was the only real objective. By the end of the 1942 season, well over 100 major leaguers were in uniform. Almost every day brought reports of players who were either called up for pre-induction physicals or actually inducted. With the decreasing numbers of available players, most of the minor leagues were forced to close down. In early 1942 the Giants owned, or had working agreements with, nine minor league franchises. By the end of the year only two of the clubs, Jersey City and Fort Smith, remained in operation, and it was considered unlikely that Fort Smith could start the 1943 season.

With this drastic shrinkage in his responsibilities, in December Bill Terry decided to resign. His statement began:

> Some months ago I suggested to both Mr. Stoneham and Mr. Leo Bondy that I did not believe the curtailed activities of the Giants in the minor league field warranted my remaining. I did not feel that I would be able under such conditions to earn my salary. So I suggested that, if it met with the club's approval, my contract for next year be terminated.

To quash any rumors that there was anything more than that to his departure from the Giants after 22 years of continual service, Terry's statement added, "...there is nothing but the friendliest relationship between the club and myself...." Stoneham confirmed that Terry was leaving on his own initiative and on friendly terms.

Larry MacPhail, always anxious to be where the action was, had left the Dodgers at the end of the season to enlist in the Army as a lieutenant colonel. He was replaced by Branch Rickey, the Cardinals' longtime trading master and farm system overseer.

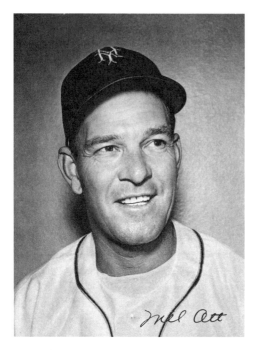

Ott in first year as manager, 1942 (author's collection).

In addition to the player shortage, transportation was another serious problems. Airplane travel had not yet come into use in the major leagues, except for special occasions, and almost all of the traveling was by train. The government asked baseball officials to look into ways to reduce transportation needs and suggested that the clubs train near their home cities. It also suggested sharp cutbacks in preseason exhibition schedules, in long road trips during the season, and increased use of off-hour trains and day coaches. The major league teams took the hint. They found training sites near home, played exhibition games locally, and reduced their travel by a variety of means, primarily by scheduling three eastern-western trips instead of the usual four.

For the duration of the war, the Giants trained at Lakewood, New Jersey, the little town in which the team had practiced during the Spanish-American War. The Giants and the Jersey City club shared an old, pine tree–covered estate formerly owned by John D. Rockefeller. Their practice fields were laid out on what had been Rockefeller's private golf course, and the players were quartered in the stately old mansion on the grounds. Bill Corum, of the *Journal-American*, described the family scene:

> The "Brannick Arms" (named for popular Giant traveling secretary Eddie Brannick) is so informal and just-one-big-family-like that an occupant of any room in the house can hear, at one and the same time of practically any evening, (*Daily Mirror* writer) Ken Smith practicing on his accordion, Billy Jurges turning the jukebox upside down every few minutes to hear the same tune, Bill Lohrman shaking the pinball machine, and Izzy Kaplan, the demon *Daily Mirror* photographer, rewiring his room so John Drebinger can hear the news on the radio.
>
> If it isn't just like home, it at least makes you wish for home

when it's bedtime. Ott doesn't need to check the players in at night.
His room is just above the entrance to the hotel, and every time
anybody closes the front door his bed jumps off the floor and floats
around like a spiritualist's table at a seance.

"Don't squawk over inconveniences," Mel told his players as they sat
indoors putting on sneakers for a rainy day workout in a small gymna-
sium in Lakewood. Ott continued, "Don't forget this is not Miami and
there's a war on. Grumbling will get out among the fans, and we can't
afford that sort of thing."

By March several of the more prominent Giants players were either
in service or were slated for induction. Young and Marshall were joined
in the service by Mize, Danning, Koslo, and Schumacher. Other players
expected to hear from their draft boards at any time. As the club began
its first outdoor practice drill on a cold, snow-fringed field, it was clear
that the team was in for a difficult year unless the other clubs had equally
serious manpower problems. The most glaring deficiency was at first base
with both Mize and Young gone. Ott tried Babe Barna at the position
with little success. Then Joe Orengo was moved over from third base.
Arthur Daley, of the *Times*, watched a succession of players work out at
first base. He wrote: "He (Ott) was a more deft operator at first than Babe
Barna, Joe Orengo or any one else. This proves that a great ball player
can do a good job anywhere. But Master Melvin just refuses to take over
the task."

With Orengo at first, the rest of the starting infield included the
improved Witek at second, a slowed-up and headache-ridden Jurges at
short, and the stocky, unproven Brooklynite, Sid Gordon, at third. Bartell
and Connie Ryan were the reserve infielders. Ott, Rucker, Barna, and
Buster Maynard were the only experienced outfielders since Hank Leiber
had decided to sit out the season on his farm in Arizona.

Danning's loss was a heavy blow. The other catchers were veterans Ray
Berres and Gus Mancuso and minor leaguer Hugh Poland. Relief pitcher
Ace Adams was the only shining light among the pitchers. The experienced
starters included Hubbell, Mungo, Lohrman, and Melton. There were sev-
eral younger pitchers on hand, including lefty Tom Sunkel and righthanders
Harry Feldman, Rube Fischer, Ken Trinkle, Bill Voiselle, Johnny Wittig,
Bill Sayles, and a grim-visaged unknown named Sal Maglie.

Ott had become much more assured in dealing with the writers. Joe
Williams wrote:

> He (Ott) is getting a youthful kick out of his contacts with the
> press. He delights in sitting around and sparring mentally with

the ink-stained wretches. They don't win many decisions over him, either. He is articulate, searching and witty. A year ago, he boyishly confesses, he was "scared stiff" when the reporters swarmed in to interview him. Now he insists it is a happy interlude, this being the only mark of eccentricity in him we have noted.

With the travel restrictions in effect, exhibition games were played only with Gabby Hartnett's Jersey City Giants and service teams from nearby installations. As the Giants prepared to open the season in Brooklyn, the AP poll picked them to finish fifth and favored the Cardinals to repeat.

Lohrman lost the opener to the Dodgers' Ed Head 5–2 before a meager Ebbets Field crowd. Starting his eighteenth season, Ott went 4 for 4 and drove in both Giants runs. But the big story of the game was the baseball itself. The new ball in play was seriously flawed. It had the resiliency of an overripe grapefruit and the unpredictable airborne characteristics of a flying saucer. Ott, brushing off congratulations on his hitting performance, commented, "This new ball is really something. I hit several in batting practice that I thought were really tagged but they all fell far short of the wall. In the outfield I couldn't be sure whether I had come in fast enough to make a catch. And the way the balls twist and dip, they're hard to catch even if you're camped under the ball."

The Cincinnati Reds conducted a rough experiment on the elasticity of the new baseball. Balls were dropped from the Crosley Field roof to the sidewalk outside of the ballpark. The balls used in 1942 bounced an average 13 feet. The new balls bounced only nine and a half feet on the average.

A few days later the Spalding Company admitted that the new balls contained a rubber-like cement of inferior quality because rubber, which had always been used, had been banned by the government because it was essential for the war effort. Instead of providing resiliency, the cement had hardened between the wool layers and deadened the ball. The problem was resolved when it was agreed to use the remaining balls left over from the 1942 season until a new stock of higher quality baseballs was available.

There were early signs that this would be a difficult year for the Giants. With the campaign less than a week old, the club moved to shore up the weak catching staff by obtaining slugging Ernie Lombardi from the Braves. The slow-footed "Schnozz" could still hit the ball as evidenced by his league-leading .330 average in 1942. To get Lombardi the Giants gave up catcher Hugh Poland and light-hitting Connie Ryan. Ironically, just after the trade, Ryan beat the Giants with a ninth-inning home run.

Ott in the Giants dugout at the Polo Grounds, 1942 (author's collection).

Big Lom, in unhappy contrast, ended the game by striking out as a pinch-hitter with the tying run on base.

The Giants went into a protracted slump, losing 16 of their next 22 games and falling to seventh place. The only bright spots were Sid Gordon's solid hitting and dependable play at third base, and a few good pitching turns by Wittig, Feldman, Trinkle, and Ace Adams. The club had a poor home stand against the western teams and dropped deeper into the second division. After trying unsuccessfully to bolster his team with trades, Mel told the writers unhappily, "We badly need to make changes, but no one wants to trade or sell players. There's plenty of money around, but there's an awful shortage of good players."

As the Giants headed west for the first time, Arthur Daley described their plight:

> The Giants, it is sad to report, are not a good team at present. With Johnny Mize, Babe Young, Willard Marshall and Harry Danning gone into service, most of the power has deserted and too heavy a burden is placed on Mel Ott's really promising corps of youthful pitchers. Maybe he can straighten out his forces in the West, but he will have to be a master magician to do the trick because he simply has not the men to juggle.
>
> Last year the Giants came to life when Young was switched to the outfield. However, there is no one like the Babe around this season to set up as a Noble Experiment. The legion of Ott admirers hope fervently that Master Melvin can get untangled even though he's snarled up right now.

But the Giants did not get unsnarled, returning from their trip mired deep in seventh place. During the trip Hubbell broke a string of seven straight Giants losses by pitching his final masterpiece. On June 5, approaching the age of 40, he threw a brilliant one-hitter against the Pirates, winning 5–1 with Elbie Fletcher's homer the only Pittsburgh hit. This was Hubbell's 250th career win.

The low esteem in which Giants hitting was held was reflected in an experience Tom Meany and Ott had in Pittsburgh. While Meany was in the Pirates clubhouse scrounging for news, he noticed a blackboard in manager Frankie Frisch's office detailing how the Pirates planned to pitch to each Giants player. Frisch came into the clubhouse, saw the writer peering into his office at the blackboard, and bellowed, "Hey, Meany, get the hell out of here. I don't want you going back to those guys and telling them what their weaknesses are. Some of those fellows don't even know themselves what they can't hit." The next day, after hearing Meany's story, Ott deliberately paid a visit to the Pirates clubhouse to chat with his old friend Frisch and, more importantly, to take a look at the blackboard.

Frisch invited Mel in and they talked about old times at considerable length. Ott told Meany later, "Tom, we had a nice social visit but don't think for a moment that I got a look at that blackboard. Frank had pulled a dark shade down over it and every once in a while he would look over at it, wink at me, and go right on talking about something else."

Despite experiencing the poorest year of his playing career, Ott was still respected by opposing pitchers. He was walked five times in a game against the Dodgers on June 17. And he was walked in his first two trips the following day.

By July 4, the Giants had sunk well into last place. The pitching was horrendous. Lombardi was slow in rounding into shape, then went out with injuries. Orengo was hitting under .200 and Rucker, Gordon, and Maynard were in deep hitting slumps. Jurges and Bartell were showing their ages. Ott salvaged a few games with late-inning home runs and even led the majors with 14 homers at midseason. Still, he was having his worst year.

Mel was selected for the All-Star game, an honor which he felt was undeserved. He told a writer, "I don't deserve it. That kid up in Boston, Tommy Holmes, should have been on our team, in my place." The writer said, "But you're leading both leagues with your 14 home runs." Mel gave his booster a smile of pity. "And all of 'em were hit at the Polo Grounds. I don't believe I really got hold of any of them, except maybe two." Meanwhile, in that year of modest expectations, the Giants manager was out to upset the prevailing view that 15 home runs would be tops in the National League.

Mel suffered the never-ending frustrations that went with managing an undermanned club in a difficult time with little help from the front office. As Joe Williams pointed out, "There is no one back of the scenes comparable to, for instance, a (Branch) Rickey or a (George) Weiss. Thus Mr. Ott is wholly on his own. He is the only solid baseball man in the organization with any authority."

Personnel changes did not help. Babe Barna was traded to the Red Sox for lefthander Ken Chase, but Chase proved to be no ball of fire. Napoleon (Nap) Reyes, a flashy Cuban infielder, was brought up from Jersey City. After a short stint at third base, he took over for Orengo at first base, but there was no discernible improvement. In mid–July the Giants picked up Joe Medwick from the Dodgers for the $7500 waiver price. Before obtaining him, the Giants had been struggling along with what the writers referred to as "three and a half" outfielders. This included Ott, Rucker, Maynard, and Gordon, who divided his time between third base and the outfield. Medwick, although only a shadow of the powerhouse he had been

Ott (left) with slugger Johnny Mize, 1942 (author's collection).

in his heyday with the Cardinals, had several good games and did manage to hit a respectable .281 after joining the club.

The Giants announced a major trade with the Dodgers on July 31. Pitchers Bill Lohrman, Bill Sayles, and infielder Joe Orengo were dealt for first baseman Dolph Camilli and fiery righthander Johnny Allen.

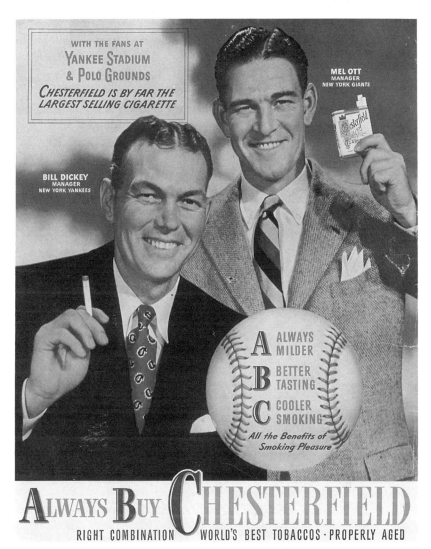

Managers Mel Ott and Bill Dickey in cigarette advertisement, 1946 (author's collection).

Camilli was the key man in the deal because of the Giants' difficulties at first base and in producing runs. Ott, while recognizing that Camilli was well past his peak, was overjoyed at getting him—overjoyed until Camilli unexpectedly announced that he did not intend to play out the season. Dolph told the writers, "I haven't been helping the Dodgers and I doubt that I can help any club. Playing for the Giants might be like taking

Mel Ott's famous hitting style from the front (author's collection).

money under false pretenses." After a two-hour meeting with Camilli, a disappointed Ott reported that Dolph would not change his mind. At least no one could question the rugged Californian's integrity as Camilli's decision cost him almost $8000 in salary. The net result was that the Giants would up with Allen and $7500 (the waiver price) since the deal had been made in good faith by the Dodgers. Brooklyn retained Lohrman, Sayles, and Orengo and a considerably lower payroll which, according to many aggrieved Dodger fans, was why Branch Rickey made the deal in the first place.

The Giants dragged on through August, sinking deeper into the cellar and suffering additional indignities. In one game against manager Freddy Fitzsimmons' Phillies, the Giants tied an old record for futility by stranding 18 men on base in a nine-inning game. Then an injury to Jurges left them with no substitute fielders; only seven able-bodied players were available to man the infield and outfield. Ott, in no condition to play because of a variety of ailments, muffed a fly ball for the first time anybody could remember. In another first, he was booed loudly for the first time ever at the Polo Grounds. Mel was asked about it after the game. He replied, "I really can't blame them. The team is doing poorly and I'm playing lousy ball. But if I don't play right field, who will?" A few days later the little manager came down with an ailment announced as a "stomach bug" which forced him to bed. The story around the Polo Grounds, though, was that Mel's problem was a nervous stomach brought on by his impossible problems.

There were only two other noteworthy items during the remainder of the season. Hubbell closed out his great career with his 253rd win on August 18, a 3–2 decision over the Pirates. And a lanky New York City native, John (Buddy) Kerr, made his major league debut at shortstop on September 8 and homered on his first trip to the plate.

As the season drew to a merciful close, Stoneham announced that Ott had been signed to a three-year, player-manager contract at a small salary increase. Stoneham told the writers that he never had any doubt about rehiring Ott despite the team's dismal year. Mel was asked whether he seriously expected to continue playing in view of his .234 batting average, the lowest of his career. He replied, "I know that I'm well past my peak, but I have to feel this was just a season when everything went wrong. As far as I'm concerned, it doesn't mean I'm through as a player. After all, I'm not even 35 yet.

The Giants lost 98 games and finished last, eight and a half games behind the seventh-place Phillies and a full 49½ games behind the pennant-winning Cardinals. Individually, Mickey Witek ranked second in the league in hits and fourth in hitting with a .314 average. Even in his subpar year, Ott finished second in homers, with a modest total of 18, and third in walks. The redoubtable Ace Adams was first in games pitched and second in saves.

Despite the Giants' awful season, Ott's popularity with the fans was undiminished. *Sports Magazine* named him the Number One Father of the Year and, in a nationwide vote by war bonds buyers, he was selected as the most popular sports hero of all time. He beat out such luminaries as Babe Ruth, Lou Gehrig, Christy Mathewson, Joe Louis, and Jack Dempsey.

Hubbell announced his retirement in November. He signed a long-term contract as the Giants' farm system director, the position that Terry had vacated. When Hubbell took over, the club's farm system consisted of the Jersey City club, the Class D Bristol team in the Appalachian League, and a small scouting staff.

Bill Terry had remained inactive during the year, tending his farm near Memphis and keeping an eye out for opportunities in the game. But in January he announced that he had abandoned his search and had become a partner in a cotton firm. Memphis Bill groused, "It's (baseball) too cheap a business and it's getting cheaper all the time." Then, completely underestimating the post-war profits and salaries to be made in the game, Terry continued, "With the low salaries they're paying managers, players, and front office men now, there's nothing in the game for me." The ex–Giants pilot said he was not worried about the game's future, concluding tartly, "No business in the world has ever made more money with poorer management. It can survive anything."

The Giants lost several players over the winter. Buster Maynard, Van Mungo, and Ken Trinkle went into the Army. Bartell enlisted in the Navy. Mickey Witek and Sid Gordon joined the Coast Guard. And Ken Chase and Johnny Allen decided to forego baseball, Chase to remain on his farm and Allen to stay on his job in a defense plant.

Ott also joined the war effort. Eager to do his part, for the first time in many years Mel took an offseason job. He went to work for the Todd-Johnson Drydocks Company in New Orleans.

Chapter 16

SURVIVING THE WAR

After a few weeks at Lakewood, Bill Voiselle emerged as the potential leader of the pitching staff with his blazing fastball and sharp curve. This despite the fact that he had pitched in a total of six major league games. Ott was desperate enough to try Ace Adams as a starter. Ewald Pyle, a 34-year-old, curveballing lefthander picked up from the Senators, showed promise. Cliff Melton still struggled with his ailing arm. Righthanders Harry Feldman and Rube Fischer were tentative starters. Two other righthanders, young Frank Seward and 43-year-old Lou (Crip) Polli, were candidates for the bullpen. The ancient Polli's major league experience, typical of that of many of the day's marginal performers, consisted of six innings of relief pitching for the St. Louis Browns in 1932. The well-seasoned catching trio of Lombardi, Mancuso, and Berres were all back.

Ott was hopeful that he had solved his first base problem when he picked up Phil Weintraub from Toledo. Since leaving the Giants in the deal for Burgess Whitehead eight years earlier, Weintraub had ricocheted around the baseball circuit—the Cardinals chain, the Reds, the Phillies, Minneapolis, and other minor league stops—before quitting the game in disgust to go into the jewelry business. When that venture failed, Phil returned to the game with Toledo in 1943. Although Weintraub was barely adequate at first base, Ott appeared to be satisfied as he watched the Chicagoan pound the ball to all parts of the field.

George Hausmann, a 28-year-old rookie, was set to replace Witek. Youthful Buddy Kerr appeared solid enough at short. Nap Reyes had taken the place of the departed Gordon at third. Other infielders in camp included 36-year-old Billy Jurges and a 30-year-old second baseman, Hal Luby, up from the Coast League.

There was no shortage of outfielders even with Maynard gone. Ott, Rucker, and Medwick were the returning regulars. Rotund Charley Mead had been called up from Jersey City. Three other vintage 1944 outfield aspirants—Bruce Sloan, Steve Filipowicz, and Danny Gardella—were in camp. Sloan was an ex–minor leaguer and a practicing accountant. The broad-beamed Filipowicz had never played baseball professionally although he was well known around the New York area as a former football and baseball star at Fordham University. Just discharged from the Marines, his chances were enhanced by his raw power at the plate, and equally important, his invulnerability to the draft.

Gardella had worked in a shipyard in 1943. He was an amusing, colorful, native New Yorker with a blithe, free-spirited approach to life in general and baseball in particular. "Dauntless Dan," as he was dubbed by the reporters, was a powerful little fellow who hit the ball with authority but whose every move in the field was fraught with uncertainty. One of the writers, after watching Gardella shadowbox with a routine fly ball, wrote that the carefree young fellow had made a "sensational catch of a routine fly ball." Another scribe wrote caustically about a long drive that Gardella had pulled down "unassisted."

Gardella had a special problem mastering the technique of using sunglasses. Johnny Rucker had shown him how to tap his sunglasses into place while pursuing a fly ball. One bright day a fly ball headed in Gardella's general direction. He tapped his glasses as instructed, but there was a problem. The sunglasses came down over his eyes, but his heavy touch brought the cap down with the attached glasses, completely covering his eyes. The fly ball dropped at his feet to the amusement of everyone except manager Ott.

The 1944 training season began on an ominous note when Ott's draft board classified the 35-year-old manager as 1-A. This meant that he could be called up for military service if he passed his physical exam. It was rumored that either Hartnett or Hubbell would replace Mel if he were drafted. However, before Mel was summoned for a physical, the military announced that men over 26 would no longer be inducted, and the Giants organization and the fans breathed a collective sigh of relief.

Hubbell's first spring as farm system director was remembered for the large number of teenagers who came to Lakewood for a tryout. Reporters wrote of Hubbell's enthusiasm for his new job as he worked hard with a small army of youngsters. All of them were eager to find a place in the Giants' depleted farm system or, miracle of miracles, a berth with the parent club as 16-year-old Mel Ott had done.

As the chilly training season ended, Ott told the writers that he expected his club to have a much better year than in 1943. "Things can't be as bad as they were last year," Mel said. "At least now we have some spare players to go around. Then, too, I think some of the other clubs have been hit a little harder than we were." But he cautioned, "Don't hold me to any prediction. If there's anything more uncertain than peacetime baseball, it's wartime baseball." The AP pollsters agreed with Ott's evaluation, picking the Giants to move up to sixth place and again projecting a Cardinals pennant win.

Bill Voiselle won the opener against the Braves 2–1 on Hal Luby's two-run double. The Giants opened with an infield of Weintraub, Hausmann, Kerr, and Luby, who had won the third base job from Reyes. Ott, Rucker, and Medwick were the outfield starters, with Lombardi catching. Typical of the times, the turnover was so great that only Ott and Rucker had played in the 1943 opening game.

The Giants took the next four games against the Braves and Dodgers but then, as the pitching sloughed off, the club fell back. Still, there was one more memorable game against the Dodgers on April 30, before more than 58,000 at the Polo Grounds, that the Giants won by an incredible 26–8 score. Some of the individual exploits were spectacular. Weintraub had 11 RBIs with a homer, triple, and two doubles. Lombardi batted in seven runs. Ott equaled his own records by walking five straight times and scoring six runs. And the Giants received 17 walks, six of them in a row, from Durocher's hapless pitchers.

But, other than their potent attack, the Giants had serious problems. The pitching was weak and Adams returned to the bullpen. Ott missed several games with an assortment of injuries, and Gardella, iron glove and all, was brought back from exile in Jersey City and inserted in the manager's place in right field. The usually patient Ott, for the first time since taking over the team, expressed his annoyance publicly at what he considered lackadaisical play. As the Giants began their first western trip, Medwick was benched for fielding lapses.

The Giants won fewer than half of their games in the West and returned home in sixth place, seven and a half games out of first place. As the trip ended with a doubleheader in St. Louis on May 21, Ott tried to instill some life into his club, giving one of his old-time performances. Returning to the lineup prematurely, both because of an injury to Rucker and the team's listless play, the little manager played right field in the first game and contributed a triple and a single in a losing effort. In the second game Ott shook up the lineup. He benched Kerr, moved Jurges from third to short, and took over at third base himself. Mel then proceeded to beat the powerful Cardinals almost single-handedly with a long home run and two ringing doubles.

With the war going well and the Allied invasion of the Continent expected any day, German submarines no longer posed a threat to shipping off the East Coast. Restrictions on night baseball in New York City were lifted, and on May 23 the Giants played their first night game in New York since the start of the war. Voiselle was well on his way to a 2–1 win over the Dodgers at Ebbets Field in the last of the ninth. With two on and two out, ex–Pirate Lloyd Waner lifted an easy fly to right center for what appeared to be the final out. Just as the ball landed in centerfielder Johnny Rucker's glove, Charley Mead, inserted in right field for defensive purposes, bumped into Rucker and jarred the ball loose. Running with two out, both Dodger runners scored and Durocher's club won 3–2. Ott rushed out to console the stunned Voiselle as he walked toward the Giants dugout. The incident reminded older fans of the 1936 game that Van Mungo lost in similar fashion when Freddy Lindstrom and Jimmy Jordan collided.

The Giants came back to win seven straight at the Polo Grounds and wound up their home stand in fourth place. The rejuvenated Ott continued his hard hitting with eight home runs during the 13-game stand although his fielding at third slipped badly, and he returned to the outfield "for my own safety as well as for the good of the club." Gardella also hit well during the home stand.

The Giants moved into a tie for third place after a strong showing against the eastern clubs. Voiselle pitched strongly and Ace Adams relieved competently. But, for the most part, the pitching was poor. Melton aggravated his ailing arm and was sent to Jersey City. Fischer, Seward, and Feldman were completely unreliable. Polli's ancient arm gave up the ghost. The final straw came when Ewald Pyle broke his thumb in an off-the-field scuffle in Boston. The infuriated Ott fined Pyle and suspended him without pay until he was able to pitch, a full month later.

The Giants picked up pitchers from every direction. They acquired 6 foot, 9-inch southpaw Johnny Gee from the Pirates where he had done little. Johnny Allen was coaxed back into uniform. Andy (Swede) Hansen and Bob Barthelmes, two young righthanders, were brought up from Jersey City. But the revamped pitching staff showed no improvement. In addition, Gardella's hitting fell off badly, and Ott, tiring of Danny's amateurish fielding, sent the colorful youngster back to Jersey City. Leon (Red) Treadway was brought up from the Little Giants to replace Gardella. Then, as a mediocre home stand ended, Ott sprained his ankle badly and was sidelined for three weeks.

Any chance for a decent season ended with the disastrous western trip which followed. The team lost its first 13 games on the trip, tying its longest losing streak since 1903, before McGraw took over. Mel missed every game and Weintraub also was sidelined. With the offense crippled, the pitching remained poor and the defense fell apart. Ott's frustration increased as he sat in the dugout helplessly watching.

The Giants pilot was particularly disturbed by his team's play in a game in Cincinnati. The Giants were leading 3–2 going into the bottom of the seventh. With Redlegs on first and second, Kerr was slow in returning to his shortstop position after a pickoff play at second base. The hitter drove a bouncer through the vacated area to send in the tying run. With two runners on later in the inning, the Reds' Frank McCormick blooped a fly ball into short left field. Medwick attempted a sliding, sitdown catch, but umpire Dusty Boggess ruled that the ball had been trapped. While the runners raced around the bases to score, Medwick foolishly held the ball aloft and raced in to protest to Boggess. Ott felt that no runs would have scored in the inning if the Giants had played routine big league baseball, and he fined each man $100 for "inexcusable mental errors." Kerr accepted the fine without complaint, but Medwick, who had a weaker case, objected furiously to the fine. However, after he had time to think it over, Joe admitted that he had pulled a boner and deserved the penalty.

Before the season ended, there was a good example of the relaxed wartime approach to the usual rules of the game. Medwick, at bat one day against the Dodgers, was hit on the elbow by a pitched ball. He sank to the ground grimacing in pain, then walked over to the dugout, apparently out of the game. In deference to the Giants' shortage of outfielders, the low standing of both clubs in the pennant race, and the desire to display all remaining resources of authentic major league talent, Ott and Durocher conferred as to what could be done to get Medwick back in the game after he had received treatment. Finally, Durocher agreed that Medwick could re-enter the game later so long as Leo could select a pinch runner for Medwick. Durocher picked the leadfooted Gus Mancuso because the even slower Lombardi was already in the game. Big Lom, the next hitter, obliged Leo by thumping resoundingly into a double play.

The Giants finished the season in fifth place with Bill Voiselle the only shining light in an otherwise lackluster Giants campaign. The big South Carolinian, with his distinguishing number 96 uniform, earned *The Sporting News* rookie of the year award with a 21 and 16 record. He tied for third in wins and complete games and led the league in strikeouts and innings pitched. Ace Adams led in games pitched and saves. Medwick was third in hitting with a .337 average, and Weintraub was well up in slugging percentage. And the doughty Ott, despite injuries and the strain of managing, ranked second in home runs with 26, third in slugging percentage, and tied for third in walks with Stan Musial.

The powerful Cardinals, who still had the services of Musial, Mort and Walker Cooper, Marty Marion, Whitey Kurowski, and other lesser players, won the pennant by 14½ games over the second-place Pirates. They went on to defeat the St. Louis Browns in the World Series.

Mel had missed the uneventful winter meetings, choosing instead to participate in a USO tour which entertained the troops just behind the combat area. In early December the tour group visited the 82nd Airborne Division in Belgium. If their itinerary had taken them to the troops just a few days later, they very likely would have been trapped by the German counteroffensive which began the Battle of the Bulge. Mel wrote Mildred, "Every day here is like the Dodgers and the Giants at Ebbets Field. Only I wish it were only pop bottles being thrown." After the tour ended, the Giants received a letter from Major Paul J. Hanna, of the 82nd Airborne. Hanna concluded, "Mel Ott's lifetime records and personality were an inspiration to us."

There were few changes when the Giants regrouped in Lakewood in March 1945. Cliff Melton decided to join Lefty O'Doul's San Francisco Seals rather than take a big pay cut. Johnny Allen retired. Mancuso had been released during the winter. Van Mungo was back from the service while Hal Luby joined it. Two new young righthanders, Loren Bain and Bill Emmerich, were in camp. And veteran righthander Ray Harrell was up from the minors where he had pitched since 1941 after spending a number of undistinguished years with several National League teams.

The pitching as usual was the big problem. Voiselle and Adams were solid. With the others Ott could only hope for the best but expect the worst. He was especially hopeful that Mungo would deliver the big season that each of his managers had envisioned since he had come up to the Dodgers in 1931. The writers referred to this as "Mungo fever," a condition characterized by sheer euphoria after watching Mungo throw his blazing fireball, followed by extreme depression when Mungo's strenuous elbow-bending and erratic performances became too painful to ignore.

There were other concerns. With Mancuso gone, only Lombardi and Berres remained to do the catching, and both men were well up in years. The infield was reasonably well set with Weintraub, Hausmann, Kerr, and Reyes the regulars. Ott was particularly high on Kerr whom he described as "potentially another Marty Marion." But he was concerned about the outfield. Medwick missed most of spring training with a back ailment. The center field job was up for grabs between the untried Red Treadway and shopworn Johnny Rucker. Mel expected to start the season, but beginning his twentieth year with the club, he assumed that his playing days were almost over.

The Giants opened in Boston with almost the same lineup that began the 1944 campaign. The only changes were Reyes, who started at third and slammed out four hits, and Steve Filipowicz in left field in place of the ailing Medwick. Voiselle won the game 11–6 following a memorial tribute to President Franklin D. Roosevelt who had died a few days before.

Ott's club went on to win 12 of its first 16 games against the eastern clubs. Almost all of the players were off to fine starts. Rucker hit safely in every game. Weintraub, Lombardi, and Reyes were hitting for distance and Ott was hitting well over .400. Hausmann and Kerr clicked around second base. Voiselle began the season with four straight wins, and Harry Feldman won three games. Mungo and the other pitchers were having difficulties, but the stocky Adams, pitching brilliantly in relief, saved a number of games.

Early May was a joyous time as the German army collapsed completely and surrendered. The war in Europe was over and interest in baseball picked up. The Polo Grounds was an especially happy place as the Giants performed admirably against the visiting western clubs. To top it off, Ott, who was leading the league in hitting, tied Lou Gehrig's lifetime home run total of 494 with a long blast off Cincinnati lefthander Arnold Carter. Lombardi was leading the majors in homers and RBIs. Voiselle had won eight straight, and Feldman was 7 and 0. The club was off to a great start.

For the first time in his managerial career, Ott felt that his club had a real shot at a pennant. In 1942 he had surprised the fans with an appealing team which played well above expectations, vaulting from deep in the second division into third place. The 1943 club, shattered by personnel losses, was a hopeless case. In 1944 the team had improved but was never in contention. But this club seemed to have a good chance to go all the way without a dominant team in the league.

The Giants left on their first western swing leading the league by three and a half games and playing at an .800 clip. They split their first ten games of the trip and moved into St. Louis, their last port-of-call, in high spirits. Voiselle, pitching in the first game, outpitched Blix Donnelly and Harry Brecheen for eight innings and went into the bottom of the ninth with a 3–1 lead, one out, and a runner on base. Then, with an 0 and 2 count, Johnny Hopp tripled to run the score to 3–2 as Ott tapped the sod angrily in right field. Suddenly, a heavy rain came up and delayed the game for an hour. When play resumed, a cooled-off Voiselle gave up a single to Ray Sanders to tie the game and a triple to Whitey Kurowski to lose it.

After the game, Ott surprised the writers with the announcement that

Voiselle had been fined $500 for "disobeying pitching instructions." The overwrought Giants skipper told reporters, "I've been telling my pitchers they would be fined for not wasting an 0 and 2 pitch. So, with 0 and 2 on Hopp, Voiselle grooves one, and the next thing you know the game is gone." Voiselle's predictable comment was that the pitch had gotten away from him. The general feeling among the surprised players and writers was that the fine was too severe. But a good deal of criticism also was directed at Mel's failure to replace Voiselle after the long rain delay, particularly since the big righthander had pitched more than eight innings.

The Giants returned home in first place by four games and things still looked bright despite the upsetting loss in St. Louis. Ott had broken Honus Wagner's long-standing National League record for career total bases when the team was in Chicago. Weintraub and Lombardi were also hitting well. Voiselle and Feldman figured to bounce back from their slumps, and Ott was still hopeful that Mungo would regain his preseason form. But Mel had soured on Medwick, and he decided to utilize Joe as trading bait for a badly needed catcher if a deal could be swung before the June 15 trading deadline.

The law of averages caught up with the Giants, and a string of losses dropped the club into fourth place behind the Cards, Dodgers, and Pirates. Ott tried to snap Voiselle out of the doldrums by rescinding the $500 fine, but it was of no help. Feldman, Mungo, and Fischer also pitched ineffectively. Weintraub was out with injuries, and Lombardi tired and had to be rested. The Giants finally completed a deal for another catcher, obtaining Clyde Kluttz from the Braves for Medwick and Ewald Pyle. Danny Gardella took Medwick's place in left field and showed his old hitting form as well as some improvement in the field. The only other bright spot was provided by manager Ott himself. Mel was hitting over .350 and playing every day despite a variety of ailments. But the team was struggling to stay up with the leaders.

On June 19, the Giants lost to the Braves at the Polo Grounds. But the big story was that Allied Commander Dwight D. Eisenhower, just back from Europe after the Allied forces' victory on the Continent, attended the game. Eisenhower was given a long standing ovation by the large crowd as his automobile circled the field. Before the game, Ike told Mel of his early days when he played for the Abilene, Texas, minor league club under an assumed name.

In late June the Giants played an exhibition game at the New London, Connecticut, naval base. Former Cubs outfielder Jimmy Gleeson, an officer at the base, raved to Ott about a stumpy catcher on the base team. Mel was equally impressed by the awkward youngster's fluid swing, his ability to connect solidly with any pitch near the plate, and his obvious baseball savvy. Learning that the young man was a Yankee farmhand, Ott contacted Larry MacPhail, then the Yankees' president and general manager. But if the Giants had any chance to obtain the young catcher, they lost it when Ott offered MacPhail $50,000 for him. Although Larry knew nothing about the obscure farmhand, the offer was high enough to alert him to the young fellow's potential. MacPhail reasoned shrewdly that if the knowledgeable Ott offered that much, the Yanks ought to keep him. The Bronx Bombers did, and Yogi Berra proved to be one of the game's great success stories. Unfortunately, the Giants didn't share in it.

The Giants managed no more than a split during their home stand against the western teams and clearly had lost their earlier spark and confidence. It was during this period that club officials learned that Harry Danning would not be back. Discharged from the Army, Danning wrote Horace Stoneham a letter which concluded dolefully, "I wish I could tell you that I was on my way to New York, but my legs are in such bad shape that I'll have to forget about ever playing ball again." On the brighter side, the Giants purchased the contract of 19-year-old outfielder Carroll (Whitey) Lockman from Jersey City. In the Lowell, North Carolina, native's first major league at-bat, he duplicated Buddy Kerr's feat by hitting a home run. In addition to his hitting, Lockman impressed with his speed on the bases and his fine fielding.

Although the war was over in Europe, there remained a serious transportation shortage as servicemen returned to the States for discharge or for transfer to the Far East. Thus, despite the end of hostilities in Europe, traveling by the major league teams was still restricted by the government ruling which banned civilian use of Pullman sleepers on trips under 450 miles. For example, before the Giants left on their second western trip, secretary Eddie Brannick noticed that the Giants were scheduled to play a Saturday afternoon game in St. Louise starting at 3:00 P.M., followed by a doubleheader in Chicago the next afternoon. The Giants requested the Cardinals to move the Saturday game up to 2:00 P.M. so that the Giants could make the last evening train at 6:00 P.M. from St. Louis to Chicago. Otherwise, the Giants would have faced the unpleasant prospect of sitting up in day coaches during the night, then playing an afternoon doubleheader.

The club fared poorly on the western swing and returned home in fifth place. The trip was best remembered for one of Danny Gardella's antics while the Giants were in Cincinnati, another antic which did not amuse Ott. Nap Reyes was Gardella's roommate. Nap went up to their hotel room one morning to pick up Gardella and head for the ballpark.

As Reyes entered the room, he noticed the window was wide open and there was a note on the bed from Gardella. "Dauntless Dan" had written that he was committing suicide because "life is too much for me." Horrified, Reyes leaped to the open window. As he approached it, he almost jumped out of his skin when Gardella's grinning countenance rose up over the window sill. Gardella had been hanging out the window by his arms, several stories above the street, "just for a laugh." Reyes was still shaking when he arrived at Crosley Field for the game.

Later in July there was an interesting game at the Polo Grounds when the Giants took on the Cubs in a doubleheader. Slugging Cubs rightfielder Bill (Swish) Nicholson hit three home runs in his first three at-bats in the first game. This gave him five homers in the series. In the second game, after Nicholson's sixth home run of the series, the Giants had a 10–7 lead in the eighth inning as Nicholson came to bat with the bases loaded and two out. Mel paid the big outfielder the supreme compliment, having him walked to force in a run and reduce the Giants lead to 10–8. The older writers recalled the 1929 game when the Phillies intentionally walked Ott to deny him a chance for the home run title. But this strategic decision, which went completely against standard baseball doctrine, worked out well for Mel as the Giants pulled out a 12–10 extra-inning win.

After missing a few weeks with injuries, Ott returned to the lineup and continued to thump the ball at a .340 clip. In a night game at the Polo Grounds on August 1, the little manager clouted his 500th career home run. It was a typical Ott home run, a sharply pulled smash into the upper right field stands. Belted off mountainous righthander Johnny Hutchings of the Braves, the ball bounced back onto the field where it was retrieved by Giants trainer Willie Schaefer. At the time, the only players with more career home runs were Babe Ruth with 714 and Jimmie Foxx with 527.

Later that night there was a big party at Toots Shor's restaurant in midtown Manhattan to celebrate Ott's milestone. Before Mel arrived at the restaurant that night, Shor sat at a table with Sir Alexander Fleming, the Scottish bacteriologist who had been awarded the Nobel prize for his discovery of penicillin. When Mel walked in the door, Shor jumped to his feet and gave Sir Alexander an inadvertent putdown. "Excuse me, Alex," he said, "I've got to greet someone who just came in who is really important."

In early August, about the time the Japanese surrender was being negotiated, there were indications that the Giants front office was taking steps to build the team for the post-war period. Stoneham announced the purchase of the Class B Trenton club. This gave the Giants outright own-ership of two minor league teams (Jersey City, of course, was the other) and working agreements with four other clubs. The Giants also announced some personnel moves. Righthander Sal Maglie and lefty Adrian Zabala were brought up from Jersey City along with young first baseman Mike Schemer. Roy Zimmerman, another first baseman, was acquired from the Newark Bears, and Phil Weintraub was optioned to the Bears.

By mid–August the Giants held onto fourth place, but they were well behind the Cubs, Cards, and Dodgers, and their chances of moving up in the standings worsened when the promising Lockman went into the Army. Still, the club seemed to have regained some of its spark, and the Polo Grounds crowds, swelled by discharged servicemen, had something to cheer about as Maglie and Zabala won their first starts, and the Giants offensive went into high gear.

Despite their improvement, the Giants were unable to close the gap on the Dodgers who swept a four-game series from Ott's club in their first meeting in more than two months. During that period the Dodgers had picked up the ultimate in wartime players, the inimitable Babe Her-man who had rejoined the Dodgers after a 14-year hiatus. Since the 42-year-old Herman left the Dodgers in 1931, he had played for the Cubs, Reds, Pirates, and Tigers before joining Travis Jackson's Jersey City club in 1938. Babe also had spent several years in the minors, never dreaming that he would be back in the major leagues. Yet here he was back in Brook-lyn, hitting an occasional long ball, taking pratfalls on the field with his old aplomb, and pleasing the Ebbets Field crowds as he had in the old days when Dodger baseball was almost indistinguishable from a Mack Sennett comedy.

For the first time in their history the Giants went over the million mark in attendance while taking a doubleheader from manager Ben Chap-man's Phillies on September 3. The Giants' best previous attendance was in 1937, their last pennant-winning year, when they drew almost 939,000. But artistically, the club was less successful, finishing the season in fifth place, two and a half games behind the fourth-place Pirates.

As late as Labor Day, Ott was hitting well over .320, high enough to rank within the top five hitters in the league. However, during the last western trip, persistent lameness in his knee worsened, and he announced that he would not play regularly for the rest of the season. As the season ended, league president Ford Frick presented Mel with a lifetime pass in honor of his twentieth year in the league. More importantly, the Giants canceled the one year remaining on his contract and signed him to a five-year contract at a substantial salary boost.

In that last wartime season a few of the Giants did well individually. Adams finished second in games pitched and tied for most saves. Rucker was fifth in triples. Voiselle was third in strikeouts. And Ott, whose batting average dropped to .308, was fifth in homers and fourth in slugging percentage.

The Cubs, almost the identical team which had finished in fourth place and under .500 in 1944, beat out the Cardinals for the pennant by three and a half games. But they lost a seven-game World Series to the Detroit Tigers. The Tigers were sparked by Hank Greenberg, just returned from the Air Corps, southpaw Hal Newhouser, and colorful righthander Dizzy Trout. Before the first game of the Series, Chicago writer Warren Brown succinctly put wartime baseball in proper perspective. As Brown sat in the press box, one of his colleagues asked him whom he picked to win. Brown looked down at the odd assortment of players warming up, thought how much the caliber of play had slipped during the war, and then turned to his questioner and answered sardonically, "I don't think either team can win!"

In December the Giants obtained pitcher-outfielder Clint (Hondo) Hartung from the Minneapolis Millers for $20,000 and three players. The purported feats of the "Pheenom," as he was referred to, were unreal. After seeing a continuing string of stories of the deeds of this latter-day Paul Bunyan, Tom Meany wrote caustically, "Hartung's a sucker if he reports to the Giants. All he has to do is sit at home, wait until he's eligible, and he's a cinch to make the Hall of Fame."

Chapter 17

ℕICE GUY FINISHES LAST

In January the Giants bought Walker Cooper from the Cardinals for $175,000, by far the largest sum the club had ever paid for a player. Big Coop was widely considered the best catcher in the game before joining the Navy after the 1944 season. Ott was jubilant as he told the writers of his high expectations for the big Missourian.

A few days later the Giants announced the signing of Carl Hubbell to a new five-year contract. When Hub took over as farm system director in 1944, the Giants had only a few clubs and scouts. Now, with the war over, the club owned franchises in Jersey City, Trenton, and Fort Smith and, within a short time, would purchase the Triple A Minneapolis Millers. The Giants also had working agreements with eight minor league teams and had a dozen scouts beating the bushes for talent.

An unusually large squad reported to the Giants' spring training camp in Miami, so large that Ott and his coaches, Red Kress, Bubber Jonnard, and Dick Bartell, had their hands full instructing and evaluating the players. There were 25 pitchers in camp alone. In addition to the holdovers from 1945, former pitching regulars returning from the service included Hal Schumacher, Bob Carpenter, Dave Koslo, and Ken Trinkle. The most prominent of the new pitchers were curveballing righthander Bob Joyce, who had excelled in the Pacific Coast League; southpaw Monte Kennedy, a wild but promising youngster from Virginia; and righthanders Mike Budnick and Marvin Grissom.

The infield was strengthened with the return of Mize and Witek and the addition of two promising rookies, Buddy Blattner and Bill Rigney. Blattner already had attained some athletic recognition—as a Ping-Pong champion. Rigney, a bespectacled Californian, was a slight, peppery young fellow who would one day manage the Giants. Outfielders Buster Maynard, Babe Young, Sid Gordon, and Morrie Arnovich were back, and

Willard Marshall was expected back from the Marines before the start of the season. Cooper would be the regular catcher with Ernie Lombardi and Clyde Kluttz the backup catchers.

For several months major leaguers had been approached to jump to the Mexican League, a newly-formed "outlaw" (not part of organized baseball) league operated by Mexican customs broker Jorge Pasquel and his brother Bernardo. A few days after camp opened, Danny Gardella announced that he had signed a five-year contract to play in Mexico. He also told the writers that other major leaguers had signed with Pasquel, including Nap Reyes, pitcher Adrian Zabala, and Dodger outfielder Luis Olmo. "Dauntless Dan" said he had been paid $4500 in 1945, and the Giants had offered him only a $500 raise despite his 18 home runs. He stated that he had no intention of letting the Giants "enrich themselves" by selling him to a minor league club, and that he had decided therefore to take his "gifted talents" to Mexico.

Ott showed little concern over the loss of Gardella (Danny's leaving was something of a relief to Mel), Reyes, and Zabala. However, a month later Sal Maglie, George Hausmann, and reserve first baseman Roy Zimmerman left for Mexico. Maglie revealed that each player would be paid at least double his 1946 salary plus a $5000 bonus and $1000 for expenses. Ott became furious with Maglie when he learned that the jumping players had placed a call to Pasquel from Maglie's hotel room. Sal claimed that the players had used his phone to call Pasquel collect only because they happened to be in his room at the time. Years later Maglie recalled:

> I was optimistic about making the team that year. I had a good winter pitching in Cuba and when I came to camp Ott seemed glad to see me. I pitched well in an early exhibition game, but after that Ott didn't seem to know I was alive. Most of the other guys weren't getting the look they deserved either.
> Mel wouldn't listen to me when I tried to explain the phone call. He accused me of setting up the whole deal, acting as Pasquel's agent. Later he came into the clubhouse and asked all the fellows if they had been contacted by the Mexicans, and if so, what their plans were.

Although several of the players admitted they had been approached, all assured Ott they would stay with the Giants. Their decisions may have been influenced by baseball commissioner Happy Chandler's edict that all jumpers would be banned from playing in the major leagues for five years.

Mel's inability to give each man sufficient opportunity to pitch in the exhibition games concerned him greatly and caused a good deal of unhappiness in the ranks, as Maglie had reported. In fact, brooding after pitching in only two games, Van Mungo showed up at the park one day in what Ott delicately called "no condition to appear on the field." As a result, he was suspended indefinitely. There would be no "Mungo fever" in 1946.

As the Giants barnstormed north with the Indians, it was apparent that pitching was still the team's fundamental problem. The catching figured to be first rate after Cooper rounded into shape. The big catcher was happy with his $25,000 contract, double the salary the Cardinals had paid him in 1944. Cooper also succeeded Billy Jurges as team captain, as the veteran shortstop had been released and picked up by the Cubs. Ott had settled on a starting infield of Mize, Witek, Rigney at short, and Buddy Kerr at third. The outfield corps of Marshall, Young, Rucker, Gordon, and Ott was slow on the bases and in the field, but it had hitting potential.

Ott, preparing to start his twenty-first season, hit well in the preseason games. But the team was frightened on the trip north when he was hit in the head by a Mike Budnick fastball in batting practice. X-rays showed no serious injury, and Ott rejoined the team after spending the night in a Norfolk hospital. Mel had escaped relatively unscathed, but he was concerned nevertheless. "My eyes!" he told a coach. "I never saw that pitch coming." But he came back to lead the club in hitting as it completed the tour with the Indians and moved into New York to start the campaign. The AP pollsters picked the Giants to finish in fifth place behind the Cards, Cubs, Dodgers, and Pirates.

The Giants opened against the Phillies at the Polo Grounds before an enthusiastic crowd of 40,000, including a large contingent of servicemen and recently discharged veterans. Voiselle outpitched southpaw Oscar Judd to win an easy decision despite the absence of Mize and Cooper. Ott thrilled the crowd in the first inning with a two-run home run to send the Giants off winging. No one minded that it was one of his least impressive home runs, a looping fly ball that barely reached the right field seats. Of greater significance, it was number 511 of his career and the last major league homer he would hit. The next day Mel dove futilely for a fly ball, injured his knee, and played only infrequently and ineffectively for the rest of the year.

Playing poorly, the Giants suffered a serious loss on April 26 when Ace Adams and Harry Feldman unexpectedly jumped down to the Mexican League. A furious Ott told the writers, "They showed up in the clubhouse before most of the other players had come to the park, packed their belongings, and left immediately. I understand that they flashed a roll of bills totaling about $15,000. Well," he went on defiantly, "I'm missing nothing." As Adams left the clubhouse, he told Ott with tears in his eyes, "Mel, I hate to quit playing for you. It's just that they're offering me too much money to turn down."

Despite his brave words, Ott knew he was missing plenty. Feldman had been erratic, but he appeared on the verge of becoming a solid winner. The loss of the rubber-armed Adams was something else. It was a body blow to a pitching staff that needed help badly, especially relief pitching.

Years later Adams explained in greater detail why he jumped to the Mexican League. "I couldn't get enough money (with the Giants). An American man came to me and offered me $50,000 to pitch one year. That was pretty hard to turn down, all expenses, an apartment. Fifty thousand in 1946 for five months' work. That's all I can save in five years. I was about to retire anyway, so why not take it? I had a good time down there, pitched good ball, got to start."

On the same day that Adams and Feldman departed, the Giants bought outfielder Goody Rosen from the Dodgers. Two days later, Rosen was the Giants' hitting star as the Giants won a doubleheader from Brooklyn. Because the Dodgers wound up the regular season tied with the Cardinals, and then lost the ensuing playoff, fans and writers speculated after the campaign that the Dodgers may well have lost the pennant by trading Rosen two days too soon.

As the Giants headed west for the first time, Arthur Daley wrote critically in the *Times* about the Giants' organizational problems:

> The Giants are one of the few remaining clubs in the majors which still operate under the archaic system whereby all the duties of running the organization devolve upon the manager…. It is a job that calls for a general manager, or a general supervisor who directs the affairs of the entire organization…. To hold Ott accountable for the woeful start the Giants have made … is uncalled for and unfair…. Given the opportunity to concentrate exclusively on directing his Giants, such as (Yankee manager) Joe McCarthy receives … and Leo Durocher receives…, Mel doubtless would more than hold his own. But the Giants still play it as they did in the horse-and-buggy age.

May 1 was a busy day on the trading block for catcher Clyde Kluttz, who was the property of three clubs within four hours. While the Giants were in St. Louis, Ott called Kluttz during breakfast and told him that he had been traded to the Phillies for outfielder Vince DiMaggio. Mel added, "You'd better stay near the phone, Clyde, because the Phillies people will be calling you very soon." Phillies general manager Herb Pennock called Kluttz two hours later to tell him to report to the Phils in Cincinnati the next day. At lunch a couple of hours later, Cardinals manager Eddie Dyer called Kluttz and told him he had been traded to St. Louis by the Phils. Kluttz returned to his cooled-off lunch, reasonably confident that he would not be traded again—before lunch.

By Memorial Day the Giants were mired in seventh place. Mize was clubbing the ball and Cooper was back after suffering a broken finger. The infield play improved as Ott finally settled on Blattner at second, Kerr at short, and Rigney at third. But the club was painfully slow afoot, and the outfield was unproductive even after the acquisition of Rosen.

Most important, other than a few acceptable outings by Koslo, Kennedy, Trinkle, and Bob Carpenter, the pitching was pathetic. Ace Adams was sorely missed. In desperation Ott picked up lefthander Tex Kraus from the Phils; righthander Gene Thompson, who had been released by the Reds; and a righthander, one John Carden, who had no professional experience. Kraus and Thompson were of some help, but Carden was cut adrift after a few weeks.

The club stumbled through June making little headway, slipping in and out of last place. Ott's frustration surfaced on June 9 in a double-header loss in Pittsburgh. In the first game, umpire Tom Dunn ejected Mel for complaining about a call on the bases. During the second game, umpire George Magerkurth bounced him for protesting too vigorously on a tipped bat call against Lombardi. Giants fans, hearing the game on the radio or reading about it the next day, could hardly believe it. Their mild-mannered idol, Mel Ott, had set a major league record, the first manager to be thrown out of two games on the same day!

Later in the season Ott and Durocher collaborated unwittingly in adding to the American idiom. The last-place Giants took on the league-leading Dodgers at the Polo Grounds. Koslo won the first game behind booming homers by Mize and Lombardi. In the second game the Dodgers won despite three more well-tagged homers by Marshall, Blattner, and Lombardi. The next day Dodgers broadcaster Red Barber sat on the Dodgers bench before the game kidding Durocher. "Leo," Barber needled, "your guys were lucky to split yesterday the way the Giants were hitting, especially those home runs." Lippy Leo scoffed, "Hell, they were nothing, just cheap Polo Grounds specials." Barber continued to needle, "Come on, Leo, be a nice guy and give credit where it's due." Durocher, better at giving the needle than taking it, shouted at Barber, "Nice guys! Do you know a nicer guy than Mel Ott? Or any of the other Giants? And where are they? The nice guys over there are in last place!" That was the way Frank Graham reported the dialogue the next day in the *Sun*, and that was the origin of the familiar tough-guy phrase, "Nice guys finish last."

The Giants' misfortunes and inept play continued for the rest of the season. Cooper suffered another broken finger and missed several weeks. Ott continued to try anything to bolster his weak pitching staff. He went so far as to sign coach Red Kress solely because of the live arm Kress displayed in batting practice. Red, a former shortstop, had pitched five innings for the Washington Senators in 1935. It took Kress only one four-inning stint to convince Ott that he could not help the Giants. Mize's hitting was one of the few bright spots. But, here again, the Giants were snake-bit as the big Georgian was beaned by the Cards' Harry Brecheen, then fractured his hand in a meaningless exhibition game with the Yankees, and then broke a toe in his first game back in the lineup. He was finished for the season.

Years later Mize told an amusing story about the Giants' retaliation against Brecheen after he beaned Mize. The Big Cat's story as he reported in Donald Honig's classic *Baseball When the Grass Was Green*:

> Well, after I was hit, Mel Ott told (Monte) Kennedy (who was pitching), "When Brecheen comes to bat, throw at him. Not at his head; hit him in the knee." He's telling this to a fellow who generally had a hard time just keeping his pitches in the ballpark. But, son of a gun, when Brecheen came up, the first pitch from Kennedy hit him right in the knee. Brecheen was out for ten days. That's probably one of the mysteries of baseball, that Kennedy, wild as he was, could hit a guy on the knee with his first pitch.

Even with the Giants out of contention, they attempted to play their traditional role in the Giants-Dodgers rivalry as they took on the Dodgers at the Polo Grounds in a three-game series just before Labor Day. The Dodgers and Cardinals were involved in a replay of their ferocious pennant fights of 1941 and 1942, and the Giants had a golden opportunity to pay the Dodgers back in kind for the 1934 debacle.

Kennedy outpitched Kirby Higbe in the first game. Goody Rosen and Eddie Stanky enlivened the game with a spirited fist fight after Rosen slid into second base with spikes high. Stanky took the throw, tagged Rosen squarely in the mouth, and the two little gamecocks went at it in fine style as the dugouts emptied rapidly. After several vicious, if ineffectual, blows were exchanged, both combatants were ejected. In the earlier McGraw-Terry-MacPhail days, this would have called for a special squad of police at the park for the next day's doubleheader. But these were different times, and Stanky and his teammates got their revenge peacefully enough by easily beating Voiselle and Trinkle before 53,000. Durocher's club wound up the day only one and a half games behind the Cards, and the Giants lost an opportunity to salvage something from their dismal season.

A few weeks later Rosen buried the hatchet publicly. On Eddie Stanky Day at Ebbets Field, Goody presented the scrappy little Dodger second baseman with a set of boxing gloves. He made the presentation with the lighthearted comment over the public address system, "Take these home and practice with them during the offseason." Then, to the applause of 30,000 fans, Goody added, "Seriously, Eddie's a great player and a good friend of mine, except when he's covering second and I'm coming in." With that, Rosen and Stanky shook hands and refrained from snarling at each other until the game began.

After Labor Day, the Giants sank into last place as Giants fans turned their attention to individual players and performances. On September 2, for the first time in the memory of Giants fans, a pinch hitter batted in place of Ott. Mel called on righthand-hitting Sid Gordon to replace him as the Braves brought in a lefthand pitcher. On September 9, Bobby Thompson made his debut for the Giants, playing third base and slapping out two hits. Righthander Sheldon Jones made his first Giants appearance and pitched five strong innings after a rocky start. But the current Giants hero was Buddy Kerr. The native New Yorker had developed into a superb shortstop and wound up the season with 52 straight errorless games and 274 chances without an error, breaking records set by Leo Durocher and Eddie Miller.

The only other development of note in 1946 was the home attendance. Although the Giants finished dead last, 36 games off the pace, the club drew 1,234,773 fans, exceeding by far the club attendance record set in 1945. Even though Mize missed one-third of the club's games because of injuries, he finished second in the league in home runs with 22, only one behind Ralph Kiner. Dave Koslo, the staff "ace" with a 14 and 19 record, tied for second in the league in innings pitched, and was third in complete games, and fourth in strikeouts. Ken Trinkle, mopping up where Adams left off, led the league in games pitched. Although Ott intended to stay out of the lineup, his club's desperate problems forced Mel to play in 31 games, mostly as a pinch hitter. After his Opening Day home run, the little manager accumulated a mere five hits, including only one double, as he hit a microscopic .074.

The Giants released Dick Bartell as the season ended. He left unhappy with Stoneham and with Ott, for whom he had great respect as a player and as a person. It was rumored that Bartell had coveted the job as Giants manager as early as 1941 when it became apparent that Bill Terry was tired of managing the club. In his book, *Rowdy Richard*, Dick wrote that he was supposed to be notified of his status with the Giants by six weeks before the end of the season. He had had some differences with Stoneham regarding the length of a contract to manage the Giants' farm team in Minneapolis, and felt he had been getting the runaround. He claimed Ott kept telling him that he couldn't find Stoneham to ask him about Dick's status. Bartell wrote:

> On the last day of the season Ott said, "I talked to Stoneham and he's going to give you your release this winter." I (Bartell) cussed him out and told him he had not lived up to his word, and Horace hadn't either. Then he asked me to go out and coach at third for the last game. I was so mad I just tore off my uniform and left the park.

(Bartell never explained why he did not deal with Stoneham directly, inasmuch as the decision as to arrangements for managing the Minneapolis Millers was that of Stoneham, and not Ott.)

After the season ended, the Giants began to clean house. Most important to Giants fans was the question about Mel's future. Still tremendously popular, he had not managed the club to a first division finish since his first year as manager in 1942. The war years were abnormal and could be written off. But what about the past season when the team had finished last? It was understood that Stoneham was asking himself the same question. A story made the rounds that the Giants owner had contacted Lefty O'Doul in San Francisco to inquire whether he would be interested in replacing Ott. But Lefty would not leave his home town.

So, the rumors had it, Stoneham had thought, pondered, and thought some more. He convinced himself that the Giants had an offensive powerhouse coming along, the likes of which the Polo Grounds had not seen in years. The crushing injuries to Mize and Cooper were unlikely to strike the team again, and a disaster like the unexpected loss of Ace Adams was even more unlikely. Also, the club had the potential for defensive improvement, and the pitching figured to improve as Carl Hubbell's farm system seemed about ready to begin producing decent pitching prospects.

Moreover, the National Exhibition Company (the Giants' corporate name) had done well financially, and there was no pressure from stockholders to replace Ott. As a matter of fact, there were four more years to go on Mel's contract, and the additional expense of paying two managers would antagonize the stockholders. In the final analysis, how could he fire his friend Ottie, the apple of his eye as a player and one of the finest men—yes, nicest guys—Stoneham had ever known. No, the personal and financial considerations favored the retention of Ott, and he would be back to manage the Giants in 1947.

Chapter 18

*T*HE *W*INDOWBREAKERS

The sad state of Giants affairs was driven home at the annual dinner of the New York chapter of the Baseball Writers Association in February. The writers lampooned the Giants with a satirical verse sung to Bing Crosby's then-popular "Swinging on a Star" as follows:

> A giant is a midget, gettin' by on his past,
> He can't hit a hook or nuthin' fast,
> His club makes money but it's gone to pot,
> The fans go there to dream of Hubbell and Ott.

As if to emphasize the point, Carl Hubbell had been elected to the Hall of Fame a few days before the dinner.

Giants fans, anticipating a major trade for establishing pitching talent, were disappointed when the team assembled in Phoenix, Arizona. Larry Jansen, a lean, jut-jawed righthander who had been a big winner in the Pacific Coast League, and Bill Ayers, a 21-game winner at Atlanta, were in camp. But, with the exception of Hal Schumacher, who had called it a career, it appeared that the Giants were saddled with the same staff that had labored so ineffectually throughout the 1946 season.

Stocky Dave Koslo was a solid southpaw starter although not the overpowering type normally considered the bellwether of a serious contender's pitching staff. Bill Voiselle had never been the same since his differences with Ott in 1945. Monte Kennedy had pitched brilliantly at times, but he still was wild and unpredictable. Bob Carpenter's arm had been ailing for some time. Mike Budnick lacked control and had won only two games in 1946. Ken Trinkle was a durable reliever, but he was hardly a satisfactory replacement for Ace Adams. Junior Thompson had become a marginal performer. And lefty Woody Abernathy had done little. Ott was so concerned that he hired old-time pitcher Walter (Dutch) Reuther to work with the pitchers.

The infield picture was brighter. Mize was a powerhouse at first base.

Blattner, Witek, and Rigney were experienced second basemen although none of the three were particularly adept at making the double play. Kerr was one of the top fielding shortstops in the league. The third base job was a three-way battle between versatile Sid Gordon, young Bobby Thomson, and Jack (Lucky) Lohrke. Brought up from Spokane, Lohrke had gained his nickname by his good fortune in narrowly escaping a series of airplane, railroad, and bus accidents.

Ott was always one of the boys with his players, including the youngsters, refusing to withdraw into an ivory tower as a manger. He urged his players to call him "Mel" or "Ottie," and he managed to maintain a one-big-family atmosphere on the club without surrendering any authority. He kidded his players, and they responded in kind. One day he was instructing Bobby Thomson at second base, a position Thomson had never played. After a couple of ground balls went through Mel's legs, Thomson put his hands on his hips in mock disapproval and told the other infielders, "They'd better get me another sparring partner out here or I'll never learn the position!"

The outfield figured to improve with the addition of speedy, talented Whitey Lockman. Many considered Willard Marshall a solid hitter and fielder although he had been a disappointment in his first year back from the service. Johnny Rucker was still around. Lloyd Gearhart and Al White were young outfielders without major league experience. Babe Young was still floundering as an outfielder because he could not dislodge Mize at first base. Joe Lafata, a promising first baseman–outfielder, was given a chance to make the team. Ott was still on the active roster although there was little expectation that he would play. And then there was the fabled Clint (Hondo) Hartung, who had spent the 1946 season at Minneapolis learning to track fly balls but with only modest success.

The catching appeared to be excellent if Cooper could avoid the injuries which ruined his first year with the Giants. Ancient Ernie Lombardi was still on hand, and Mickey Grasso was back after a short stint with the Giants at the end of the 1946 season.

After a few weeks in Phoenix, an upbeat Mel told the writers, "This is the first Giants team I've seen in a long time that reminds me of Mr. McGraw's clubs. We have more speed than we've shown in a long time with fellows like Thomson, Lockman, Rigney, and Lafata. And we have established power hitters like Mize, Cooper, and Marshall, and some of the other boys can powder the ball." He continued, "I also like the spirit and morale. They remind me of the old bunch—Terry, Youngs, Lindy, Jackson, and the rest. If only a few of the younger players come through, we should do all right." As the writers left the clubhouse, one was heard to mutter to another, "Mel may have something there but you notice he didn't mention there was anyone around who reminds him of Hub, Schumacher, or Fitzsimmons!"

The Giants' exhibition game schedule included a series with Lefty O'Doul's San Francisco Seals in Hawaii before the club began its long barnstorming trip east with the Indians who also had moved their training camp to Arizona. Severe injuries to Giants players marked the exhibition games. Mickey Witek broke his arm and was sent home to recuperate. Larry Jansen suffered a broken cheek bone and narrowly escaped a fractured skull when he was hit by a line drive off Bob Feller's bat. But the cruelest blow of all came on April 8 in Sheffield, Alabama. Lockman, who was playing brilliantly, broke his right leg sliding into second base. His season was virtually over before it began.

Mel's special concern for the well-being of his players was recognized throughout the league. Jansen told writer Al Stump that Ott demanded and got the best of care for Larry's damaged face regardless of the cost. Years later, Lockman told Stump that Ott was suspicious of the bone-setting job done on his leg, and Mel had Whitey flown from Alabama to Johns Hopkins in Baltimore where a specialist operated on the badly injured leg. The empathetic Ott even traveled from New York to Baltimore on off-days to visit the lonely young outfielder.

Just a week before the season opened, commissioner Happy Chandler stunned the baseball world by suspending Leo Durocher for the season for "accumulated unpleasant incidents." Giants fans reacted to the hated Durocher's ouster with surprising compassion. In addition to the consensus that the one-year suspension was unduly severe, Giants rooters realized they would miss Durocher in the same way that Dodgers fans missed Bill Terry when he left the Giants dugout for good. They had lost a choice target for their boos.

Brooklyn general manager Branch Rickey sought out several baseball men before finding a replacement for Durocher. He was reported to have contacted ex–Yankees manager Joe McCarthy and former Braves and Reds manager Bill McKechnie. Finally, the name of a prominent Giants alumnus surfaced as a candidate, none other than Bill Terry. But before the fans could react to this potentially astonishing development, Rickey replaced Durocher with a longtime associate, 62-year-old Burt Shotton. Polo Grounds old-timers remembered Shotton unfondly for the game in 1929 when he denied Ott a chance for the home run title.

Picked to finish sixth, the Giants opened in Philadelphia with an infield of Mize, Thomson at second, Gordon at third, and Rigney at short in place of the ailing Kerr. Willard Marshall started in right field with

Al White in center and Hartung in left. Cooper and Voiselle rounded out the opening game lineup. Voiselle pitched well but lost on a wild throw by Gordon, one of five Giants errors. Hartung belted a double and single, but the big fellow ignominiously bobbled the first ball hit to him. The Giants lost again the next day as Ayers and Jansen were driven from the mound in their major league debuts, and the Giants committed three more errors.

The Polo Grounders came home to open against the Dodgers and to play for the first time against the Dodgers' heralded black rookie, Jackie Robinson. Ott, a proud son of the South, but a man noted for his sense of fair play, called a team meeting before the game to discuss how to deal with Robinson. Many years later, Buddy Kerr told a writer that Mel had told his players not to heckle Jackie or to make any racist or other inflammatory remarks. Ott instructed his players to "treat him as you would any other rookie." Bobby Thomson confirmed that the Giants had followed their manager's dictum, writing in his book, *The Giants Win the Pennant*, "I interacted with black people all the while I was growing up, so Jackie was no big deal to me. I knew later there were guys who didn't want to play with or against him, but I don't recall any talk on the Giants about it then." Red Barber, the great Dodgers (and later Yankees) broadcaster, confirmed Mel's treatment of Robinson. In Barber's book, *1947—When All Hell Broke Loose in Baseball*, he wrote: "And let it be noted that manager Mel Ott, a former Giant hero of genuine worth, and his players did not give Robinson a hard time in any way except when trying to get him out during the game. Sometimes they did, sometimes they didn't."

Mel's fair treatment of Robinson was in sharp contrast to the cruel taunting of Phillies manager Ben Chapman and some of his players. A number of players around the league, notably some of Robinson's teammates and several members of the Cardinals, also treated Robinson with well-publicized bigotry and general unfairness. But that was not Mel Ott's way.

Just before the first Giants-Dodgers game, Branch Rickey announced the appointment of Burt Shotton. He sat in the dugout, Connie Mack–style, in street clothes with a pearl gray hat and a topcoat. Koslo won, despite three more errors, behind a six-homer Giants barrage. John Drebinger wrote:

> Just where the Giants will finish this season is still a matter over which the experts are at considerable variance. But all are agreed the 1947 cast should prove one of the most colorful in years. They have committed 11 errors so far, but Ott seems to have assembled a group of dashing youngsters who are not bothered by misplays. They can belt the ball a mile and run like blue streaks.

The club fell into a slump, and Ott shook up the lineup drastically. He moved Thomson from second base to center field to replace the ineffective alternates, Gearhart and White. Buddy Blattner took over at second base. Rigney moved from short to third to replace Lohrke, who was not hitting. Kerr returned to shortstop. In left field Sid Gordon supplanted Hartung who was having his problems at the plate as well as in the field.

Convinced that Hartung was not yet a big league outfielder, Mel brought the "Pheenom" in to pitch a game against the Braves with the Giants losing 6–0 after three innings. Hartung, fast and wild enough to keep the Braves from taking toeholds at the plate, for once really was phenomenal. He pitched six scoreless innings and gave up only two hits. The next day Jansen, in his first start, won a slick six-hitter over the Braves.

The club reacted magically to the changes, winning 14 of its next 19 games and vaulting into first place by Memorial Day. Mize, in particular, was overpowering, clubbing home runs, batting in runs in clusters, and setting a National League record by scoring at least one run in 16 consecutive games. Hartung won his first start, against the Cubs, and then came through with another complete game win over the Reds. Koslo, Kennedy, and Jansen also chipped in with well-pitched games. The fielding improved with Thomson and Gordon playing well in the outfield and with Kerr in top form. Buddy handled 383 chances in a row before fumbling a hard ground ball drilled directly at him by the Braves' Bob Elliott.

The Giants' pitching faltered in June. Yet, their murderous hitting pulled out game after game, and as the month ended, the club was one one and a half games behind manager Billy Southworth's league-leading Braves. Then the Giants fell back as the pitching worsened. Jansen continued to win, but Koslo and Kennedy turned erratic. Hartung, after winning his first four starts with complete game efforts, suddenly lost his touch and couldn't buy a win. To make matters worse, Kennedy was put out of action with an injury.

Ott continued his efforts to deal with his pitching problems. Babe Young was traded to the Reds for veteran righthander Joe Beggs. Bill Voiselle went to the Braves for Mort Cooper. One of the game's foremost pitchers at one time, Cooper had lost much of his effectiveness since an arm operation in 1945. Still, Ott was willing to gamble that Cooper's arm would come around in time. Besides, Mel was glad to unload Voiselle who had been of little use all season. Voiselle was equally glad to leave, confirming that he had "strained relations" with Mel for some time. Although some of the fans and writers felt that Ott had mishandled the sensitive Voiselle, it is worth noting that the big righthander did not pitch

.500 ball in any season for the remainder of his major league career under other managers.

One other pitcher joined the club during the month. On June 22 the Giants picked up southpaw Clarence (Hooks) Iott from the St. Louis Browns. Winless in six big league games, Iott (immediately dubbed "One Ott" in deference to the manager) joined the Giants in Chicago two days later. Mel greeted him with a hearty handshake and the brisk announcement, "You're pitching today." Two hours later Iott took the mound against the Cubs and, with little apparent effort, pitched a two-hit shutout to everybody's amazement. Unhappily, visions of another badly-needed starting pitcher arriving out of nowhere faded very soon. A few days later Iott lost to the Dodgers, and the big lefty won only two more games during the rest of the season.

By the All-Star break the Giants were in third place but only because the powerful attack continually bailed out the weak pitching staff. Ott's club broke a National League record by homering in 16 straight games with a total of 37 home runs during that stretch. After the first 77 games (exactly half the season), the Giants had hit the remarkable total of 118 home runs, and on August 2 they broke the old Giants record of 144 set in 1930. The National League club home run record for a season at that time was 171, held by the Cubs of the Hack Wilson–Gabby Hartnett era. The American League record of 182 was held by the fearsome Yankees of 1936. It appeared certain that the Giants would far exceed these totals, and the Polo Grounds was packed game after game to watch Mel's "windowbreakers," as club secretary Eddie Brannick affectionately referred to them. As early as July 20, the club drew its one millionth customer, an unheard-of attendance at the old park under Coogan's Bluff.

The Giants slipped to fourth place in August. Through it all, Ott displayed a new serenity. One writer theorized, "Mel has built a terrific offense in his own image. If the club can trade some of that surplus power for some pitching help during the offseason, the Giants will be something to reckon with in 1948. Mel feels that way and that's why he's calmed down."

But Mel had not calmed down completely. His relations with a few writers had become strained. An example was the reporter who lambasted Ott each day in print. He dropped into Mel's office along with other writers for the usual post-game highball. Ott had not reacted publicly to his columns for several weeks. Then one day he raised his voice above the din in his office. "Joe," he said to the writer, "I can't see how you can call me a dumb bastard and still drink my whiskey every day." The writer, who had never become that personal in print, arose, put down his glass, and left. He continued to find fault with Mel's managing.

Arthur Daley, one of Ott's most devoted writer-friends, remained loyal to the little manager. He wrote about Ott's empathy for his players:

> During his first few years as manager, Ott, for a time, tried to play out of character. Self-conscious of ... the reputation of being a shy, retiring sort of bloke ... he got pretty tough with ... umpires as well as his own players. But that has long since worn off. Back to his natural self he works quietly, makes the best moves as he sees them, and lets it go at that. If he makes a mistake, he accepts the blame. If the player slips up, he accepts it as another tough break, providing of course, the player tried his best.

Ott's feelings for his players was matched by their fondness for him. This personal, one-of-the-boys relationship (criticized by some of Mel's detractors as "friendly disrespect") was reflected in the practical jokes the players pulled on him. St. Louis writer Bob Broeg, in a 1976 column in *The Sporting News*, told of an incident involving Walker Cooper recounted by Buddy Blattner:

> What he (Cooper) did ... when we were playing for Ottie was so funny it was almost obscene. Time and again, with Ottie deep in thought, Cooper would slip a lighted cigarette in the boss' hip pocket seconds before Ottie would reach into his pocket to draw out his lineup card. So one day Ott pulled out his pockets, but Cooper was ahead of him. He'd snipped off the pocket linings. So when Ott stuck the batting order cards in his hip pocket, oops! Blattner imitated an embarrassed Ott standing at the plate before 40,000 at the Polo Grounds, trying to fish down the inside of his pants for the lineup cards.

From mid–August on, all hopes of contending for the pennant ended as the Dodgers and Cards pulled further ahead of the Giants. Nevertheless, the fans continued to pour into the Polo Grounds, and the 1946 home attendance record was broken on August 22. Home runs kept exploding off the Giants bats, and the Cubs' old National League record was surpassed on August 24. The Yankees' record was broken on September 1 on a homer by Lucky Lohrke, who was not one of the Giants' big guns.

The combination of the Giants' explosive hitting and the Dodgers' struggle for the pennant brought out tremendous crowds in a four-game set at the Polo Grounds in early September. Although the Giants were mired in fourth place, 14 games behind the league-leading Dodgers, more than 166,000 fans poured into the horseshoe-shaped ballpark in four days. Little lefthander Vic Lombardi shut out the Giants in the first game before nearly 50,000 on a Thursday afternoon. The next day Larry Jansen,

THE WINDOWBREAKERS   171

who had pitched ten straight complete game wins, was knocked out of the box in a tense, nip-and-tuck loss before another large weekday gathering. On Saturday, before 43,000 roaring fans, Ray Poat, a righthander just acquired from Baltimore, beat the Dodgers' Ralph Branca on a two-out, last-of-the-ninth homer by Walker Cooper.

On Sunday the fans started to queue up at the gates at six in the morning. By the time the gates opened at 11 o'clock, the lines extended all the way out to Old Manhattan Field, the large, vacant field outside the ballpark behind the first base and right field stands. Koslo started against righthander Clyde King before more than 51,000 frenzied fans. The Giants went off to a three-run lead in the first inning when Marshall clubbed his thirty-fifth home run. Kerr drove in three more runs with another homer. Big Johnny Mize, his round, red face bulging with an oversized chew of tobacco, rammed his forty-sixth four-master into the upper right field stands in the bottom of the seventh to give the Giants a 7–2 lead. But the determined Dodgers clawed their way back on homers by Cookie Lavagetto and Gene Hermanski to cut the Giants lead to 7–6 with only one out in the eighth inning. In desperation, Ott brought in Ken Trinkle, the last pitcher left in whom the little manager had any confidence in a spot like this. With the fans roaring on every pitch, Trinkle outdid himself. He rubbed out Eddie Stanky and Pee Wee Reese to end the inning, then polished off Pete Reiser, Bruce Edwards, and Dixie Walker in the ninth to end the game.

Playing no favorites, the Giants knocked the second-place Cards out of the race the following week in St. Louis by sweeping a three-game set in characteristic style. Jansen beat righthander Jim Hearn easily behind homers by Cooper and Thomson. Trinkle beat lefty Alpha Brazle in relief in the second game as Cooper supported him with another homer. In the final game Ray Poat outpitched southpaw Harry Brecheen as Gordon and the red-hot Cooper backed him with circuit blasts. Big Coop carried it off with a flourish, finishing off his old club with a booming, 450-foot drive that seemed to have lost little velocity as it crashed into the bleachers in dead center field.

The Giants moved on to Chicago and, with nothing at stake, Ott started two rookies just up from Minneapolis. One was Bobby Rhawn, a second baseman who would have a short, uneventful major league career. The other youngster, catcher Wes Westrum, spent ten years as a player with the Giants and then managed the club after its move to San Francisco. That same day Whitey Lockman, getting back into shape, appeared in his first game of the campaign. The Giants finished their home season on September 21 as Jansen won his twentieth game. The club ran off with a record-breaking string of 18 consecutive games with at least one home run, and the fans continued to respond as the Giants' home attendance soared to 1,599,784, almost 380,000 more than in 1946.

On September 20, Ott announced his retirement as a player after 22 years with the club. Mel had made only four unsuccessful pinchhitting appearances during the season. His last turn at bat had come against the Pirates on June 11 when he batted for Trinkle and popped to short. Mel had to appreciate the glowing stories about him in the New York newspapers over the next few days although he reacted with typical self-deprecation. He told Arthur Daley, who had written a particularly laudatory column about him, "Thanks for the kind word. I mailed your piece home to my wife, and I told her this was my obituary notice and I hoped she liked it." A writer asked Ott when he knew he was finished as a player. Mel answered, "Last summer for sure. The ball was beginning to play tricks. It would jump on me in flight." Alluding to his career-long problems with his legs, which had always given him trouble, he said, "Funny thing, my eyes went before my legs. I knew what to do, but I just couldn't do it."

The Polo Grounders wound up the season in fourth place, 13 games behind the pennant-winning Dodgers and five games in back of the third-place Braves. Mel's "windowbreakers" hit 221 home runs, 39 more than the 1936 Yankees' record. Ironically, none of them were contributed by Ott, the greatest National League home run hitter up to that time. The new record stood until the Cincinnati Reds tied it in 1956 when the league home run total was much higher, indicative of a livelier ball. Then, with a long schedule of 162 games, the Yankees hit 240 homers in 1961. By 1997, the Seattle Mariners had extended the record to 264 home runs.

Individually, the 1947 Giants were not a colorful group. There was no team pixie like Danny Gardella, no battling gamecock like Dick Bartell. It was essentially a team of strong, silent men who did their talking with their bats. Still, they were fun to watch, and some of their individual performances were outstanding. Mize tied the Pirates' Ralph Kiner for the home run lead with 51, and Marshall, Cooper, and Thomson ranked third, fourth, and fifth in homers in that order. Mize led the league in RBIs and runs scored; Cooper and Marshall were in the top five in RBIs. Jansen led the league in winning percentage with a sparkling 21 and 5 record and was in the top five in wins and complete games. Koslo won 15 and lost 10; Trinkle led in games pitched and was third in saves. And Kerr led all the shortstops in assists. Despite these excellent performances, many observers dismissed the team as "sluggish" and "uninspired." The simple truth is that the club would have been in the thick of the pennant fight with only one or two more competent starting pitchers.

Stoneham and Ott, looking forward to better things in 1948, went to another subway series between the Yanks and Dodgers. They saw the Bronx Bombers win a classic seven-game set. It featured Yankee Bill Bevens' one-hit game loss to the Dodgers on Cookie Lavagetto's two-out-in-the-ninth double and Al Gionfriddo's famous catch of Joe DiMaggio's long drive in front of the left field bullpen at Yankee Stadium. Many fans watched the Series on small, seven-inch television sets, then coming into wide use.

During the Series, it was announced that Danny Gardella had sued the Giants, the Commissioner, the major league presidents, and the head of the minor league for $300,000, charging that the reserve clause "is monopolistic and tends to restrain trade and commerce." Gardella's suit, which was dismissed a year later, was nothing new then, and the issue remained unresolved until almost 30 years later.

Chapter 19

EXIT OTT—
ENTER DUROCHER

As the Giants gathered in Phoenix to start their 1948 campaign, writer Al Stump described the scene in an article in the book, *Sports Magazine's All-Time All Stars*:

> The New York Giants, led by a stocky, wind-burned little man wearing number 4 on his back, jogged out on the field and began to throw and hit baseballs. It was a routine spring training drill, except for the commotion in the third-base bleachers. School was out that March day in Phoenix, Arizona, and the Municipal Stadium stands were jumping with eager, wild-eyed, vociferous kids.
>
> In the batter's cage, huge Georgian John Mize was hoisting 350-foot drives against the right-field wall. Behind him, others of the Giants' wrecking crew—Willard Marshall, Bobby Thomson, Walker Cooper—waited their turn to give the ball a ride. Nearby, lazy-eyed Larry Jansen … unlimbered his $100,000 arm. And the hawk-nosed, greying figure in civvies, taking outfield throws and clowning, was Frankie Frisch, perhaps the greatest of second-basemen.

Stump noted that none of these players held the attention of the kids. The youngsters were more interested in forming a circle around the stocky man wearing No. 4. Mel Ott was doing nothing more spectacular than leaning on a bat on the sidelines as he chatted quietly with the young fans, none of whom had been born when he broke into baseball. As a famed performer, to most of them he was only a dim, legendary figure who had played in far away ballparks. Still, they flocked around Mel as they would around a Babe Ruth or a Ty Cobb.

Stump continued, "Sitting in the grandstand with Eddie Brannick, secretary of the Giants, I watched Ott. He started to walk away. Then he noticed other kids. One of them had a ball. Ott stopped to sign it. He talked to them, mussed the hair of a little Mexican boy, cracked a joke, and at last tried to go back to work. The youngsters trooped along, unwilling to let him go.

"Better than a volume of words, the springtime scene told the story of Mel Ott's place with anyone who is, or ever was, a baseball fan. I said as much to Brannick and he smiled. 'That's the way it's always been,' he said. 'They all love him, from the old-timers to the kids. Here or anywhere he goes.'"

Stump made the point that Ott had yet to prove that he was as great a manager as he had been a player. Stump discussed the pressures Ott faced as he began his seventh season as the Giants' manager. The writer concluded: "The future is troubled, with much depending on the results of the present campaign. Until another bright bit of bunting flies from the Polo Grounds, there will be no peace for McGraw's boy."

Over the winter it had been the same old story, plenty of talk about trading for established pitchers, but nothing had come of it. Jansen, coming off a great rookie year, was expected to be the staff ace. Ken Trinkle was a solid receiver, but there were no other heavyweights on the staff. Ray Poat, Andy Hansen, and Sheldon Jones had not proven their worth. Hartung had been erratic. Monte Kennedy was still wild and inconsistent. Joe Beggs had been of little use since coming over from the Reds. Bill Ayers and Hub Andrews were back for another try, but Mort Cooper had retired. Then there were a number of anonymous pitchers up from the farm clubs.

As spring training moved along, the Giants began to collect veterans who had been cast adrift by other teams. They signed 41-year-old lefthander Thornton Lee, released by the White Sox after 15 years in the American League. They obtained southpaw Vern Olsen, an ex–Cub, who had not pitched a major league inning in 1947. Then Ott picked up the well-traveled, 39-year-old Bobo Newsom. Since 1929, the righthander had pitched for eight major league clubs, including several tours of duty with the Washington Senators.

There was another category of Giants pitcher—anyone with a strong arm regardless of his qualifications or experience. In this case it was catcher Jim Gladd who had caught in four games with the Giants in 1946. Gladd was a weak hitter, but his rifle arm attracted the attention of Ott and his coaches. He was given a trial as a pitcher for a couple of weeks, just long enough for him to develop a bad sore arm which ended the experiment abruptly. Over all, the pitching situation seemed hopeless, and Ott knew it although characteristically he was never heard to complain publicly about the lack of help provided him by the front office.

The rest of the team was pretty well set. Mize was a fixture at first, and Rigney played second base with increased assurance. Kerr, after a determined holdout, was at shortstop, and Jack Lohrke appeared to have the inside track at third although he had yet to prove that he could handle major league pitching. Other infielders in camp included Mickey Witek, Buddy Blattner, Bobby Rhawn, Jack Conway from the Indians, and ex–Cub Lou Stringer. Johnny McCarthy, who had been selected as Bill Terry's successor at first base 12 years before, had been brought up from Minneapolis.

The regular outfield was expected to include Marshall in right field with Thomson, Lockman, and Gordon competing for the other two outfield slots. Don Mueller, Joe Lafata, Lloyd Gearhart, and Les Layton, up from Minneapolis, were other outfielders in camp. Walker Cooper, of course, was the regular catcher. Wes Westrum, Mickey Livingston, Ben Warren, and "good throw–no hit" Jim Gladd were the other catching hopefuls. The new Giants pitchers showed little as the club barnstormed east with the Indians, and it was clear that Ott would have to rely upon his veterans. Still, the writers were impressed by the Giants' powerful offense, and the Associated Press polls projected a fourth-place finish for the Giants, behind the Cards, Braves, and Dodgers.

Leo Durocher had been reinstated and was managing the Dodgers as the Giants opened the season against them before more than 48,000 at the Polo Grounds. It was a bad day all around for Ott's club. Buddy Kerr, hit on the head by an outfield throw in one of the final exhibition games, did not play. His loss proved to be crucial as Whitey Lockman collided with Bobby Rhawn, Kerr's inexperienced replacement, permitting a blooper to fall safely and drive in the winning Dodgers run. The next day Mel suspended Kerr for refusing to play despite doctor's reports that he was in shape to play. But all was forgiven a few days later when Buddy returned to the lineup and flashed his old form.

The Giants were in second place after completing their first series with the eastern clubs. The pleasant surprise was the impeccable pitching of Jones and Poat which matched first-rate outings by Jansen. But even with the pitchers doing better than expected, and the offense coming along, the Giants had a serious catching problem. The indispensable Cooper had sustained a chipped bone in his knee in the first week of the season, and the big Missourian underwent surgery that was expected to sideline him for two months.

The club played slipshod ball on its first western trip as the pitching and hitting slipped. To make matters worse, the Giants were guilty of a number of errors that cost ball games. Typical was a game in Chicago when they blew a 6–0 lead to lose the game on a succession of mechanical and mental miscues. The Cubs' winning run scored on an incredible lapse by Ken Trinkle. With the game tied, two out in the bottom of the ninth, and Cubs runners on second and third, Trinkle got Peanuts Lowrey to hit a soft bouncer back to the mound. Instead of throwing to first for the routine third out, Trinkle threw home thinking there was only one out. The throw to an amazed Mickey Livingston was too late, almost skulling the surprised catcher, as Eddie Waitkus scored the winning run. After the game, Ott gave his blundering charges a blistering that would have done credit to John McGraw.

The Giants did poorly on their next home stand and slipped down to fourth place, four games out of first. The club struggled through to the All-Star break, eight games off the pace with a 36 and 37 record. Cooper returned to the lineup, but even having him back did not help the pitching, which reached a new low. Twice in a week Mel called upon seven pitchers in futile attempts to win games.

Early on the morning of July 16, a bombshell hit. Bill Corum, in an exclusive story in the *Journal-American*, reported that Ott had been fired, Durocher had been named to replace him, and Burt Shotton again had been called out of semi-retirement to take over the Dodgers. Beginning with the Giants' unimpressive play in June, there had been a resurgence of the old rumors that Mel was on the way out, but they were not taken seriously. With the Dodgers floundering after their pennant win in 1947, there also had been rumors of Durocher's dismissal, but here too, little credence was placed in the stories. Even then, if either manager had been let out in unrelated moves, this would have been accepted as part of the game. But Leo Durocher, the new boss at the Polo Grounds! To Giants fans this was unthinkable. As Ken Smith wrote in the *Daily Mirror*, "Giant fans hate Durocher because he was a Dodger. To drop him suddenly in the Polo Grounds, where the feats of McGraw, Terry, Ott, Matty, and the others are a sacred memory, was a shock too abrupt for acceptance." Smith, a personal friend of Leo's, was so upset at Mel's dismissal that he told the new manager flatly, "I loved Mel Ott and I'll tell you right now I'm gonna knock your brains out in the paper."

The Giants held a news conference at the club offices later in the morning with Stoneham, Durocher, Ott, Hubbell, and publicity director Garry Schumacher on hand. The questions flew thick and fast.

When had Stoneham decided to make the change? At about one o'clock the day before. It was shortly before the doubleheader with the Pirates in Pittsburgh. Ott, of course, was with the club. Durocher was in Montreal looking over Dodgers farm talent.

Was the change a surprise to Ott? Stoneham told the writers, "I had already discussed this with Ottie. He was the one who suggested getting Durocher if it were possible."

What about getting the okay to talk to Durocher? Stoneham responded, "I called (Commissioner) Ford Frick and obtained his approval. I then contacted Rickey and told him we would like to have Leo manage the Giants. I was agreeably surprised when Rickey gave me permission to negotiate with Leo. I met with Leo about 10:30 last night at his apartment, and we came to terms pretty quickly."

What was Durocher's reaction? The Lippy One started off like a diplomat. "I feel the change will do me a lot of good because I have always liked Ott and Stoneham and their organization. Of course," he added quickly, "I was also very happy in Brooklyn and I definitely was never asked to resign." This did not square with a United Press story from Pittsburgh datelined July 17, the next day, in which the UP quoted Durocher as saying that on July 4, Dodgers press secretary Harold Parrott told Durocher, "The boss wants you to resign, Leo." Durocher told Parrott that he "…would not resign. They'd have to fire me."

What changes would he make in the Giants? Durocher looked at the writers, their pens poised as if to impale him, and he turned uncharacteristically reticent. "I have nothing to say on that one. I have some ideas, but I want to talk them over with Mel before I make any changes."

And what about Mel, whose contract ran through the 1950 season? Stoneham answered, "Ottie will work with Hub in his farm system operation."

A few more questions and the press conference was over. Durocher, Stoneham, Hubbell, and Garry Schumacher left immediately for Pittsburgh to join the team. And Mel, after a few quiet good-byes, walked somberly out of the Giants offices and disappeared in the crowd on 42nd Street. The next day the Giants permanently retired his number 4 uniform. After almost 23 years, that was the last field job Mel would have with the Giants although he took on a variety of tasks with Hubbell through the remainder of his contract.

James P. Dawson, of the *New York Times*, wrote of the players' reaction to the change in leadership:

> The end of Master Melvin's reign, although not unexpected, nevertheless, came with bombshell-like effect on the squad. The engagement of Durocher aggravated the shock. The change finds the Giants playing under orders of a leader on whom they have been riding hard since his return from last year's exile.
>   That the players regretted the passing of Ott was plain, parti-

cularly the startling manner in which the Ott reign ended. It was generally held that the change was influenced by the front office, that something had to be done and, as is generally the case in such circumstances, Ott became the sacrificial goat.

Most Giants fans fumed about having Durocher at the Polo Grounds although there were some who thought it was a stroke of genius on Stoneham's part. Still, it was hard to find a Giants fan who was not saddened by Ott's departure. In today's sports world, managerial changes rarely cause much excitement. But in 1948 New York was a city that took its baseball, and its emotional involvement with long-standing heroes like Ott, very seriously. Fans gathered everywhere—offices, bars, restaurants, streets—to discuss the change.

Some Giants rooters were against the change without reservation. "Hell, they should have got Mel some pitchers. That's all he needed," said one. A fashionable Park Avenue matron snapped, "From now on, I'm an ex–Giant fan." George Chefalo of Peekskill, New York, a leading Giants rooter for nearly 25 years, said emphatically, "That settles it, brother. I'll never go to the Polo Grounds again." He was asked, "What if Durocher leads them to the pennant?" Chefalo rejected the idea out of hand with a curt, "That's impossible!" Other Giants fans saw it differently. One rejoiced, "It means the pennant. With that power, Durocher will blow the league apart." Another commented, "We couldn't beat the Dodgers under Ott, so we had to get a manager who can. Personally, I don't care for Durocher, but we had to make a change."

Durocher was out of favor with most Dodgers fans. One said, "I never wished the Giants anything but bad luck, but I didn't think they'd get it wrapped up in one neat package." Another Dodgers rooter related the change to his finances with the comments, "It's like taking a pay cut. I haven't spent a dime in Ebbets Field this year. But with Durocher gone, I'll be buying four or five tickets soon." Another Brooklynite analyzed the change in terms of the Dodgers' finances. "That Rickey is a smart guy. He gets rid of Durocher who's liked by less than half of the people and who gets a big salary, and he brings back a guy that everyone likes who gets a much lower salary."

A couple of interesting details on the managerial upheaval came out later. One had to do with Stoneham's strategy in obtaining Rickey's agreement to release Durocher. After Ott recommended Durocher as his successor, Stoneham pondered how best to gain Leo's release. Stoneham felt that the Dodgers would be glad to see Durocher go, but the Giants owner was afraid that Rickey would turn down a direct request for the Giants to approach Leo. So Stoneham attacked the matter more indirectly.

The late, long-time Giants broadcaster Russ Hodges described Stoneham's tactics in his book, *My Giants*. According to Hodges, Stoneham's chance came as he flew to St. Louis for the All-Star game two weeks before Ott's ouster. On the plane Stoneham met Frank Shaughnessy, the president of the International League and a close friend of Rickey's.

"Frank," said Stoneham, "do you think Burt Shotton might be available to manage the Giants?"

"I don't know," Shaughnessy answered, "but I can ask Rickey. Do you want me to sound him out?"

Stoneham told Shaughnessy to go ahead. A few days later Shaughnessy brought back word that Shotton wasn't available, but would Durocher do instead? Stoneham said that Leo would do very nicely indeed, and that paved the way for the deal. If Hodges' account was accurate, it contradicted Stoneham's press conference response that he was "agreeably surprised" on July 15, the day he said that Rickey informed him that Durocher was available.

Then there was the matter of Bill Corum's exclusive story. Rickey and Stoneham agreed to release the story simultaneously on July 16 from New York and from the Giants' hotel in Pittsburgh. Rickey was enraged when Corum's scoop appeared in advance of the agreed-upon time. Although both the Giants and the Dodgers had taken precautions to guard against a news leak, Garry Schumacher, who knew Durocher well, was positive that the story would come out prematurely. According to Russ Hodges' account, Schumacher deliberately spent the night of July 15 with Stoneham to make sure that he (Schumacher) would not be held responsible for any leak. Just as Schumacher anticipated, Durocher called Corum as soon as the deal was set with Stoneham to ask Corum what he thought of it. Presumably, Corum expressed his opinion and then immediately filed the story. The net result was a big scoop for Corum and, more importantly, a new manager at the Polo Grounds.

Although he never showed it publicly, Mel took his dismissal hard. Sportswriter Arnold Hano wrote:

> His managing did not always work out well, and when the news broke…, Ott walked manfully to the phone to call his wife. The abruptness of the move had pained him, but he carefully hid his hurt. Until his wife, at the other end of the phone, began to cry, then he, too, cried. Why not? He never knew how to act out a false role.

A few days after Mel was replaced, he went to the Polo Grounds to clean out his office. He saw Giants clubhouse man Eddie Logan whom he had met when he joined the Giants in 1925. Both men had been close since that time. Several years ago Logan recalled:

> Mel had a great sense of humor, even under such circumstances. The first thing he said when I came in to offer sympathy was that he was glad to get out of there because I was the worst clubhouse man he had ever seen. I told him, "Yeh, but I haven't been fired," and then he laughed and took out the bottles of Scotch and Bourbon that were always in the manager's office, and we sat down and polished them off. When they were gone, we sent out for a couple more, and finished them up at two in the morning, crying on each other's shoulders.

Logan remembered Mel fondly. "He was a gentleman, that's what Mel was. But he was never nice to opposing pitchers, or to anyone on the other side of the field. He was always a winner, a terrific competitor, a real man. A class act."

Chapter 20

"THE GIANTS IS DEAD"

When Ott was deposed, the Giants were in a fourth-place tie with the Dodgers, eight and a half games behind the first-place Braves and playing at a .493 clip. The club spurted briefly in the first few days under Durocher but then fell back, burdened by its inescapable pitching shortcomings. The team played at a .519 pace under Durocher and finished in fifth place as the Braves held on to win the pennant. In effect, Durocher did no better with the team than Ott. As the season ended, one of the reporters wrote, "Maybe nice guys and not-so-nice guys finish in pretty much the same place—just as far as their talent takes them."

Giants fans came back in 1949 to see how Durocher would fare in his first full year of managing the club. But 1949 was a repeat of 1948 as the club finished in fifth place again. Mize and Cooper slumped badly, and only Bobby Thomson and Sid Gordon had good years. Lippy Leo was exasperated by the Giants' failure, and he was further pressured by a strong Dodgers showing that brought another pennant to Brooklyn. He proclaimed during the late summer that he was going to build "my kind of team," one built on speed and aggressiveness rather than power. He handed Horace a four-word report: "Back up the truck." In other words, he felt the Giants needed a drastic overhaul.

Durocher wrote in his provocatively titled book, *Nice Guys Finish Last*:

> Horace couldn't believe I was serious. The Giants had set an all-time record for home runs the year before I got there and had easily led the major leagues again. "We can win the championship with this team next year," he insisted. "And you're the manager who can do it."
>
> "It ain't my kind of team," I told him. We had Johnny Mize, who could hit the ball a mile and couldn't run. We had Walker Cooper, who could hit the ball out of sight and couldn't run. We had Willard Marshall and Sid Gordon who could hit the ball out of the park and could run a little but not very much.

182

"Horace, you're throwing your money away when you pay me. A little boy can manage this team. All you do is make out the lineup and hope you get enough home runs. You can't steal, they're too slow. You can't bunt. You can't hit and run. I can't do anything. I can only sit and wait for a home run."

Durocher began to clean house long before the season ended. Cooper, having a poor year and never a Durocher admirer, was traded to the Reds for catcher Ray Mueller. Mize, hitting .263 with a mere 18 home runs, was sold to the Yankees in time to star in the World Series as the Bronx Bombers beat the Dodgers. During the winter the Giants made a whopper of a deal that completed the transformation begun with the Cooper trade. Willard Marshall, Sid Gordon, and Buddy Kerr were dealt to the Braves for second baseman Eddie Stanky and shortstop Alvin Dark. Durocher was building his kind of team.

In 1950 the Giants moved up to third place, finishing only five games behind manager Eddie Sawyer's pennant-winning Whiz Kid Phillies. Robin Roberts, Curt Simmons, and reliever Jim Konstanty supplied the Phils' pitching, and Del Ennis and Willie (Puddinhead) Jones were the big hitters. Still, things were looking up for the Polo Grounders. The team had more pep and speed. Stanky and Dark solidified the club around second base. After a so-so year in 1949, Larry Jansen rebounded with 19 wins. And Durocher got a big break as Sal Maglie returned from Mexico a tough, seasoned pitcher who had learned a lot from Dolph Luque. Durocher himself had calmed down to the point where the writers referred to him tongue in cheek as "the Little Shepherd of Coogan's Bluff."

Ott helped Carl Hubbell manage the Giants' farm system in a number of ways. He traveled extensively and visited each farm club several times in 1949 and 1950. He worked closely with the farm club managers and scouts, and he instructed individual players, all of whom he impressed with his wide knowledge of the game and his easy manner. Although Mel devoted much of his instruction effort to batting techniques, he made it a point not to encourage the adoption of his distinctive high leg kick because he felt that a player had to hit in the style most comfortable to him.

Mel had little input to the parent club after giving Durocher his opinions of the players Leo had inherited. However, at Durocher's request, Mel worked with Bobby Thomson in August 1950 when Thomson went into a severe hitting slump. Ott helped Thomson break out of his slump by shortening his stance and making him more conscious of the fact that he was putting his weight on his front foot instead of the back. Although Ott and Durocher were totally different in style and demeanor, Mel knew that Leo meant him no harm in his "nice guys" comment in 1946 and, as a matter of fact, the two men got along well.

During the period that Mel worked with Hubbell, he unfortunately missed an opportunity to manage the Atlanta club of the Southern Association. In his book, *Tuned to Baseball*, announcer Ernie Harwell wrote that club owner Earl Mann told him, "I tried to get in touch with Stoneham to discuss a deal, but I couldn't locate him. Nobody else in the Giants' organization had the authority to make the deal, so I was never able to hire Ott as my manager."

As Mel had predicted, his tenure with the Giants ended when his contract expired after the 1950 season. His only appearance of note in New York after his dismissal had come in January 1949 when his old friends in the New York chapter of the Baseball Writers Association threw a party in his honor. The writers presented him with a magnificent sterling silver ice bowl, after which Dan Daniel, Tom Meany, Frank Graham, and the other reporters expressed their warm regard for him in a number of speeches. The dinner was attended by nearly 100 of Ott's baseball friends, including such baseball officials as Horace Stoneham, the Dodgers' Branch Rickey, Yankees owner Dan Topping and general manager George Weiss, and many of Ott's old teammates including Carl Hubbell and Frankie Frisch.

After all of the laudatory speeches had been made, an emotional Ott stood up to speak. He looked around the banquet hall and managed to choke out the words, "It's good for a man to know he has so many friends." Mel was so touched that he could only look around the room tearfully before sitting down to a loud round of applause.

In December 1950 Mel attended the minor league meetings in St. Petersburg. While there, Brick Laws, the owner of the Oakland Oaks of the Pacific Coast League, offered Mel the managership of his club. He accepted the offer enthusiastically and signed a two-year contract.

A few weeks later Mel's older daughter, Lyn, married Philip Loria, a young doctor. After the wedding, Ott left on a tour of veterans hospitals in the Southeast. He told Mildred, "These fellows need to see a friendly face to tide them over the bad days." Mel also toured children's hospitals in the New Orleans area, playing catch with the young patients and talking baseball with the thrilled youngsters. He was visiting patients at a leprosarium on January 21 when the Baseball Hall of Fame announced that he had been voted into the Hall. Mel did not attend his induction on July 25, preferring to stay with his Oakland club.

Ott's plaque reads:

ONE OF THE FEW PLAYERS TO JUMP FROM A HIGH
SCHOOL TEAM INTO MAJORS. PLAYED OUTFIELD
AND THIRD BASE AND MANAGED CLUB (the Giants)
FROM DEC. 1941 THROUGH JULY 1948. HIT 511 HOME
RUNS, N.L. RECORD WHEN HE RETIRED. ALSO LED
IN MOST RUNS SCORED, MOST RUNS BATTED IN,
TOTAL BASES, BASE ON BALLS, AND EXTRA BASES ON
LONG HITS. HAD A .304 LIFETIME BATTING AVER-
AGE. PLAYED IN ELEVEN ALL STAR GAMES AND IN
THREE WORLD SERIES.

In March 1951 Mel made his managerial debut with the Oakland
club. The season was a social success as he joined other former major leaguers who were managing on the Coast—Lefty O'Doul, ex–Yankees second baseman Joe Gordon, former Cubs third baseman Stan Hack, and
Rogers Hornsby. But his two-year tenure with the Oaks was an artistic
failure as Ott's club fared poorly, and he announced his retirement from
baseball after the 1952 season. There was no hope of his return to the
major leagues as a manager. As a result, he went into the building construction business in 1953, becoming vice president of the Milan Engi-
neering Company in New Orleans.

The Giants' fortunes had improved impressively in 1951. This was
the year of the "Miracle of Coogan's Bluff." The Giants opened the season with their first black players, Monte Irvin at first base and Hank
Thompson at third, both of whom had joined the club in 1949. Stanky
and Dark rounded out the infield. Don Mueller, nicknamed "Mandrake
the Magician" because of his deft bat control, was the right fielder. Thomson was in center with Lockman in left. Wes Westrum was the regular
catcher. The starting pitchers were Jansen, Maglie, Koslo, righthander
George Spencer, and Jim Hearn, who was acquired from the Cardinals
in 1950.

The club started slowly and Durocher made some changes. He
switched positions between Lockman and Irvin and replaced Thomson
in center with a young fellow just up from Minneapolis where he was hitting a cool .477, the incomparable Willie Mays. Durocher had been
handed a real prize. Thomson alternated between the outfield and third
base for the remainder of the season. After a slow start, Mays began to
spark the club with his spirited play and infectious good nature. Yet, on
August 11, the Giants were a distant 13½ games behind Charlie Dressen's
league-leading Dodgers. Durocher's club bounced back dramatically and
cut the Dodgers lead to five games with a 16-game winning streak, then
pulled dead even as the regular season ended.

In the three-game playoff for the pennant, Hearn beat Ralph Branca

3–1 in the first game, but the Dodgers squared matters as Clem Labine won 10–0. The famous deciding game came the next day at the Polo Grounds as Maglie faced big Don Newcombe. The Dodgers held a 4–1 lead going into the bottom of the ninth, and Newcombe seemed to be throwing hard as he had all day. Dark and Mueller opened with singles, but Irvin popped out. Lockman doubled in Dark and sent Mueller to third. With the Giants behind 4–2 and one out, Thomson stepped up.

Dressen waved in Branca from the bullpen, and the ensuing scene is as familiar to today's fans, who have viewed the film so often on television, as to those at the Polo Grounds on that long-ago, early October afternoon. Thomson swung mightily at Branca's second pitch and the ball buzzed on a line into the lower left field stands. Giants announcer Russ Hodges screamed, "The Giants win the pennant. I don't believe it, Oooh boy, the Giants win the pennant!" Stanky sprinted out of the Giants dugout, headed straight for Durocher who was coaching at third, and ecstatically wrestled the Giants manager to the ground. The Giants greeted Thomson en masse at the plate, while the stunned Branca walked slowly off the mound, barely comprehending that the pennant had been lost on one pitch. The Giants' loss to the Yanks in the World Series was strictly an anticlimax.

The Giants finished in second place in 1952 as the Dodgers came back to win. Irvin missed most of the year with a broken ankle, and Mays was called up by the Army early in the season. Hearn, Maglie, and reliever Hoyt Wilhelm carried the pitching load as Jansen faltered, but the Giants were outclassed.

With Mays in the service for the entire season, 1953 was a leaner year, and the Giants fell back to fifth place. Maglie, Jansen, and Hearn had poor years. Wilhelm was less effective, and the only bright spot was provided by rookie pitcher Ruben Gomez, who won 13 games. The Giants were out of the race by midsummer, and Charlie Dressen counted them out emphatically in August with the accurate, if ungrammatical, pronouncement, "The Giants is dead."

The year 1954 provided a pleasant surprise as the Giants came back to win the pennant. The offense was paced by the booming bat of the returned Willie Mays. Lockman, Dark, and Hank Thompson had good seasons, and a colorful Alabaman, Jim (Dusty) Rhodes, had a remarkable year as a pinch hitter, coming through in the clutch time after time. Lefthander Johnnie Antonelli, a former bonus baby obtained from the Braves (then based in Milwaukee), led the pitching staff with a brilliant 21 and 7 record. Gomez, Maglie, righthander Marv Grissom, and Wilhelm were the pitching reliables as the Giants beat out the Dodgers by five games.

This was Walter Alston's first year managing the Dodgers, as Dressen and Dodgers owner Walter O'Malley were unable to agree on a multi-year contract for Dressen. Durocher's most successful year with the Giants was 1954, as his team beat a strong (111 regular-season wins) Cleveland club in four straight in the World Series. This Series is best remembered for Mays' remarkable over-the-shoulder catch of Vic Wertz's long drive almost to the right center field bleacher screen at the Polo Grounds.

Durocher's last year with the Giants was 1955, as the club slipped back to third place, 18½ games behind another powerful Dodgers club. The Giants had three new regulars: first baseman Gail Harris, second baseman Wayne Terwilliger, and catcher Ray Katt. None of them came through, the pitching was mediocre, and another great season by Mays was wasted. Durocher's contract ran out and was not renewed.

After his retirement, Ott spent the next two years in the construction business. This was the first time since before 1925 that he spent full years at home in Louisiana, and he appeared to enjoy the change. He did more hunting and fishing than he had in years. An excellent golfer, he brought his scores down to below 80, spending more time than ever on local golf courses with friends and business associates. It was a congenial life style, and he seemed completely relaxed and happy. He was sufficiently content that he turned down an offer to enter politics as a candidate for parish (county) sheriff.

But during the spring of 1955 he showed his first signs of missing an active role in baseball although he had no interest in managing again. He contacted friends in broadcasting and was pleasantly surprised to learn that there was interest in him as a baseball announcer despite his lack of broadcasting experience. The Mutual Network offered him a job as one of its major league "Game of the Day" announcers. The work involved recreating an important game later that day. Mel enjoyed his role although it involved little contact with live activities, which was his primary interest. He told a writer:

> My new undertaking came about by chance, but it has given me a real thrill because it puts me back in baseball. After being connected with the game for so many years, it sort of got in my blood, and I guess I wasn't really happy outside of it.

In 1956 Mel took a broadcasting job more to his liking, that of radio-television broadcaster of the Detroit Tigers games. He worked with Van Patrick, a big favorite in Detroit. Ott was a natural for the job with his warm, friendly, down-to-earth style and slight Southern accent complementing Patrick's smooth, professional delivery. The Tigers received many favorable comments, and Detroit reporter Watson Spoelstra wrote about a long-time ballpark regular who had been unable to attend games because of a serious illness. The fan observed, "Ott did the best reporting job of any radio man I ever knew. He has a way of presenting baseball so that it can be understood by all. His words carry authority because he knows the game so thoroughly."

Mel was well liked by the Detroit players, particularly the younger men like Al Kaline and Harvey Kuenn who came to him with their problems on and off the field. He was especially helpful to Paul Foytack, a strong-armed righthander with a world of stuff but with severe control problems, very reminiscent to Mel of Monte Kennedy. Ott observed that Foytack, who was having a poor early season in 1956, appeared to exhibit less concentration on the mound than he did in playing cards with teammates in the clubhouse. Mel approached him privately one day and asked: "Paul, how could you be so serious about a game of cards that doesn't mean a thing, and so casual about a game that reflects on your pride, your skill, and your livelihood?" Foytack thought for a minute, then said, "Mel, I think you're right. Thanks for pointing that out." Foytack apparently took Mel's suggestion to heart as he came back to win 15 games that season.

Mel remained on the Detroit broadcasting team through the 1958 season. Meanwhile, he retained his interest in the Giants, and he was especially pleased when the Giants selected Bill Rigney to manage the Giants in the 1956 season. Mel told acquaintances with considerable pride, "Rig was one of my boys, and I'll be rooting for him."

But Rigney's tenure with the Giants was even less successful than Ott's had been. The Giants finished sixth as Walt Alston's "Boys of Summer" won again. The peppery Rigney had little to work with. Antonelli had another great year. Otherwise, the pitching staff's ineptitude reminded fans of Ott's tribulations years before. Mays, after a slow start, belted 36 home runs, and young Bill White, a rookie first baseman and future National League president, showed promise. Giants rooters were unhappy with the team's performance but concerned even more about rumors that the franchise might be moved.

The story was the same in 1957. A sixth-place finish, inept pitching except for Ruben Gomez who won 15 games, and a generally mediocre club with weaknesses relieved only by the brilliant play of Mays and the occasional power hitting of outfielder Hank Sauer, who had come over from the Cardinals.

In 1955 it had become public knowledge that Walter O'Malley wanted to move the Dodgers out of Ebbets Field with its limited capacity. He signaled his frustration with the situation by announcing that the

Dodgers would play seven games in 1956 in larger, more modern, Roosevelt Stadium in Jersey City. This had been the home field of the Jersey City Giants who had ceased operations. At the same time that O'Malley was taking steps to move the Dodgers, Stoneham was looking for another home for his team. With the Polo Grounds slated to be demolished and replaced by a housing development, it was rumored that Stoneham was considering renting Yankee Stadium, full cycle from the early 1920s when the Yankees were ousted from the Polo Grounds by John McGraw. But it was clear that the eventual decision as to where to transplant the Giants would depend upon where the Dodgers went.

After long, unproductive negotiations began between the Dodgers and Brooklyn borough officials, O'Malley openly expressed his disenchantment with the Brooklyn situation and his interest in moving his team to Los Angeles. (There were many who thought that this had been O'Malley's intention all along and that his dealings with Brooklyn officials were simply a smoke screen.) At the same time, Stoneham told the writers that he had received an attractive offer to relocate the Giants to San Francisco. Finally, in August 1957, with arrangements all but completed to move the Dodgers to Los Angeles, the Giants announced they would move to San Francisco in time for the 1958 season. To Giants and Dodgers fans, it was little consolation to know that the historic Giants-Dodgers rivalry would continue almost 3000 miles away. Giants and Dodgers fans would recognize that baseball, like all professional sports, is at bottom a business.

The Giants played their last home game at the Polo Grounds on September 29 and lost to the Pirates 9–1. Just after Dusty Rhodes grounded out to end the game, most of the 11,606 fans raced out on the field while the players fled for the safety of the clubhouse. The crowd ripped out home plate, the pitching rubber, the bases, the bullpen fixtures—almost anything that wasn't steel, concrete, or otherwise fastened down. Fans gathered in forlorn groups in center field, many shouting unsuccessfully for the players to come out of the clubhouse. Others screamed insults at Stoneham's empty office over the clubhouse.

Ott's broadcasting work prevented him from attending the last Giants game at the Polo Grounds. But he was remembered with many other former Giants players who were at the game along with Mrs. John McGraw. She had remained a devoted Giants rooter in the many years since her husband's death, and she was the last "official" fan to leave the ballpark. She lamented tearfully, "I can't believe it. This would have broken John's heart. New York will never be the same." Many of the other Giants fans just stood there silently for a while and then trudged sorrowfully out of the Polo Grounds.

Chapter 21

T*HE* W*ORST* H*APPENS*

Mel returned home to Metairie after another pleasant season of broadcasting Tigers games. (He had a much better year than the Detroit club which finished in fifth place in an eight-club race.) After three years of broadcasting live games, he had become completely proficient and relaxed behind the microphone, and his easy delivery showed it. Mel had continued to enjoy his rapport with the players and the fans throughout the league. He returned home and resumed his work with the building construction firm and his usual offseason recreational pursuits—hunting, fishing, golfing, and socializing with business and personal friends. He was a happy man.

Mel and Mildred purchased a cottage in Bay St. Louis, Mississippi, a couple of hours driving distance from their home. On Friday, November 14, they drove to Bay St. Louis to inspect the cottage which was under construction. On the trip home that evening, they encountered heavy fog, and they decided to stop off at a restaurant near Bay St. Louis, hoping that the fog might lift before they finished dinner. But the fog was still heavy as they left the restaurant, and Mel drove their station wagon slowly onto the foggy highway. Suddenly they were hit head-on by a smaller sedan whose driver had lost the middle of the road in the fog. The two vehicles smashed together, locked and spun crazily, and shattered metal and glass covered the highway.

By the time help arrived, Mel and Mildred were alive but badly injured as they were extricated with extreme difficulty from their station wagon. The driver of the lighter sedan, 50-year-old Leslie Curry, was killed instantly. The Otts were rushed to the emergency room of nearby Hancock County Hospital. Both were in deep shock. Mel suffered from kidney damage, multiple fractures, six broken ribs, broken legs, a broken arm, head injuries, and internal injuries. Mildred sustained a bad concussion, multiple fractures, and internal injuries.

Mel and Mildred's families rushed to the hospital, and the Otts' son-in-law, Dr. Philip Loria, assisted in the care of the badly injured couple. On Saturday, the following day, they were both operated on at Memorial Hospital in Gulfport, and physicians reported at the time that their chances for recovery were good. They both appeared improved for a few days, but Mel's condition suddenly worsened on the following Wednesday as a serious kidney malfunction developed. Mel was rushed to Touro Infirmary in New Orleans where he underwent seven and a half hours of surgery on Thursday. After the surgery, physicians said his chances for survival were slim despite the use of an artificial kidney. Mel was being prepared for another emergency operation on Friday when he died shortly after noon on November 21. His death was attributed to uremia, a kidney function breakdown, and the effects of injuries that resulted in a "massive failure." After several days of treatment in Gulfport, Mildred was brought to New Orleans where she underwent surgery. She survived after a long recuperation period.

Ott's funeral was held on Saturday with Lutheran religious rites conducted at his home. In addition to Mildred, he was survived by his two daughters, Lyn and Barbara; his mother (his father Charles having died some time before); his brother and sister; and Lyn's son, Mel's only grandchild. At the same time as the funeral, more than 81,000 people at the Tulane–Louisiana State football game in New Orleans rose to pay a one-minute, silent tribute to Mel. All during that weekend, the family home in Metairie was bombarded with telegrams and phone calls as friends expressed their heartfelt condolences.

In the evening before Mel's death, the New York reporters who had cared so deeply for him gathered at Toots Shor's restaurant to talk in hushed tones about Mel's accomplishments and the kind of man he was. Many of them wept openly after Mel's death. Shor called Horace Stoneham who was vacationing in Ciudad Trujillo in the Dominican Republic, and they shared their loss. Stoneham broke down and lamented to Shor, "Toots, the worst has happened." He broke short his vacation to attend the funeral, after which he told reporters, "I'm so shocked. Mel was not only a great Giant player but also a very dear personal friend."

Ott's death sent the entire baseball world into mourning. Baseball commissioner Ford Frick said, "As a player, manager, and broadcaster, he was a credit to himself and to baseball. He was a true gentleman and one of whom baseball was most proud." Carl Hubbell noted, "Mel was one of my closest friends, and we remained close through the years. He was one of the great ones, and his passing is a great loss to baseball." A stunned Bill Terry commented, "His death is a great shock to me because we were such good friends." Giants secretary Eddie Brannick could hardly speak, but he told a writer who called him, "He was a credit to the game and a great man. I've lost a friend and I'll miss him. A lot of people will."

Garry Schumacher said that Ott had to be rated as "the greatest of all Giants, with the exception of McGraw." Casey Stengel commented, "Ott proved a player could go direct to the major leagues if he tries hard enough. He never had an enemy, and I never heard him speak bad about anyone." Mel's old comrade in arms, Fred Lindstrom, said, "My first impression of Mel was that he couldn't make the grade on account of his heavy, fat legs. But through constant play his legs tapered and he became, I think, about the greatest ballplayer we've ever seen."

Mel was honored in a number of ways. Boston sportswriters announced a new "Mel Ott Memorial Award" for the outstanding Red Sox player of the year. The New Orleans City Council recommended that the newly constructed Mississippi River Bridge at New Orleans be named in Mel's honor. And, to the present day, the National League honors its leading home run hitter each season with the "Mel Ott Award."

Arnold Hano wrote feelingly of Mel in his book, *Greatest Giants of Them All*:

> When he died, he held fourteen baseball records, a little man with a bashful smile and a silken swing, baseball's legendary nice guy. His death was the worst that could have happened to baseball, but his playing career had been the best.

Chapter 22

TEAMMATES

In the late 1950s there was a round, swarthy man in his sixties known only as Louie, whose deep knowledge of the game as a Polo Grounds bleacherite made him master of all he surveyed. Louie held court from a seat near the Giants bullpen in deep right field. He impressed his younger bleacher friends mightily. They were not necessarily impressed by his unusual custom of coming to the ballpark a full two hours before the start of a game and occupying himself by reading Shakespeare and other classics not considered a normal pregame diversion. But Louie's bleacher colleagues were impressed by the recognition accorded him by the players before games as they walked to and from the dugout to the center field clubhouse.

All of the bleacher occupants expected to be ignored by the players when the fans shouted encouragement and criticism to them. No surprise then that Louie's cohorts were thrilled, if only vicariously, by the recognition he received—"Howdy" from Dick Bartell, an agreeing nod from Harry Danning when Louie reminded him of a mental error in the previous game, or a pleasant smile from Ott.

Louie had been occupying his bleacher seat since 1924, almost a quarter of a century before Ott was deposed as manager. Louie was a walking encyclopedia of information of the Giants for all of those years, and the fans who sat with him loved to hear him talk about the Polo Grounds figures he had seen, many of whom had played roles of varying importance in Mel Ott's career.

John McGraw, of course, was the single most important person in Ott's development as a player. McGraw's wide circle of friends, in and out of baseball, had sent him unsolicited a number of excellent prospects, among them players like Larry Doyle, Frankie Frisch, Travis Jackson, Bill Terry, and Hank Leiber. And so Harry Williams followed a well-worn path when he sent Ott to McGraw.

Mel was a special case because of his extreme youth and lack of experience in organized baseball. McGraw had the exceptional foresight to visualize the future greatness of the unprepossessing 16 year old after seeing him hit in batting practice. And McGraw had the patience to keep the youngster with him for his personal supervision and very careful insertion into the Giants lineup. The usual steps would have been either to send Ott back home to grow up or to send him to the low minors. Instead McGraw converted the sturdy little catcher into an outfielder because of his small size and kept him with the Giants. Jimmie Foxx was the only other player who comes to mind who was handled similarly but, even in the case of Foxx, he had brief minor league experience before Philadelphia Athletics manager Connie Mack played him in a few games with the A's when Foxx was 17. Mack returned Foxx to the minors again before bringing him up to stay when he was 19.

McGraw saw the wisdom of not changing Ott's unorthodox hitting style (he lifted his right leg before stepping into a pitch, but not as much as he would a few years later), and he was concerned that a minor league manager would attempt to change that style. And McGraw was astute enough to correct the problem Mel's heavy, still-growing legs could have presented. Hiring a track coach to teach Mel to run properly in his first spring training camp was credited with minimizing leg cramps and charley horses which could have ended Ott's career prematurely.

Mel had the benefit of almost three years of on-the-job training before he became a regular in 1928. During this period he was obliged to sit on the bench next to the salty-tongued McGraw for a continuous lecture on game situations. McGraw restricted Mel's at-bats to righthand pitching until the manager was convinced that the left-hand-hitting Ott had gained confidence in his ability to hit left-hand pitching. McGraw also watched over his young protégé like a hawk off the field. He forbade Mel from playing cards, or otherwise fraternizing with the older players who McGraw thought might lead Mel astray. As a result, Mel was often referred to as "John McGraw's little boy." Years after McGraw's death, his widow told writers that her husband's all-time favorite Giants players were Christy Mathewson, Ross Youngs, and Ott.

Louie recalled a conversation he had with journeyman Giants righthander Tim McNamara in 1926 shortly after the club returned north from spring training. McNamara told Louie, "The kid is a real hitter and we feel he has a great future. But he's got to learn how to play the outfield and keep that strong arm under control. He's a nice, quiet kid, though, and all of us are very fond of him."

Louie told his bleacher friends that he could recall seeing Mel sitting next to McGraw on the bench during Mel's first few years with the

Giants. And Louie was there when Ott his his first, inside-the-park homer in 1927. Louie talked about McGraw's special feeling for the youngster the writers also called "Master Melvin." He theorized, "The McGraws did not have children, and I think McGraw thought of Mel as the son he never had. I also heard that Mel's hitting reminded McGraw of himself when he was a young infielder back in the 1890s."

Ross (Pep) Youngs had a career similar to Ott's in many respects. He joined the Giants in September 1917 at the age of 20. Small in size like Ott, he stood a mere 5 feet 8 inches and weighed 162 pounds, but he was powerfully built. Similar to Ott, he reminded McGraw of himself although in Young's case it was his aggressiveness and toughness. The Giants had bought Youngs' contract for $2000 in 1916, and he joined the parent club after a great year with Rochester in the International League.

Again similar to Mel, Young was moved to the outfield after he convinced McGraw that he was not cut out to be an infielder. In a short time, he proved he could do anything it took to win except hit home runs. There was one special quality that endeared him to McGraw—his unconquerable will to win. As an example, one day he slid hard into Cincinnati third baseman Babe Pinelli, another fierce competitor, and he told the protesting Pinelli, "Hey, Babe, don't get excited, we're not playing marbles, you know."

By 1918 Youngs, barely 21 years old, was the Giants' regular right fielder, a difficult position at the Polo Grounds that he mastered after considerable effort. Youngs was the Giants' chief spark plug as they won four straight pennants from 1921 through 1924. He had his only sub–.300 season in 1925 when McGraw noticed that he had lost some of his pep and durability. In spring training the next year, Youngs was diagnosed with Bright's Disease, a usually fatal kidney disease. So McGraw hired a male nurse to accompany Youngs through the 1926 season. Ross responded heroically despite his weakening condition, hitting .306 in 95 games and doing something that endeared him even more to McGraw. He unselfishly taught the fine points of playing right field at the Polo Grounds to 17-year-old Mel, who Youngs knew would be his successor. He also befriended the youngster off the field, and Mel always spoke of him with great affection and respect. The man McGraw called his "greatest outfielder," died on October 22, 1927, leaving behind a lifetime .322 average, eventual election into the Hall of Fame, and the admiration of anyone who ever saw him play.

As the Giants traveled north to start the 1922 season, Norman (Kid) Elberfeld, an old friend of McGraw who managed the Little Rock club of the Southern Association, recommended his shortstop, Travis Jackson, to McGraw. The bone-thin, 21-year-old Jackson was signed shortly after, and he joined the Giants at the end of the 1922 season, becoming their regular shortstop in 1924. He played for the Giants for 15 years, serving as their field captain the last five seasons.

The 5-foot, 10-inch, 160-pound Waldo, Arkansas, native, nicknamed "Stonewall," excelled at shortstop, possessing one of the most powerful throwing arms and widest ranges in the game. He led the league several times in assists, total chances, fielding average, and in double plays. In 1934, with knee injuries reducing his mobility, he played his last season at shortstop. He moved to third base for his last two seasons.

Jackson could hit with power, considering his slight build, with 135 home runs to go with his .291 career average. And he did the things that do not show up in the box score. He was hard to strike out and was an expert bunter and skilled hit-and-run man. And above all, he was what every manager wants, a model of steadiness and consistency.

Writer Arnold Hano captured the essence of the popular, workman-like Jackson in the following description:

> All through his career, one picture remains vivid, and that is the lean, dark-haired young man gliding to his right and rifling out runners at first. But he also ripped his share of base hits into the left-field corner, and he had another trait that nearly equaled his arm. On a team always known for its ability to bunt and squeeze out runs one at a time, Jackson was a master. He could sacrifice with deadly skill; better (despite the fact that he was a right-hand hitter), he was one of the finest drag-bunters, for base hits, the game ever saw.

Louie often told his bleacher friends that the underrated Jackson was the consummate "ballplayers' ballplayer." The Veterans Committee at the Hall of Fame agreed with Louie belatedly, voting in Jackson in 1982.

Ott and Jackson, two of a kind in temperament, personality, and playing skill, admired each other tremendously. Long after their playing days, Jackson said of Ott, "Mel was always in the background, not saying much but listening good." He smiled and recalled, "I remember him reading detective story magazines on trips. He must have gone through 10,000 of those things." After Mel took over the Giants, he hired his old friend as a coach as soon as he could. Jackson served the Giants in that capacity in Mel's last two seasons at the helm.

Third baseman–outfielder Fred Lindstrom was Mel's closest friend on the Giants during Ott's first four years when the two young men roomed together on the road. The spirited Lindstrom and the shy, diffident Ott were naturals to become roommates because both were McGraw's "boy wonders." The roommates were split up in midseason of 1929 when McGraw thought it advisable.

Although only 16 in 1922, Lindstrom hit .304 for Toledo in the American Association. He became the Giants' regular third baseman in 1924, and at 18 years and two months of age, he became the youngest player ever to appear in a World Series game. He belted ten hits in that Series against the Washington Senators, including four in the deciding seventh game. However, Lindstrom's fine performance was overshadowed when a twelfth-inning ground ball hit to him struck a pebble and bounced over his head letting in the winning run. Lindstrom never let the heartbreaking loss get to him. He had a fine arm, great hands, decent speed, and good bat control. And he was McGraw's kind of player. Even though Lindstrom was one of the few Giants who had the courage to talk back to the imperious McGraw, the Giants manager was willing to take Freddie's backtalk for what he could accomplish on the field.

While Lindstrom had his share of sensational moments, he also was a model of steadiness. His .318 career batting average with the Giants is the seventh highest in franchise history. He twice had 231 hits in a season, collected nine hits in a doubleheader, and he had five hits in a game three times in 1930. The Veterans Committee of the Hall of Fame elected him to the Hall in 1976.

Left-hander Carl Hubbell began his professional career at 20 in 1923 with Cushing of the Oklahoma State League. In 1925 he began to throw his famous reverse curve, or screwball, and the Detroit Tigers signed him after a 17 and 13 season in the Western League. Hubbell's first spring training with the Tigers was a disappointment as Tiger manager Ty Cobb ordered him not to throw his screwball, cautioning him that the unnatural use of his wrist, turning it to the right, would hurt his arm. After two disappointing years in the Tiger farm system, and deprived of the use of his best pitch, the Tigers gave up on Hubbell early in 1928, selling him to Beaumont in the Texas League. On the strength of a well-pitched game in Houston, the Giants obtained him for $30,000 that summer, and he joined the Giants in July 1928. McGraw encouraged him to throw his best pitch, and Carl had a fine 10 and 6 record over the rest of the season.

Hubbell won 18 games in 1929, including a no-hitter on May 8, and he was on his way. Carl's brilliance shone through most strikingly in 1933 and 1936, his MVP seasons. He was at his peak during the five seasons beginning in 1933, during which time he won 115 games and led the Giants to three pennants. His most sensational performances came in 1933 when he won an incredible 1–0, 18-inning game without issuing a

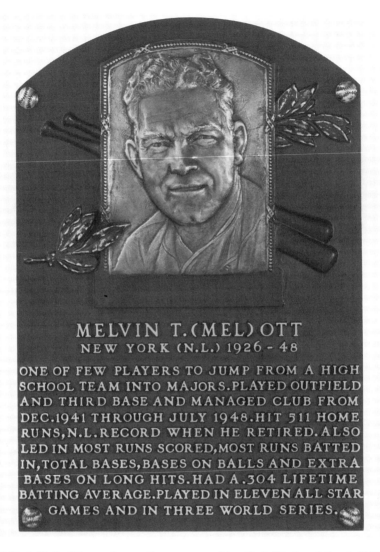

Mel Ott's Hall of Fame plaque, Cooperstown, New York (National Baseball Hall of Fame).

walk, and in the 1934 All-Star game when he struck out five great hitters in a row.

Pitching great Waite Hoyt provided a professional analysis of Hubbell's considerable talent. Hoyt told a writer:

> Hubbell is one of the great pitchers, yet he represents no mystery to the onlooker. The source of his skill is his matchless control in

using his curveball to set up his screwball. Emotions, if he has any, never affect him. His timing, his conservation of energy, and influence on the ball club are other factors in rating him among the great pitchers of all time.

One day one of the younger bleacher fans, who was too young to have seen Hubbell pitch, asked Louie what he remembered about Hubbell. Louie responded:

When most people talk about Hubbell, they usually have in mind his screwball, his 18-inning masterpiece, his All-Star game strike-outs, that kind of stuff. I don't think of his individual games. I think of an artist painting a portrait, every stroke of the brush with a purpose. Or a chessmaster who studies every move with the same detached concentration, whether he's playing or just watching. Hub would start a batter off with a curve, and it was usually a beaut, always low and on the corner. Then, with that uncanny control and that good speed of his, he'd bust one in, either on the fists or high and outside. Then maybe a changeup. Next, the screwball. Jeez, what a pitch! It gave those right-hand hitters fits.

Louie's eyes sparkled as he thought of the lanky Oklahoman with the number 11 uniform and the trouser legs bloused well below his knees. Hubbell said that this means of dress was natural for someone "without a behind." Louie continued,

Hub was great in the clutch. He won for years with a low-scoring team, and he won the big games consistently. Also, he won more than he lost against the best pitchers of his time—Dizzy Dean, Lon Warneke, Paul Derringer and the other great ones. His only weakness was that the Dodgers were his jinx team, and that was rough, the Giant-Dodger rivalry being what it's always been.

Louie went on,

Hubbell had the perfect temperament. He never got excited or lost his concentration when we blew an easy chance behind him. And I used to get a kick just watching him in the dugout on days he wasn't pitching. Even at the end of his career when he'd seen it all, he would sit there quietly and never take his eyes off the batter or the pitcher. I think he knew their strengths and weaknesses better than they did themselves. All in all, Hub was the greatest left hander I've ever seen, and most of the players I know feel the same.

Hubbell, voted into the Hall of Fame in 1947, remained in charge of the Giants' farm system until the Stoneham group sold the club in 1976.

Mel Ott memorabilia at Hall of Fame (National Baseball Hall of Fame).

Hubbell and Ott were roommates from midway through the 1929 season until Mel took over as manager in 1942. The *World-Telegram*'s Joe Williams wrote, "Carl Hubbell is so much like Ott that it was inevitable that they would be intimate friends and long-time roommates." After Ott was replaced, it was particularly fitting that Mel worked with his closest baseball friend in his last years with the Giants.

William Harold (Bill) Terry joined the Giants in September 1923 at age 25 after having pitched and played first base in semi-pro and minor league baseball since 1915. McGraw was taken aback by Terry's independence when McGraw gave him an offer to join the Giants in the spring of 1922. McGraw asked, "How would you like to come to New York with us?"

"For how much?" Terry asked.

McGraw sizzled. "Do you understand that I'm offering you a chance to play with the Giants?"

Terry replied confidently, "Excuse me if I don't fall all over myself, but the Giants don't mean a thing to me unless you can make it worth my while."

"All right," said McGraw. "I'll think it over." A few weeks later McGraw offered Terry a generous (for that time) $5000-a-year contract and, after Terry accepted, he was sent to Toledo to improve his play at first base.

A straightaway hitter, Memphis Bill drove the ball to all parts of the field rather than aiming for the nearby right field wall at the Polo Grounds. In 1927 the handsome Atlanta native had his first of six straight seasons with at least 100 runs scored. He enjoyed his best year in 1930, hitting .401 and tying the National League record with 254 hits. Terry was named the National League's MVP that year despite the Giants' third-place finish. Besides having an outstanding .341 lifetime batting average over 14 major league seasons, Terry ranked among the all-time great fielding first basemen and was the premier National League player at the position for most of his playing career. Although it was not well recognized by fans, the 6-foot, 200-pound Terry was one of the fastest players in the league.

Bill Terry's brilliant playing career was complemented by his successful reign as Giants manager, as the Giants won three pennants during his 11½-season tenure. He was at odds with many of the reporters covering the Giants, some of whom he contemptuously referred to as "25 dollar-a-week clerks." The writers reacted by delaying the proud Terry's election to the Hall of Fame for 18 years after his retirement as an active player.

Terry was one of the few Giants players who never acknowledged Louie's presence. Still Louie talked of him with respect:

> Terry was a different kind of guy than Hubbell and Ott. He was a mature man with a family when McGraw brought him up, and he was never awed by the big city like Hub and Ott were for a time. To Terry, the money was right and the Giants were just another big league team. I always thought his attitude was strictly

a matter of "what's in it for me?" I think a lot of his independent attitude stemmed from his ability to make a lot of money outside of baseball.

Terry was a great player, though. He was a smart, line drive hitter, and he didn't try to pull the ball unless the situation demanded it. He always hit for a high average because he scattered those line shots so well. His .401 average in 1930 was no fluke. Terry had lots of guts, too. I'll never forget the way he forced himself to play in 1936 when his knees were in such bad shape. And he was the best fielding first baseman I ever saw. He was a big guy, but he covered a lot of ground and no one could make that first-to-second-to-first double play any better. The man also was exceptionally graceful around the bag.

One of the fans interjected, "He was a good manager, too." Louie responded,

I thought Terry was a hell of a manager. I heard that some of his players didn't care for him. They thought he didn't care about their problems, and he could be a tough guy to deal with at contract time. Some of the players who didn't go back to the old McGraw days thought that Bill was a cold fish. And he wasn't a colorful guy, although I always thought he provoked the Dodgers on purpose just to build up the gate receipts. Another rap was that he won only as long as the players McGraw left him were still around—Hubbell, Ott, Fitzsimmons, Jackson, and Terry himself. That's true up to a point. After all, he won three pennants before those guys wore out and none after 1937 when Ott was the only fellow with much left. But, don't forget, Terry made those pennants possible with three big trades. Getting Mancuso won the 1933 pennant, and the Bartell and Whitehead deals brought us the pennants in 1936 and 1937.

Terry was one of the best field strategists of his time. In 1933 he brought back the idea of playing for one run early in the game, and it really worked. He knew how to handle his pitchers, too. And his teams were drilled in the fundamentals—the cutoff play, throwing to the right base, bunting, sliding, and general heads-up play. He got the most out of his players, or they didn't last long with the Giants. His personal relations with writers were lousy, though. He alienated them by playing hard to get, and he made it worse by discouraging his players from talking to reporters. He got away with it while the team was winning, but he got a terrible press when we stopped winning. That was why the fans never really warmed to the guy.

Terry and Ott were good friends, and they frequently visited each other during the offseason. Terry was 11 years older than Mel, and he sometimes appeared to treat Mel as he would a much younger brother. On Mel Ott Night in August 1940, a writer asked Terry, "What was the first thing you remember Mel doing?"

Mel Ott's mausoleum in Metairie (Louisiana) Cemetery (courtesy Jay Gauthreaux).

Terry responded, "Catching batting practice at the Polo Grounds. He was around for a while before I even knew his name."

The writer continued, "Did his name mean anything to you?"

"No," answered Terry. "I had played in the same towns where he played, but he was a baby then. But in time he became a great player. He had a tough act to follow in Ross Youngs. And he wasn't as aggressive as Youngs. But even without that aggressiveness, Mel was a better ballplayer and that's saying a lot."

Mel played with several other Hall of Famers but, with the exception of George Kelly and Frankie Frisch, none of them were primarily associated with the Giants. In Mel's first year, Kelly was the Giants first baseman and Frisch was at second. In following seasons, Rogers Hornsby, Edd Roush, and Burleigh Grimes were Mel's teammates. Later, Mel played with and managed Johnny Mize, Ernie Lombardi, and Joe Medwick.

Louie told his fellow bleacherites that of these players only Frisch, Mize, and Lombardi could be considered to have found identities as Giants. Said Louie:

We loved big Lom. He was a sweetheart, and he always had something to say to me as he walked by. He could still hit when we got him, and he was a rock behind the plate.

One day he was catching Van Mungo when Mungo could still throw hard. Mungo threw a fast ball that was too far to Lom's right for him to get his mitt on the ball. I'll be damned if he didn't spear the ball in his bare hand, and toss it back to Mungo nonchalantly as though it was a simple game of catch. I understand he did the same thing before with Johnny Vander Meer who was almost as fast as Mungo. I never saw a catcher do that before, and I haven't seen it since.

There were other Giants teammates who were especially important to Mel. He was a close friend of Hal Schumacher, and both men, along with Hubbell, spent a lot of time together when the Giants were on the road. Mel and Joe Moore also were close. Mel talked about this and his difficulty in releasing Moore after Mel took over as manager. He told the *Sporting News*:

> Maybe you don't think it was tough getting rid of Joe Moore. You couldn't meet a finer fellow, or a player who gave more. But then Joe understood the situation. If a fellow you've got to give the bad news to is really the fine guy you think he is, he'll understand and make the nasty job easier for you. That's what Joe did.

Dick Bartell wrote in *Rowdy Richard*:

> Everybody loved Mel as a man and a player, nobody liked him as a manager…. He was a great guy and a real family man. We went on picnics together. He and his wife were close to the Meltons and Hubbells and other couples on the club…. He had the disposition that all managers look for in a player: loved to play, played to win, kept going even when he lost, short on vanity and long on loyalty, willing to do whatever he's asked to help the team…. Ott was born a man. Spirit. Disposition. Attitude. He had them all.

Lefty O'Doul was one of the most important teammates Mel ever had although O'Doul was with the Giants only during the 1928 season and the 1933–1934 seasons. After Mel died, O'Doul told a writer:

> We were close friends from the start. One of the things that made him a great hitter was practice. We used to spend hours, just the two of us, practicing hitting the ball down the right field foul line. We got so we could keep it fair by just a few inches. I've always been proud to have had the chance to help him in 1928 because that was the first year that he started to hit home runs. He was a wonderful man, one of the finest I ever met.

Chapter 23

$\mathcal{P}$ERSPECTIVE

Mel Ott was surprisingly small for a home run hitter. He was built like a middleweight fighter, five feet, nine inches and compact. In his playing prime he weighed only about 170 pounds, and for years his playing weight remained around 165. Although he was about the size of an average-sized American man, he was 30 to 50 pounds lighter than the other great hitters of his era, such sluggers as Lou Gehrig, Babe Ruth, Jimmie Foxx, Hank Greenberg, Johnny Mize, Joe DiMaggio, and Ted Williams. Yet when Mel retired as a player in 1947, of his contemporaries, only Ruth and Foxx, and eventually Williams, hit more balls out of the park.

When asked where he got all that power, Mel shrugged, "Timing, I guess. Mostly it was a matter of connecting at exactly the right place in the swinging arc. That way I was able to get every pound into the swing. I think that raising and lowering my front leg before the pitch also gave me more momentum to hit for distance." He smiled and continued, "Pulling the ball down the line at the Polo Grounds also helped."

Near the end of Ott's managerial career, his face was unlined, strong, and deeply tanned from continual exposure to the sun. He had only a slight suggestion of a double chin and his thick, curly hair was almost black. His bright eyes were a deep brown peering out from behind his glasses, and his features were regular and remarkable only for an outsize pair of ears. He had a pleasant smile.

Mel had a quiet, sly sense of humor. Mildred Ott said he was the most even-tempered and approachable of men, even when a nervous stomach sent him to bed in 1943. Mildred said that if there was one thing that characterized her husband, it was his consideration of others.

Mel was a heavy smoker who liked the plain way of life. He usually dressed for comfort, favoring sports clothes although he had a wardrobe of a dozen fairly conservative, expensive suits. He was a fine party companion and poker player when he was in the mood. An intelligent man, he was an interesting, though not a scintillating, conversationalist.

Writer Bob Broeg, who knew Mel well, wrote:

> Ottie drank, all right, but the little guy with the passive southern accent and an active taste for crayfish bisque, New Orleans style, was too well-disciplined to do anything reckless.
>
> Ott was a movie addict, a crossword puzzle devotee and partial to gin rummy, bouillabaisse and oysters Rockefeller. He didn't mind betting a few bucks on the horses now and then. He played golf very well, shooting in the mid–70s, and he played the way he threw, right-handed. He chopped wood the way he batted, left-handed.

The Otts never really left the South. Their home was a sprawling ten-room house in Metairie. They had built the house in the late 1930s and spent the offseasons there with their two daughters. During the baseball season, Mel and Mildred rented an apartment in Greenwich Village, and sent their girls to a summer camp in Pennsylvania.

The shift that moved Bill Terry into the front office and Ott into the managership changed the Giants' persona. Terry's teams had won three pennants, but he was not personally liked. The writers found him surly, independent, and sometimes insulting. After Terry's teams began to slip in the standings, newspaper coverage of the Giants reflected the writers' dislike of Terry. Typical was the case of the woman reporter who was assigned to write a feature story about Terry. "I don't give interviews to women," he said curtly, and walked away. As a result, the woman's story was uncomplimentary. When manager Mel was placed in the same situation, he stood politely, offered the lady writer a seat, and chatted with her for half an hour. The resulting article was highly favorable. There was no doubt that Mel appreciated the importance of good public relations, but it also was his nature to be courteous and obliging. There was no manager in the game who was easier to interview, and the writers loved Mel for it.

Stan Musial mentioned Mel's unselfishness when Musial spoke at ceremonies in July 1969 at his induction into the Hall of Fame. He said:

> When I was moving in on his (Mel's) records for extra base hits, total bases, and others, he'd not only wish me well, but he'd actually encourage me to spur me on. I was impressed then by Ottie's sense of honor, his sportsmanship. When my records fall, I hope I'm as gracious as Ottie was.

Melvin Thomas Ott was only 49 when he died. He left behind memories of one of the most productive baseball careers. He would remain, until 1966, the greatest home run hitter the National League had produced with 511. When he died, he held league records with 1860 RBIs, 1859 runs scored, 5041 total bases, and 1708 bases on balls, all of which have been surpassed. He hit two or more home runs in 50 games, and in six seasons he either led or tied for the league lead in home runs. No National Leaguer had ever scored six runs in a game. Mel did it twice.

In 1929, at age 20, Mel hit 42 home runs and drove in 151 runs. No other 20 year old has ever driven in that many runs in a season. Nor has any Giants player ever driven in that many runs in a single season, and that includes hitters like Johnny Mize, Willie Mays, Willie McCovey, and Orlando Cepeda. Mel played in the era of National League sluggers which included players like Chuck Klein, Joe Medwick, Wally Berger, Hack Wilson, Dolf Camilli, and Ernie Lombardi. These men terrorized the league, and the pitching of that time was as good as it has ever been. Of all those players, no one equaled Mel in terms of consistently high production over a long period.

In addition to his power, Mel brought to the plate enormous patience and a keen eye for the strike zone. Pitchers walked him because they feared him, and he refused to join the many sluggers who swing at anything. Once Mel walked seven times in a row. The only other slugger who approached him in this regard was Ted Williams. Both men looked upon hitting as a science, and not a brutish pleasure. With Williams, it was an adjunct to all his other talents and his large, rangy body. With Ott, it was a necessity because of his relatively small size. Players of Mel's modest physical stature have tended to specialize in choking their bats and poking hits over the infield or to the opposite field. Unlike them, Mel was no Punch-and-Judy hitter. But he was small, and he had to use his total hitting potential. He could not waste swings. As a result, he became one of the most disciplined hitters ever to play the game.

Mel was especially adept at waiting for his pitch. Like all sophisticated hitters, he waited on pitches within a certain area in the strike zone, pitches that he could drive for distance. Giants pitcher Cliff Melton remembered the many times when Ott returned to the dugout after hitting a long drive which was caught. Mel would take a seat in the dugout and tell his teammates, not boastfully but confidently, "If he (the pitcher) throws me another in that spot, I'll hit it out." Melton said that it was remarkable how often Mel would wait patiently for a pitch in that spot and deliver on his promise.

This is a school of thought that takes the view that Ott's many hitting feats were due in large part to the convenient right field wall at the Polo Grounds. A breakdown of his hitting records at home and away indicates that this is the case only in regard to his home runs. The first edition of *Total Baseball* contained a section on home vs. away hitting for a number of great hitters. A discussion of Mel's hitting figures led to the following comments in that book:

> One looking at Ott's home run breakdown is liable to think that the Polo Grounds (257-foot foul line in right) kept him in the major leagues. He hit a startling 323 of his 511 career home runs at home, and another 40 (in about 110 games) in friendly Baker Bowl (in Philadelphia). In Ott's last seven seasons, 100 of his 123 homers (including all 18 in 1943) were hit at home. Additionally, this analysis showed that Ott slugged .589 at home and only .370 on the road during this period, and that he didn't score a run in his last 37 road games.
>
> The Polo Grounds may have extended Ott's career and turned him into a world-class home run hitter, but he was a world-class *hitter* all by himself. Over his first nine seasons Ott averaged a resounding .343 on the road, as compared to .286 at home. In 1929 he set National League records for runs (79) and RBIs (87) on the road. For his career he batted 14 points better on the road and hit significantly more singles, doubles, and triples away from home.
>
> It is interesting to note that Ott's record at home and away can be viewed as essentially the same, except that about 130 doubles on the road were turned into homers by the short dimensions of the Polo Grounds.

Especially in his earlier seasons, Mel hit some mammoth drives at the Polo Grounds and on the road. At home he drove many homers far from the right field foul pole and deep into the upper stands. And he blasted many balls over the Polo Grounds roof. In other parks he hit with the best of them. For example, in 1930 he hit a home run at vast Braves Field in Boston which was the longest drive into the right field bleacher section at that park since it had opened in 1915. In his first World Series at-bat in 1933 Ott homered off Washington Senator left-hander Walter Stewart (he hit left-handers as well as right-handers after he became a regular). Mel blasted the drive so far and deep into the stands that a reporter wrote, "It would be a home run in any park in America, including Yellowstone."

But had all of Ott's home runs been hit into the lower deck in short right field, what difference would it have made? Other players had their shots at the Polo Grounds walls, and only Ott beat such a steady tattoo. Mel tailored his game to his home park just as Babe Ruth and Roger Maris accommodated themselves to the friendly, low-walled right field stands at Yankee Stadium. Duke Snider had done the same at intimate Ebbets Field, and Chuck Klein took deadly aim at the convenient tin wall at Baker Bowl.

Most of the great hitters had higher career batting averages at home than on the road. The only notable exceptions were Lou Gehrig, Hank Aaron, Joe DiMaggio, and Ott. Mel had a lifetime .297 average at the Polo Grounds and a .311 average on the road. In almost the same number of games at home and away, Mel had many more home runs, RBIs, runs scored, and walks at home.

Ott was a much more powerful hitter in his first 11 full seasons than he was in the following seven seasons but he took more advantage of the cozy Polo Grounds right field wall during the latter period. From 1928 through 1938 just over 57 percent of his 341 home runs were hit at home, for an average of 31 homers per season. From 1939 through 1945, 75 percent of his 168 homers were hit at the Polo Grounds, a reduced average of 24 homers per season. Mel hit his largest number of out-of-town home runs in Philadelphia with 40 (all of them at Baker Bowl before the Phillies moved to larger Shibe Park in midseason in 1938). Ott's lowest road production came in Cincinnati, where he hit 13 home runs.

The little outfielder carried the Giants offensive for most of his career. Mel led the Giants in home runs for an incredible 18 consecutive seasons, from 1928 through 1945, and he also was the club RBI leader in nine of those years. Most significantly, Mel was by far the leading RBI producer in each of the Giants' three pennant-winning years in the 1930s. In 1933 he had 31 more RBIs than club runner-up Johnny Vergez. He had a remarkable 68 more RBIs than Hank Leiber who was the Giants' second best RBI man in 1936, and 29 more than runner-up Jimmy Ripple in 1937. Mel also was the Giants leader in drawing walks for 17 years in a row, testimony to the respect given him by opposing pitchers and the way in which they pitched around him.

In light of Ott's hitting heroics, there is a tendency to forget that he was the best right fielder of his era and one of the best in the history of the game. Mel was one of the surest-handed outfielders to play for the Giants, and he caught everything within his reach. Very seldom did he leap or dive for a ball only to have it trickle off his glove. There was an astonished surprise at the Polo Grounds one day in 1943 when Mel dropped a routine fly ball. It was the first fly ball he had dropped in nearly 20 years and, by this time, Ott also was presiding over a team of inferior bumblers, the worst Giants club in history.

Like Ross Youngs before him, Mel learned the right field wall at the Polo Grounds, and he played caroms off the wall with unerring skill. And when he did come up with those caroms and straighten up to fire the ball to third, rival third base coaches had their runners advance with extreme caution. Trolley-wire throws whistled out of that right field corner. With his quick release, Mel threw with a short motion. The ball seemed to fly from his hand, shoulder-high across the grass and into the infield. It usually took one hop to the waiting baseman or the catcher, dead on target.

William Curran, in his authoritative *Mitts—A Celebration of the Art of Fielding*, rated Ott and Roberto Clemente as the best-fielding right fielders. He rated Clemente just above Mel by a hair, writing:

> I spent a couple of hours pacing the floor mumbling Ott, Clemente, Ott, Clemente. Clemente was the faster of the two, though neither could have stayed within Rickey Henderson's shadow in a ten-yard dash. They both had enough speed to cover right field with something to spare. Mel may have had a slightly more accurate arm, though here we are splitting hairs. Bobby was a more aggressive fielder, probably took more chances. In a very close decision I must go with Clemente.

Defensive statistics often can be misleading. A poor fielder may be charged with few errors simply because he did not reach balls that a better fielder would reach. But this was not the case with Ott and Clemente, both of whom were superior fielders who covered their assigned territory thoroughly. Ott and Clemente had very similar statistics as right fielders, according to figures presented in *The Bill James Historical Baseball Abstract*. Both players had very comparable numbers for putouts, assists, and fielding range. But Mel had a significant advantage in errors, fielding average, and double plays.

Travis Jackson speculated that Ott may have missed his calling by not being a regular third baseman. Jackson told a writer, "What a swell infielder he would have made. But his arm was just too good in that outfield. His throws were always right to the bag when a runner was coming in." Dick Bartell wrote, "He (Ott) always played ground balls in the outfield like an infielder, charging them and getting the throw away faster than any other outfielder in the game."

Mel did not have great speed because of his short, stocky legs, but he was a smart base runner. Early in his career he learned that a quick jump compensated largely for lack of blazing speed. That quick jump enabled him to advance from first to third on routine singles, and it also helped Mel race to the right field wall on short drives, or almost to the Giants bullpen in deepest right center field at the Polo Grounds.

Despite Mel's "nice guy" image, he was a brutal slider coming into a base. Here his short, compact body was advantageous. He demonstrated this with that well-remembered play in 1942 when he body-blocked Pee Wee Reese and broke up a double play attempt. That was how Mel introduced Reese to the rough play which characterized the Giants-Dodgers rivalry in the many years before both clubs left for the West Coast.

Ott was never really happy as a manager, and certainly not after his successful first season in 1942. Mel's regime began on a high note. The New York fans, writers, and players rejoiced in the likable slugger's appointment, and his trade for Johnny Mize made a big hit. It also paved the way for an unexpectedly strong third place finish as Ott and Mize blasted the pitching-poor Giants to win after win. But Giants fortunes plummeted in 1943 as the club lost a disproportionately large number of regulars to the military draft. The undermanned Giants sank deep into the basement early in the season, and Mel personally had his worst year, hitting a meager .234 and was sidelined with a nervous stomach brought on by his team's impossible situation. As the season drew to a merciful close, Stoneham signed his good friend Ott to a three-year, player-manager contract despite the Giants' loss of 98 games and a finish well behind the seventh-place Phillies. The 1944 club managed a fifth-place finish, reflecting the simple fact that other National League clubs had lost more talent to the military than the Polo Grounders. The Giants repeated their 1944 performance in 1945, again finishing in fifth place with no real chance for the pennant.

Things looked better as the Giants grouped to start spring training in 1946, especially with the purchase of Walker Cooper, then considered the best young catcher in the game. Then, without warning, just before the season opened, several Giants jumped to the newly-formed Mexican League. Within a six-week period, the Giants lost eight players, including Ace Adams, their standout reliever. The pitching was woeful, and Adams was missed badly as game after game slipped away because of poor relief pitching. The club stumbled through June making little headway, then settled in last place to stay. The 1947 club, which finished in fourth place, was a reinforced version of the 1946 team but without the same problems. This was the year when Ott's "windowbreakers" wound up with a then-record 221 homers in a 154-game season.

Giants fans, despite their unshakable fondness for Mel, continually debated his merits as a manager. Some said he couldn't handle pitchers. Others faulted his tendency to play for one run late in the game despite his pitchers' inability to hold leads. Many simply felt that he was "too nice" to win. But, in retrospect, many of his problems could have been overcome with better pitching. The 1948 season began with Ott's future in doubt. In mid–July, with the Giants tied for fourth place, eight and a half games behind the first-place Braves, Ott was replaced by Leo Durocher.

It should be noted that the Giants teams that Mel managed were never competitive with the ultimate pennant winners. Ott's clubs never came closer to the pennant winner than a margin of 13 games. This came in 1942. In Ott's other five full years, his clubs finished no closer than 19 games from the pennant winner. It is clear that the Giants under Ott were destined to be also-rans no matter who managed them.

In the book *Legends of Baseball*, Carl Hubbell told author Walter M. Langford:

> Mel Ott was too good a guy to be a really effective manager. And Horace Stoneham had a good deal of influence on him. But Horace was a baseball fan and a fan has likes and dislikes, and so his influence wasn't always the wisest.

Dick Bartell was sharply critical of Ott as a manager. Some of Dick's criticisms, expressed in *Rowdy Richard*, appear valid, but other seem self-serving and erroneous. Bartell wrote:

> He (Ott) couldn't wear authority easily. He didn't know how to handle players. He was a quiet, easy-going guy. Maybe somebody got to him and convinced him that he was too easy, he'd have to get tough. But he didn't know how. It was against his nature. When he tried it didn't work. He didn't know what to do or how to do it, to be something he wasn't.

Bartell added a comment which appears unfair and inaccurate. He wrote, "Cliff Melton had been one of his (Mel's) closest friends. ... He released Melton just before Cliff became eligible for a pension, then begged him to come back." Bartell's point is confusing inasmuch as Melton left the Giants after the 1944 season and the pension plan was not developed and in place until after the players' strike in 1946. I spoke with Melton in 1978, and I asked him why he left the Giants. He told me that he left the Giants simply because he got a significantly higher salary offer from Lefty O'Doul's San Francisco club. Also, Melton spoke warmly of his relations with Ott. So it would appear that Mel did not release Melton in cold disregard of his pension situation, as implied by Bartell.

Bartell also wrote: "The players felt Mel was more concerned about himself than his players." This statement is contradicted by Mel's strenuous efforts to get the best possible treatment for injured Whitey Lockman and Larry Jansen in the spring of 1947, and his attentiveness to Lockman during his recuperation.

Bartell wrote that the umpires didn't have much respect for Ott and that one of them called him "the whiner." Presumably, Bartell would have his readers believe that the umpires would have had more respect for the likes of Leo Durocher and Billy Martin who thought nothing of kicking dirt all over umpires and showing them up in other ways.

There were other cases of Giants players who were not happy with manager Ott. The Bill Voiselle case, after which some players and writers felt that Mel had acted too impulsively, has been discussed earlier along with the observation that Voiselle did not pitch very well subsequently for other managers. The Danny Gardella case, also discussed earlier, was a matter of a wartime player not taking his job seriously enough for a manger who always took his responsibilities seriously. The Sal Maglie situation was unfortunate because Ott assumed logically that calls to Jorge Pasquel placed from Maglie's room had been placed by Maglie. It also was unfortunate for Ott because the relatively inexperienced Maglie of 1946 was nothing like the pitching-smart Maglie who learned his trade before returning to the Giants in 1950.

The veteran Giants players such as Mize, Cooper, and Lombardi were fond of Mel and enjoyed playing for him, so much so that they were openly apprehensive when Durocher replaced Ott. Among the younger players, Bobby Thomson, Mickey Witek, Bill Rigney, and Jack Lohrke loved Ott. Before Ott's dismissal, Lohrke told a writer:

> When I came up from the West Coast, there were two or three guys ahead of me at third base. Mel told me in the spring that on his club, nobody had a position sewed up. He said it went to the best man. He helped me from the start, and I was a green hand. I wouldn't be hitting like I have if it wasn't for Mel. For my money, he's a great manager and a wonderful man.

Ott, who had a deep knowledge of the game, was appointed to succeed Terry largely because of his great popularity and the club's need to win back its old fans. He had not had the chance to show whether he was ready to be a major league manager. Personalities aside, Ott's failings as a manager can be attributed to two basic factors, neither having to do with being "too nice" to his players.

First, Mel tended to emphasize the offensive game at the expense of the club's defense and speed. Durocher had a valid point when he told Stoneham that there was little flexibility in the club he inherited. He proved it by his inability to improve the Giants' performance immediately after he replaced Ott. That club could hit and score runs, but it was painfully slow in the field and on the bases.

Second, the Giants' pitching was woefully deficient throughout Ott's regime, and the Giants had neither a capable general manager nor sufficient money to engineer deals for better pitchers. Stoneham was Mel's biggest admirer but, other than the purchase of the very effective Larry Jansen, Stoneham never exhibited the wherewithal to obtain competent pitchers. In retrospect, maybe Mel's problem was that he was "too nice" a guy with his own boss rather than with his players.

Ott had a mediocre .467 record as a manager, winning 464 games and losing 530. Managing was not Ott's happiest task. Temperamentally he was unfit for the job. He couldn't act up, scream or fuss, or flail his arms at an umpire. When he did, it never looked real.

Bleacher authority Louie was talking about Ott with his fellow fans some years later. "I don't like to think about Mel as a manager," he said. "He didn't have the temperament, the ruthlessness, the front office support, or the luck. But as a player, that's something else!"

His audience listened as the perceptive Louie continued.

> Talk about Ott as a player and what do most people think about? The unorthodox batting style, the short right field wall and all those home runs. How young he was when he started, what a natural he was, and how small he was to be such a big hitter. But to me, that's not the real story of Ott.

Louie paused and went on.

> I think Mel was one of the most underrated of the great players I've seen. For one thing, he was so quiet and unassuming that he never got the publicity he deserved even though he played in New York. He wasn't flashy, and he played almost every game every year no matter how he felt with those charley horses and other injuries. He was just a solid little guy with an uncanny ability to make the big play at bat or in the field more consistently than any player I've ever seen. He was a great clutch hitter, particularly in the late innings, and I mean all kinds of hits, not just homers.

Louie was just getting warmed up talking about his favorite player.

> There's so much more to say about Ottie. He was so versatile and unselfish that he would play anywhere he was needed. I've always thought we won the pennant in 1937 only because he volunteered to play third so we could get Jimmy Ripple's bat in the lineup. Remember, the Giants were a weak-hitting team for so many years and that put a big strain on Ott because they could pitch around him. Don't forget that Terry batted ahead of Mel, not after him. Besides Hank Leiber in 1935 and Johnny Mize in 1942, Ottie didn't have the protection of a good hitter behind him like all of the home run hitters I can think of—Gehrig behind Ruth, DiMaggio or Dickey behind Gehrig, Cronin after Foxx, just for a few examples. That's why Mel got so many walks.

There were other things I remember. Ott could hit to left field when it was necessary. McGraw made sure he learned that when he was a kid. And, for a home run hitter, he was an excellent bunter, and Terry often had him sacrifice. Another thing people don't realize was that very few of the other sluggers struck out as infrequently as Ott in relation to the number of walks he drew. That's important because, except for a double play, nothing kills a rally as fast as a strikeout. You don't advance runners when you don't hit the ball.

Then, of course, Mel was the best right fielder in the game for a long time: judging flies, playing the wall, throwing, and keeping the runners close to the bases. He was no speedboy. But even then he was a smart, tough base runner, and he hit into very few double plays because they played him for a sharp pull hitter, way to the right side and deep. No, great as he was, I don't think Ott was fully appreciated except by the guys who played with him or against him and by people who watched him closely year after year. On top of that, he was a sweet guy. Just a wonderful, unspoiled kid when he came up, and he never really changed.

Sportswriter Jack Mann wrote a thoughtful column in the Washington (D.C.) *Daily News* in August 1970 about players he had idolized when he was growing up who had disappointed him when he met them years later in his professional capacity. As a youngster, Ott and Hubbell had been his favorite players.

Mann was a 33-year-old writer when he learned of Ott's death over an office teletype machine. He wrote that "the little boy in him grieved because Ott had kept the faith with the little boy (himself)." Before he met Mel, Mann had met such players as Yogi Berra and Mickey Mantle in their glory days. In interviewing them, Mann had found many of them to be rude and unpleasant. Berra, for example, had responded to a question with, "How the hell would I know?" Mantle had answered another question with the response, "What difference does it make?"

Mann told of the time he entered the press room at Yankee Stadium for something to eat. He surveyed the crowded room and saw that there was one empty seat at a table for four. The other three seats were occupied by Hall of Famers Dizzy Dean, Frankie Frisch, and Rogers Hornsby. Mann decided he didn't have to eat just then. He had already discovered that Dean was an "overbearing boor," Frisch was a "blabbermouth," and Hornsby was a "super-negative man with a kind word for nobody." Had Mann been offered the fourth seat at the table when he was 15, he would have jumped at the chance. At age 25 he would have paid $50 for the seat. But he had found out that they were not the gallant heroes they were portrayed to be in the purple prose that Mann had read in the 1930s, and he wanted no part of them.

At the time Mann turned down the seat at the table, he already had met Carl Hubbell, his erstwhile co-hero, and had found him "dull." So he concluded that not meeting Mel Ott was the only safe way to protect his fanciful youthful delusions. But in the course of his work, Mann happened to meet Ott, just a few weeks before Mel's death. And they had a nice conversation. Mel told Mann that in a few months he would be 50, and would begin drawing his baseball pension. His younger daughter, Barbara, had just married, and he and Mildred had plans to enjoy their middle age. Mann wrote, "He was a pleasant man who took himself not too seriously to acknowledge that he was a superior player who had become an inferior manager, and why. Or to be needled about the 257-foot, right field line at the Polo Grounds without pointing out that he (had hit many homers out of larger ballparks). He was, it turned out, for real."

And that is the way the "Little Giant" is remembered by anyone who ever knew him or who ever saw him play. In the fullest and best sense, Mel Ott was for real.

*A*PPENDIX: *STATISTICS*

Melvin Thomas Ott
b. 3/2/09, Gretna, La.; d. 11/21/58 New Orleans; BL/TR

Regular Season Record
(All with N.Y. Giants)

	G	AB	R	H	2B	3B	HR	RBI	BB	SO	AVG	TB	SLG
1926	35	60	7	23	2	0	0	4	1	9	.383	25	.417
1927	82	163	23	46	7	3	1	19	13	9	.282	62	.380
1928	124	435	69	140	26	4	18	77	52	36	.322	228	.524
1929	150	545	138	179	37	2	42	151	113	38	.328	346	.635
1930	148	521	122	182	34	5	25	119	103	35	.349	301	.578
1931	138	497	104	145	23	8	29	115	80	44	.292	271	.545
1932	154	566	119	180	30	8	38	123	100	39	.318	340	.601
1933	152	580	98	164	36	1	23	103	75	48	.283	271	.467
1934	153	582	119	190	29	10	35	135	85	43	.326	344	.591
1935	152	593	113	191	33	6	31	114	82	58	.322	329	.555
1936	150	534	120	175	28	6	33	135	111	41	.328	314	.588
1937	151	545	99	160	28	2	31	95	102	69	.294	285	.523
1938	150	527	116	164	23	6	36	116	118	47	.311	307	.583
1939	125	396	85	122	23	2	27	80	100	50	.308	230	.581
1940	151	536	89	155	27	3	19	79	100	50	.289	245	.457
1941	148	525	89	150	29	0	27	90	100	68	.286	260	.495
1942	152	549	118	162	21	0	30	93	109	61	.295	273	.497
1943	125	380	65	89	12	2	18	47	95	48	.234	159	.418
1944	120	399	91	115	16	4	26	82	90	47	.288	217	.544
1945	135	451	73	139	23	0	21	79	71	41	.308	225	.499
1946	31	68	2	5	1	0	1	4	8	15	.074	9	.132
1947	4	4	0	0	0	0	0	0	0	0	.000	0	.000
Total	2730	9456	1859	2876	488	72	511	1860	1708	896	.304	5041	.533

Runs-Led League in 1938 and 1942.
Home Runs–Led League in 1932, 1934, 1936, 1938, and 1942 and tied for lead in 1937.
RBIs-Led League in 1934.
BB-Led League in 1929, 1931–33, 1937, and 1942.
Slugging Percentage–Led League in 1936.

World Series Record

Hitting

	G	AB	R	H	2B	3B	HR	RBI	BB	SO	SB	AVG
1933	5	18	3	7	0	0	2	4	4	4	0	.389
1936	6	23	4	7	2	0	1	3	3	1	0	.304
1937	5	20	1	4	0	0	1	3	1	4	0	.200
Total	16	61	8	18	2	0	4	10	8	9	0	.295

Fielding

	POS	PO	A	E	AVG
1933	RF	10	0	0	1.000
1936	RF	12	0	1	.923
1937	3B	5	9	1	.933
Total		27	9	2	.947

Miscellaneous Offensive

	OBP	HBP	SB	GIDP	PO	A	E	FA	POS
1926	.393	0	1	N/A	18	3	2	.913	O-10, 3-150
1927	.335	0	2	"	52	2	1	.982	O-32
1928	.397	2	3	"	214	14	7	.970	O-115, 2-5, 3-1
1929	.449	6	6	"	335	26	10	.973	O-149, 2-1
1930	.458*	2	9	"	320	26	11	.969	O-146
1931	.392	2	10	"	332	20	7	.981	O-137
1932	.424*	4	6	"	347	11	6	.984	O-154
1933	.367	2	1	10	283	12	5	.983	O-152
1934	.415	3	0	10	286	12	8	.974	O-153
1935	.407	3	7	4	304	42	6	.983	O-137, 3-15
1936	.448	5	6	8	250	20	4	.985	O-148
1937	.408	3	7	4	198	126	10	.970	O-91, 3-60
1938	.442*	5	2	8	163	241	15	.964	3-113, O-37
1939	.449*	1	2	5	190	45	11	.955	O-96, 3-20
1940	.407	6	6	9	240	92	12	.975	O-111, 3-42
1941	.403	3	5	2	256	19	9	.968	O-145

	OBP	HBP	SB	GIDP	PO	A	E	FA	POS
1942	.415	3	6	8	269	15	3	.990	O-152
1943	.391	3	7	4	219	12	6	.975	O-111, 3-1
1944	.423	3	2	3	200	19	7	.969	O-103, 3-4
1945	.411	8	1	6	217	11	4	.983	O-118
1946	.171	0	0	1	23	2	0	1.000	O-16
1947	.000	0	0	0	0	0	0	.000	-
Total	.414	64	89	82	4716	766	144	.974	O-2313, 3-256
									2-1

Fielding—Right Field Only

	G	PO	AS	ER	DP	AVG		G	PO	AS	ER	DP	AVG
1926	10	18	3	2	0	.913	1937	91	156	13	0	1	1.000
1927	32	52	2	1	1	.982	1938	37	65	3	0	0	1.000
1928	115	214	14	7	4	.970	1939	96	175	6	5	2	.973
1929	149	335	26	10	12	.973	1940	111	210	9	4	2	.982
1930	146	320	23	11	6	.969	1941	145	256	19#	9	3	.968
1931	137	332	20	7	4	.981	1942	152	269	15*	3	3	.990
1932	154	347	11	6	5	.984	1943	111	219	12	6	1	.975
1933	152	283	12	5	3	.983	1944	103	199	6	3	0	.986
1934	153	286	12	8	1	.974	1945	118	217	11	4	1	.983
1935	137	285	17	3	7	.990*	1946	16	23	2	0	1	1.000
1936	148	250	20	4	3	.985							
Total	2313	4511	256	98	60	.980							

*Denotes league leadership   #Denotes tie for league leadership

All-Star Game Record

Hitting

	AB	R	H	2B	3B	HR	RBI	BB	SB	AVG
1934	2	0	0	0	0	0	0	0	1	.000
1935	4	0	0	0	0	0	0	0	0	.000
1936	1	0	1	0	0	0	0	0	0	1.000
1937	1	0	1	1	0	0	0	0	0	1.000
1938	4	1	1	0	1	0	0	0	0	.250
1939	4	0	2	0	0	0	0	0	0	.500
1940	0	1	0	0	0	0	0	1	0	.000
1941	1	0	0	0	0	0	0	0	0	.000
1942	4	0	0	0	0	0	0	0	0	.000
1943	1	0	0	0	0	0	0	0	0	.000
1944	1	0	0	0	0	0	0	0	0	.000
Total	23	2	5	1	1	0	0	1	1	.217

Fielding

	POS	PO	A	E	AVG
1934	OF	0	1	0	1.000
1935	OF	1	0	0	1.000
1936	OF	0	0	0	.000
1937	PH	-	-	-	-
1938	OF	3	0	0	1.000
1939	OF	4	0	0	1.000
1940	OF	0	0	0	.000
1941	PH	-	-	-	-
1942	OF	1	0	0	1.000
1943	PH	0	0	0	.000
1944	PH	0	0	0	.000
Total		10	1	0	1.000

Managerial Record
(All with N.Y. Giants)

	G	W	L	PCT	Team Standing
1942	152	85	67	.559	Third
1943	153	55	98	.359	Eighth (last)
1944	152	67	87	.435	Fifth
1945	154	78	74	.513	Fifth
1946	154	61	93	.396	Eighth (last)
1947	154	81	73	.526	Fourth
1948	75	37	38	.493	Fourth*
Total	1004	464	530	.467	

*Replaced by Leo Durocher on 7/16/48

Home-Road Offensive Statistics

Home

	G	AB	R	H	TB	2B	3B	HR	RBI	BB	AVG	OBP	SLG
1926	12	14	3	7	7	0	0	0	0	0	.500	.500	.500
1927	37	79	1	26	36	3	2	1	9	9	.329	.398	.456
1928	59	204	29	59	98	8	2	9	33	26	.289	.372	.480
1929	75	266	59	79	153	12	1	20	65	54	.297	.417	.575
1930	76	257	67	92	169	10	2	21	64	62	.358	.484	.658
1931	70	245	49	57	126	7	1	20	57	46	.233	.354	.514
1932	77	270	53	77	168	15	2	24	66	57	.285	.415	.622

	G	AB	R	H	TB	2B	3B	HR	RBI	BB	AVG	OBP	SLG
1933	74	267	45	70	120	9	1	13	48	39	.262	.360	.449
1934	75	270	49	69	127	8	1	16	49	46	.256	.366	.470
1935	79	292	59	99	171	11	2	19	60	51	.339	.442	.586
1936	75	250	58	83	151	12	1	18	64	59	.332	.463	.604
1937	75	263	48	71	128	10	1	15	45	52	.270	.390	.487
1938	71	241	65	76	152	12	2	20	58	67	.315	.469	.631
1939	64	198	46	61	117	7	2	15	44	58	.308	.465	.591
1940	75	256	42	71	120	13	0	12	39	48	.277	.399	.469
1941	73	236	51	82	150	11	0	19	50	63	.347	.488	.636
1942	77	269	70	94	173	10	0	23	62	59	.349	.468	.643
1943	65	211	41	50	110	6	0	18	34	56	.237	.399	.521
1944	65	203	51	51	121	5	1	21	46	53	.251	.409	.596
1945	72	242	52	83	150	13	0	18	49	37	.343	.440	.620
1946	18	41	2	3	6	0	0	1	3	7	.073	.208	.146
1947	4	4	0	0	0	0	0	0	0	0	.000	.000	.000
Total	1368	4578	953	1360	2553	182	21	323	945	949	.297	.421	.558

Away

	G	AB	R	H	TB	2B	3B	HR	RBI	BB	AVG	OBP	SLG
1926	23	46	4	16	18	2	0	0	4	1	.348	.362	.391
1927	45	84	9	20	26	4	1	0	10	4	.238	.273	.310
1928	65	231	40	81	130	18	2	9	44	26	.351	.419	.563
1929	75	279	79	100	193	25	1	22	87	59	.358	.478	.692
1930	72	264	55	90	132	24	3	4	55	41	.341	.431	.500
1931	68	252	55	88	145	16	7	9	58	34	.349	.431	.575
1932	77	296	66	103	172	15	6	14	57	43	.348	.432	.581
1933	78	313	53	94	151	27	0	10	55	36	.300	.372	.482
1934	78	312	70	121	217	21	9	19	86	39	.388	.459	.696
1935	73	301	54	92	158	22	4	12	54	31	.306	.370	.525
1936	75	284	62	92	163	16	5	15	71	52	.324	.434	.574
1937	76	282	51	89	157	18	1	16	50	50	.316	.424	.557
1938	79	286	51	88	155	11	4	16	58	51	.308	.416	.542
1939	61	198	39	61	113	16	0	12	36	42	.308	.432	.571
1940	76	280	47	84	125	14	3	7	40	52	.300	.413	.446
1941	75	289	38	68	110	18	0	8	40	37	.235	.324	.381
1942	75	280	48	68	100	11	0	7	31	50	.243	.361	.357
1943	60	169	24	39	49	6	2	0	13	39	.231	.381	.290
1944	55	196	40	64	96	11	3	5	36	37	.327	.438	.490
1945	63	209	21	56	75	10	0	3	30	34	.268	.378	.359
1946	13	27	0	2	3	1	0	0	1	1	.074	.107	.111
1947	0	0	0	0	0	0	0	0	0	0	-	-	-
Total	1362	4878	906	1516	2488	306	51	188	916	759	.311	.407	.510

Home Runs

	Home	Away		Home	Away		Home	Away
1926	0	0	**1934**	16	19	**1941**	19	8
1927	1	0	**1935**	19	12	**1942**	23	7
1928	9	9	**1936**	18	15	**1943**	18	0
1929	20	22	**1937**	15	16	**1944**	21	5
1930	21	4	**1938**	20	16	**1945**	18	3
1931	20	9	**1939**	15	12	**1946**	1	0
1932	24	14	**1940**	12	7	**1947**	0	0
1933	13	10						

Total   Home—323   Away—188

Pitchers Yielding Most Homers to Mel Ott

Pitcher	Threw	HR	Pitcher	Threw	HR	Pitcher	Threw	HR
Lon Warneke	R	13	Ray Benge	R	8	Dizzy Dean	R	7
Paul Derringer	R	12	Guy Bush	R	8	Bob Smith	R	7
Larry French	L	12	Ben Cantwell	R	8	Al Javery	R	6
Max Butcher	R	11	Phil Collins	R	8	Van Mungo	R	6
Charlie Root	R	10	Curt Davis	R	8	Claude Passeau	R	6
Bill Lee	R	9	Red Lucas	R	8	Rip Sewell	R	6

- Of Ott's 511 home runs, 410 were hit off righthand pitchers and 101 were hit off lefthanders.
- Ott had 50 multi-home run games. This included one three-homer game (8/31/30) and 49 games in which he had two home runs.
- Ott had eight home runs with the bases loaded.
- Ott hit 83 career home runs against Pittsburgh, his highest total against any team. His other career home runs are as follows: Philadelphia—82, Chicago—77, Boston—73, Brooklyn—71, St. Louis—66, and Cincinnati—59.

BIBLIOGRAPHY

Following are the sources of information used in the writing of this work.

Newspapers and Periodicals

Baseball Digest
Baseball Magazine
Baseball Weekly
Bronx Home News
Brooklyn Eagle
(N.Y.) Giants Jottings
Gretna (LA) Times-Picayune
New York American
New York Daily Mirror
New York Daily News
New York Herald-Tribune
New York Journal-American
New York Post

New York Sun
New York World-Telegram
Liberty Magazine
Life Magazine
Look Magazine
PM
Saturday Evening Post
Sport Magazine
The Sporting News
Time
Washington (DC) Daily News
Washington (DC) Post

Interviews

Leo Durocher, in Washington D.C.
Roy Hughes, in Arlington, Va.
Hank Leiber, in Phoenix.
Gus Mancuso, by telephone.
Cliff Melton, in Baltimore.
Mrs. Mel Ott, by telephone.
Mrs. Lyn Ott Loria, through correspondence

Hal Schumacher, in Cooperstown, N.Y.
Warren Spahn, in Washington, D.C.
Bill Terry, in Washington, D.C.
Bobby Thomson, by telephone.
Burgess Whitehead, in Charlotte, N.C.

Books

Alexander, Charles C. *John McGraw* (New York: Viking, 1988).

Allen, Lee, and Thomas Meany. *Kings of the Diamond* (Mel Ott) (New York: G.P. Putnam, 1965).

Barber, Red. *1947—When All Hell Broke Loose* (New York: Doubleday, 1982).

Bartell, Dick. *Rowdy Richard* (Berkeley, CA: North Atlantic Books, 1987).

Bjarkman, Peter C., ed. *Encyclopedia of Major League Baseball Team Histories—National League* (Westport, CT: Meckler, 1991).

Bonner, Mary G. *Baseball Rookies Who Made Good* (Mel Ott) (New York: Alfred A. Knopf, 1954).

Broeg, Bob. *Super Stars of Baseball* (Mel Ott) (St. Louis: *The Sporting News*, 1971).

Carmichael, John P. *My Greatest Day in Baseball* (Mel Ott) (New York: A.S. Barnes, 1945).

Curran, William. *Mitts—A Celebration of the Art of Fielding* (New York: William Morrow, 1985).

Daley, Arthur. *All the Home Run Kings* (Mel Ott) (New York: G.P. Putnam, 1972).

Durocher, Leo. *Nice Guys Finish Last* (New York: Simon and Schuster, 1975).

Graham, Frank. *McGraw of the Giants* (New York: G.P. Putnam, 1944).

Graff, Henry F., ed. *Dictionary of American Biography* (Mel Ott) (New York: Scribners, 1980).

Hano, Arnold. *Greatest Giants of Them All* (New York: G.P. Putnam, 1967).

Hodges, Russ. *My Giants* (New York: Doubleday, 1963).

Hynd, Noel. *The Giants of the Polo Grounds* (New York: Doubleday, 1988).

James, Bill. *The Bill James Historical Baseball Abstract* (New York: Villard Books, 1986).

Kiernan, Thomas. *The Miracle at Coogan's Bluff* (New York: Thomas Y. Crowell, 1975).

Langford, Walter M. *Legends of Baseball* (South Bend, IN: Diamond Communications, 1987).

Meany, Thomas. *Baseball's Greatest Hitters* (Mel Ott) (A.S. Barnes, 1950).

Nason, Jerry, et al. *Famous American Athletes of Today*, 7th series (Mel Ott) (New York: Page, 1940).

Porter, Daniel L., ed. *Biographical Dictionary of American Sports* (Mel Ott) (Westport, CT: Greenwood, 1987).

Shapiro, Milton J. *The Mel Ott Story* (New York: Julian Messner, 1959).

Shatzkin, Mike, ed. *The Ballplayers* (Mel Ott) (New York: William Morrow, 1990).

Smith, Ira L. *Baseball's Famous Outfielders* (Mel Ott) (New York: A.S. Barnes, 1954).

Stein, Fred. *Under Coogan's Bluff* (Glenshaw, PA: Chapter and Cask, 1981).

Stein, Fred, and Nick Peters. *Giants Diary* (Berkeley, CA: North Atlantic Books, 1987).

Stump, Al. *Sport Magazine's All-Time All Stars* (Mel Ott) (New York: Atheneum, 1977).

Thomson, Bobby. *The Giants Win the Pennant! The Giants Win the Pennant!* (New York: Kensington, 1991).

Thorn, John, and Pete Palmer, eds. *Total Baseball*, 1st ed. (Warner, 1989).

Williams, Peter. *When the Giants Were Giants* (Chapel Hill, NC: Algonquin, 1994).

Selected Articles

Daley, Arthur. "Mel Ott's Luckiest Moment," *Baseball Digest*, Sept. 1958.

Drebinger, John. "Will Mel Ott Make a Successful Manager?" *Baseball Magazine*, Feb. 1942.

_____. "Mel Ott: Take a Bow," *Baseball Magazine*, Nov. 1942.

"Everybody's Ballplayer: Mel Ott of the Giants," *Time*. July 2, 1945.

Gold, Eddie. "Mel Ott Still the Majors' One-Park Homer King," *Baseball Digest*, June 1975.

Graham, Frank. "Listening in on Ott and French," *Baseball Digest*, Feb. 1944.

_____. "Mel and Mr. (John J.) McGraw," *Sport*, Sept. 1946.

Lane, Frank C. "The Big Little Man of the New York Giants," *Baseball Magazine*, July 1934.

_____. "The Greatest Individual Punch in the National League," *Baseball Magazine*, Feb. 1937.

Miller, Hub. "Matchless Mel, Master Mauler and Manager," *Baseball Magazine*, March 1947.

Peters, Nick, and Fred Stein. "The Giants' All-Stars": Mel Ott, in *1984 San Francisco Giants Yearbook*. Woodford Associates, San Francisco, CA, 1984.

Rice, Grantland. "Ott, Williams 'Most Valuable' in Rice's Book," *Baseball Digest*, Dec. 1942.

Russell, Fred. "This Is Who Mel Ott Was," *Baseball Digest*, July 1966.

Smith, Lyall. "Mel Ott: He Was Big League All the Way," *Baseball Digest*, Feb. 1959.

Steiger, Gus. "McGraw's Proxy Bawl-Outs Helped Mold Ott," *Baseball Digest*, July 1958.

Stump, Al. "Mel Ott on the Hot Seat," *Sport*, June 1948.

Wood, Wilbur. "Why All the Barbs Against Ott?" *Baseball Digest*, Jan. 1948.

INDEX